Taste of Home RECIPE MAKEOVERS

TASTE OF HOME BOOKS • RDA ENTHUSIAST BRANDS, LLC • MILWAUKEE, WI

© 2023 RDA Enthusiast Brands, LLC.
1610 N. 2nd St., Suite 102, Milwaukee, WI 53212-3906
All rights reserved.
Taste of Home is a registered trademark of RDA Enthusiast Brands, LLC.

Visit us at **tasteofhome.com** for other Taste of Home books and products.

International Standard Book Number:
978-1-62145-826-5

Chief Content Officer, Home & Garden: Jeanne Sidner
Content Director: Mark Hagen
Associate Creative Director, Editorial Products: Raeann Thompson
Senior Editor: Christine Rukavena
Senior Art Director: Courtney Lovetere
Editors: Amy Glander, Hazel Wheaton
Art Director: Maggie Conners
Senior Designer: Jazmin Delgado
Deputy Editor, Copy Desk: Dulcie Shoener

Copy Editor: Kara Dennison
Senior Food Editor: Peggy Woodward, RDN
Contributing Designer: Jennifer Ruetz

Cover
Photographer: Mark Derse
Set Stylist: Stephanie Marchese
Food Stylist: Josh Rink

Pictured on front cover: Lasagna Deliziosa, p. 73
Pictured on title page: Chicken Florentine Meatballs, p. 130
Pictured on back cover: Greek Sloppy Joes, p. 74; Ginger Plum Tart, p. 203; Air-Fryer Coconut-Crusted Turkey Strips, p. 131; Grilled Southwestern Steak Salad, p. 74

INSTANT POT® is a trademark of Double Insight Inc. This publication has not been authorized, sponsored or otherwise approved by Double Insight Inc.

Printed in China
1 3 5 7 9 10 8 6 4 2

Table of Contents

MORE WAYS TO CONNECT WITH US:

About Our Nutrition Facts

Recipe Makeovers provides a variety of recipes that fit in a healthy lifestyle. Here's how we arrive at the serving-size nutritional information at the end of each recipe.

- Whenever a choice of ingredients is given (such as ½ cup sour cream or plain yogurt), we use the first ingredient in our calculations.

- When a range is given for an ingredient, we calculate using the first amount.

- Only the amount of a marinade absorbed is calculated.

- Optional ingredients are not included in our calculations.

- Sugars provided in the Nutrition Facts represent both added and naturally occurring sugars.

AT-A-GLANCE ICONS
Refer to these 6 icons to easily locate recipes that suit your needs.

- = A nutritionally complete "power-packed" recipe that is a good source of fiber, lean protein and a healthy dose of fruits or vegetables

- = Breakfast, lunch, dinner and snack-time options that don't use meat or meat products

- = Finished in 30 minutes or less

- = Made in a slow cooker

- = Made in a pressure cooker

- = Made in an air fryer

Here's What "Healthy" Means at *Taste of Home*

We're here to help you navigate the options in *Taste of Home Recipe Makeovers*.

We all love comfort food, but not the fat and calories that go with it. With *Taste of Home Recipe Makeovers*, you can indulge in all your feel-good favorites, because each recipe has been given a healthy reboot. But what exactly is healthy? We have a lot of factors to consider; research is constantly uncovering new information and science still has a lot to discover about how food and nutrition affect our health. With all this in mind, the editors and dietitians at *Taste of Home* have created a set of guardrails to help our readers stay on track.

Since the concept of healthy covers a wide spectrum, we take a middle-of-the-road approach at *Taste of Home*. Organizations that make recommendations rooted in proven science like the USDA, FDA, WHO, NIH plus the American Heart Association, the American Diabetes Association and the Academy of Nutrition and Dietetics help guide us.

WHAT HEALTHY IS

The idea that healthy foods should nourish us with vitamins, minerals, protein, fiber and healthy fat is so important that we added a new "power-packed" icon used throughout *Recipe Makeovers*. These recipes are made up of multiple healthy ingredients, such as vegetables, fruits, whole grains, lean meats, legumes, low-fat or fat-free dairy, and healthy fats.

WHAT HEALTHY ISN'T

The big picture isn't just about what's in our food, but also what's not in our food. Experts widely recommend that we limit saturated fat, trans fat and sodium for optimal health and disease prevention, so we steer away from those in our healthy recipes. At the same time, healthy eating doesn't mean cutting out entire food groups, feeling deprived or eating food that doesn't taste good!

IT'S ABOUT BALANCE

Healthy eating is about balance: a recipe that's made mostly of healthy ingredients; a meal that's made up mostly of healthy recipes; a day that includes mostly healthy choices. This will provide us with all the nutrients we need to function our best. Nutritious recipes can include butter and sugar, just as healthy meals can include an indulgent dessert—it's all about moderation and keeping a healthy big picture in mind.

Use the Test Kitchen-approved dishes inside *Recipe Makeovers* to help you find your balance. Whether you're looking for a power-packed weeknight dinner, such as  **BOW TIES WITH SAUSAGE & ASPARAGUS (P. 142),** or a special-occasion dessert such as **CHOCOLATE SWIRLED CHEESECAKE (P. 194),** you'll find a great combination that works for you and your family.

Happy Cooking,

Peggy

Peggy Woodward, RDN
Senior Food Editor

Healthy Food Impostors

These foods may seem like virtuous choices, but they usually aren't.

GRANOLA BARS

We usually equate granola with wholesomeness, but it isn't necessarily healthful, especially granola bars. They may contain whole grains and some healthy fats in the form of nuts or seeds, but most bars are packed with added sugar, more like candy than health food. Make your own to control sugar and add good health.

SMOOTHIES

While smoothies may seem like health food in a glass, many aren't. In addition to the natural sweetness from fruit, they often have added sugar in the form of fruit juice concentrate, honey or agave nectar. Make your own, leave out the extra sugar, and remember to count the calories from your smoothie in your day's intake.

BREAKFAST CEREAL

The cereal aisle has become overrun with sweetened flakes, marshmallows and other ingredients you might find in dessert. Check out the ingredient list; if sugar's one of the first, that means it's mostly sugar. Look for whole-grain, low-sugar cereal with protein-packed ingredients such as nuts and seeds.

VEGGIE CHIPS

Better than potato chips, right? Well, potatoes are vegetables, too. And just like potato chips, most veggie chips are highly processed, with added fat and salt. Some also have preservatives and artificial colors to give them their vibrant color. If you love them, eat them (a few anyway), but don't think it's the same as eating a serving of raw veggies.

AGAVE NECTAR

Syrup from the agave plant sounds too good to be true–and it probably is. While it might be more "natural" and lower on the glycemic index than some sweeteners, it's still heated, processed and full of fructose, and it's still added sugar. Treat agave nectar the same way you would any other sweetener— always use it in moderation.

LOW-FAT FOODS

Processed foods that are marketed as low-fat or fat-free typically have more of what we don't want—added sugar and processed ingredients to help them taste more like the full-fat versions. Remember that fat isn't off-limits; we need healthy mono- and polyunsaturated fat in our diets to help absorb certain nutrients and provide essential fatty acids.

Power Up with Power-Packed Foods Such as These

Start the day right with a breakfast bowl that has it all: health, convenience, comfort and amazing taste. 🥕🍗 **POACHED EGG BUDDHA BOWLS** from *Amy McDonough* warm up the chilliest morning in Oregon, and they're loaded with chewy, nutty whole grain wheat berries. **P. 12**

While it tastes like pure comfort food, 🍲🍗 **CONTEST-WINNING MUSHROOM POT ROAST** from Kansas cook **Angie Stewart** boasts a bevy of vegetables and 30g of satisfying protein in every portion. Reduced-sodium broth keeps salt at bay, and the best part is that this classic dish is conveniently made in the slow cooker. This family-pleaser will become part of your regular rotation. **P. 78**

Summertime is the prime time for healthy eating, and Astoria, New York's **Rosalyn Nguyen** incorporates zesty marinated grilled pork into a fresh salad that's perfect for lunch or a light dinner. 🍗 **GRILLED PORK NOODLE SALAD** is bursting with rice noodles, ripe garden produce, fresh herbs and a homemade dressing. **P. 107**

Smart Ways to Eat Healthy on a Budget

Eating right doesn't have to be expensive. Here are some of our favorite ways to cook healthier meals for less.

1 Enjoy oats for breakfast. When it comes to eating healthy on a budget, oats are a go-to choice for a quick, substantial breakfast. Because oats are a whole grain and low on the glycemic index, they can satisfy your hunger for longer than many other foods. **TEX-MEX GRAIN BOWL** from Athena Russell of South Carolina is power-packed with oats, black beans, cheddar cheese and avocado. Her hearty, surprisingly savory dish offers a unique take on the morning staple. **P. 15**

2 Shop seasonally. Not only are in-season ingredients at their tastiest and most nutritious, they are also at their best price. So stock up on hearty root veggies and winter squash in cold months, and celebrate spring and summer with well-priced asparagus, salad greens, fruits and berries. **BLUEBERRY & PEACH COBBLER** from Laura Jansen of Michigan is a flexible treat that uses fresh seasonal fruit. **P. 196**

3 Buy nuts in bulk. Nuts are healthy and cost less when bought in larger quantities. Buying them in bulk saves more money than buying a few ounces at a time from the baking aisle. To extend their shelf life, keep nuts in a resealable bag in the freezer. Look to stock up on nuts during and after the holiday baking season. **RASPBERRY-WALNUT PORK SALAD** from Florida's Virginia Anthony is enriched with a satisfying sprinkle of crunchy walnuts. **P. 97**

4 Go for frozen vegetables. Fresh vegetables can be expensive, but frozen veggies provide a lot of bang for your buck. Not only are they cheaper, but also frozen veggies do not run the risk of spoiling before you get to them, as fresh ones do. Throw in the fact that frozen veggies contain comparable vitamins and minerals to fresh, and you'll see why it's nice keeping them on ice! **SPINACH BURRITOS** from Dolores Zornow of Wisconsin have a short prep time and lots of nutrients thanks to frozen spinach. **P. 164**

5 Count on beans. Beans are one of the best healthy foods to eat for cheap. For around $1, you can get a can of ready-to-eat beans or 1 pound of dried (makes about 4 cups of cooked beans). Rich in iron, they are also one of the best sources of plant-based protein. **PRESSURE-COOKER SMOKY WHITE BEANS & HAM** from Christine Duffy of Kentucky is hearty and makes economical use of pantry staples. **P. 187**

6 Plan those leftovers. Even a few minutes of planning your meals ahead for the upcoming week can save you a lot of money at the grocery store. Make a shopping list and stick to it. Plan to eat dinner leftovers for lunch the next day, and to reinvent leftovers in other dishes. **THAI CHICKEN PASTA** from Jeni Pittard of Georgia is a quick, easy and tasty way to use up leftover cubed chicken breast. **P. 141**

DOWN-HOME BREAKFAST STAPLES

SAUSAGE & EGG GRITS

I always eat my sausage, grits and eggs together, so I thought it would be fun to mix them up in the same skillet. The resulting breakfast bombshell is loaded with down-home flavor—and it doesn't even use butter!
—*Jeannine Quiller, Raleigh, NC*

- -

Prep: **15 min.** • Cook: **20 min.**
Makes: **6 servings**

- 4 **breakfast turkey sausage links, casings removed**
- 1½ **cups egg substitute**
- 1¼ **cups whole milk, divided**
- 3 **cups water**
- ⅛ **tsp. salt**
- 1 **cup quick-cooking grits**
- ¾ **cup shredded reduced-fat cheddar cheese, divided**
- 2 **green onions, chopped**
- ⅛ **tsp. pepper**

1. Crumble sausage into a large skillet; cook over medium heat until no longer pink. Remove to paper towels with a slotted spoon. Whisk egg substitute and ¼ cup milk; add to same skillet. Cook and stir until set; remove from the heat.
2. Meanwhile, in a Dutch oven, bring water, salt and remaining milk to a boil. Slowly stir in grits. Reduce heat; cook and stir until thickened, 5-7 minutes.
3. Stir in half of the cheese. Add sausage, eggs, green onions and pepper; heat through. Serve in bowls; sprinkle with remaining cheese.
1 CUP: 208 cal., 6g fat (3g sat. fat), 25mg chol., 369mg sod., 24g carb. (4g sugars, 1g fiber), 16g pro. **DIABETIC EXCHANGES:** 2 lean meat, 1½ starch.

SUNSHINE CREPES

My family wanted something light to go with coffee for a special breakfast, so I whipped up these sweet and fruity crepes. They were a big hit! Fill them with whatever canned or fresh fruit you happen to have available.

—*Mary Hobbs, Campbell, MO*

Prep: **15 min. + chilling**
Cook: **15 min.** • Makes: **6 servings**

- 2 large eggs, room temperature
- ⅔ cup 2% milk
- 1 Tbsp. canola oil
- ½ cup all-purpose flour
- 1 tsp. sugar
- ¼ tsp. salt

FILLING

- 1 can (20 oz.) crushed pineapple, drained
- 1 can (11 oz.) mandarin oranges, drained
- 1 tsp. vanilla extract
- 1 carton (8 oz.) frozen whipped topping, thawed Confectioners' sugar

1. In a large bowl, whisk eggs, milk and oil. In another bowl, mix flour, sugar and salt; add to egg mixture and mix well. Refrigerate, covered, 1 hour.

2. Heat a lightly greased 8-in. nonstick skillet over medium heat. Stir batter. Fill a ¼-cup measure halfway with batter; pour into center of pan. Quickly lift and tilt pan to coat bottom evenly. Cook until top appears dry; turn crepe over and cook until bottom is cooked, 15-20 seconds longer. Remove to a wire rack. Repeat with remaining batter, greasing pan as needed. When cool, stack crepes between pieces of waxed paper or paper towels.

3. For filling, in a large bowl, combine pineapple, oranges and vanilla; fold in whipped topping. Spread ⅓ cup over each crepe; fold into quarters. Dust with confectioners' sugar.

2 CREPES: 299 cal., 11g fat (7g sat. fat), 64mg chol., 139mg sod., 43g carb. (31g sugars, 1g fiber), 5g pro.

MULTIGRAIN CINNAMON ROLLS

This simple recipe is sure to become a family favorite. Whole wheat flour adds a hearty twist. The wholesome cinnamon rolls will fill your kitchen with a warm, wonderful aroma.
—*Judith Eddy, Baldwin City, KS*

Prep: **30 min. + rising** • Bake: **15 min.**
Makes: **1 dozen**

1   pkg. (¼ oz.) **active dry yeast**
¾   cup **warm water**
     (110° to 115°)
½   cup **quick-cooking oats**
½   cup **whole wheat flour**
¼   cup **packed brown sugar**
2   Tbsp. **butter, melted**
1   large **egg, room temperature**
1   tsp. **salt**
1¾ to 2¼ cups **all-purpose flour**
FILLING
3   Tbsp. **butter, softened**
⅓   cup **sugar**
2   tsp. **ground cinnamon**
GLAZE
1   cup **confectioners' sugar**
6½ tsp. **half-and-half cream**
4½ tsp. **butter, softened**

1. In a large bowl, dissolve yeast in warm water. Add oats, whole wheat flour, brown sugar, butter, egg, salt and 1 cup all-purpose flour. Beat on medium speed until smooth. Stir in enough remaining flour to form a soft dough (dough will be sticky).
2. Turn dough onto a lightly floured surface; knead until smooth and elastic, 6-8 minutes. Place in a bowl coated with cooking spray, turning once to coat the top. Cover and let rise in a warm place until doubled, about 1 hour.

3. Punch dough down. Roll into an 18x12-in. rectangle; spread with the butter. Combine sugar and cinnamon; sprinkle over dough to within ½ in. of edges.
4. Roll up jelly-roll style, starting with a short side; pinch seams to seal. Cut into 12 slices. Place cut side down in a 13x9-in. baking pan coated with cooking spray. Cover and let rise until doubled, about 45 minutes.
5. Bake at 375° for 15-20 minutes or until golden brown. For icing, in a small bowl, beat confectioners' sugar, cream and butter until smooth. Drizzle over warm rolls.
1 CINNAMON ROLL: 240 cal., 7g fat (4g sat. fat), 35mg chol., 251mg sod., 40g carb. (20g sugars, 2g fiber), 4g pro.

CINNAMON PULL-APART LOAF: Follow method for cinnamon rolls but do not roll up jelly-roll style. Instead, cut into thirty-six 3x2-in. rectangles. Make 2 stacks of 18 rectangles. Place, cut sides up, in a 9x5-in. loaf pan coated with cooking spray. Cover and let rise until doubled, about 45 minutes. Bake at 375° for 25-30 minutes or until golden brown. Cool for 10 minutes before removing from pan to a wire rack. Make glaze; drizzle over warm bread. Yield: 1 loaf (12 slices).
1 SLICE: 240 cal., 7 g fat (4 g sat. fat), 35 mg chol., 251 mg sod., 40 g carb., 2 g fiber, 4 g pro.

TWISTED CINNAMON RING: Follow method for cinnamon rolls and roll up jelly-roll style, starting with a long side. Cut roll in half lengthwise. Place doughs side by side on a baking sheet coated with cooking spray. Twist together, cut side up, and shape into a ring. Pinch ends together. Cover

and let rise until doubled, about 45 minutes. Bake at 375° for 20-25 minutes or until golden brown. Remove from pan to a wire rack. Make glaze; drizzle over warm bread. Yield: 1 ring (12 slices).
1 SLICE: 240 cal., 7 g fat (4 g sat. fat), 35 mg chol., 251 mg sod., 40 g carb., 2 g fiber, 4 g pro.

TYPICAL	MAKEOVER
365 Calories	**240** Calories
11g Fat	**7g** Fat
60g Carbohydrates	**40g** Carbohydrates
294mg Sodium	**251mg** Sodium

MAPLE BACON WALNUT COFFEE CAKE

The sleepyheads will roll out of bed when they smell this sweet and savory coffee cake baking. Nuts and bacon in the crumbly topping blend with maple, nutmeg and cinnamon.
—*Angela Spengler, Niceville, FL*

- -

Prep: **25 min.**
Bake: **35 min. + cooling**
Makes: **24 servings**

- 2½ cups all-purpose flour
- 1 cup packed brown sugar
- ½ tsp. salt
- ⅓ cup cold butter
- 2 tsp. baking powder
- ½ tsp. baking soda
- ½ tsp. ground cinnamon
- ¼ tsp. ground nutmeg
- 2 large eggs, room temperature
- 1½ cups buttermilk
- ½ cup maple syrup
- ⅓ cup unsweetened applesauce
- 5 bacon strips, cooked and crumbled
- ½ cup chopped walnuts

1. In a large bowl, combine the flour, brown sugar and salt. Cut in butter until crumbly. Set aside ½ cup for topping. Combine baking powder, baking soda, cinnamon and nutmeg; stir into remaining flour mixture.
2. In a small bowl, whisk the eggs, buttermilk, syrup and applesauce until well blended. Gradually stir into flour mixture until combined.
3. Spread into a 13x9-in. baking pan coated with cooking spray. Sprinkle with reserved topping, then bacon and walnuts. Bake at 350° until a toothpick inserted in the center comes out clean, 35-40 minutes. Cool on a wire rack.
1 PIECE: 160 cal., 5g fat (2g sat. fat), 27mg chol., 183mg sod., 25g carb. (14g sugars, 1g fiber), 3g pro.
DIABETIC EXCHANGES: 1½ starch, 1 fat.

POACHED EGG BUDDHA BOWLS

My husband and I celebrate the arrival of spring with this dish, enjoying it in the backyard. I often include fresh peas and even a few other spring delights.
—*Amy McDonough, Carlton, OR*

- -

Prep: **10 min.** • Cook: **65 min.**
Makes: **2 servings**

- ¾ cup wheat berries
- 2 Tbsp. olive oil
- 2 Tbsp. lemon juice
- 1 Tbsp. thinly sliced fresh mint leaves
- ¼ tsp. salt
- ⅛ tsp. freshly ground pepper
- ½ cup quartered cherry tomatoes
- ½ cup reduced-fat ricotta cheese
- 2 Tbsp. sliced Greek olives
- 2 large eggs
  Optional: Additional olive oil and pepper

1. Place wheat berries and 2½ cups water in a large saucepan; bring to a boil. Reduce heat; simmer, covered, until tender, about 1 hour. Drain; transfer to a bowl. Cool slightly.
2. Stir in oil, lemon juice, mint, salt and pepper; divide between 2 bowls. Top with tomatoes, ricotta cheese and olives.
3. To poach each egg, place ½ cup water in a small microwave-safe bowl or glass measuring cup. Break an egg into the water. Microwave, covered, on high 1 minute. Cook in 10-second intervals until white is set and yolk begins to thicken; let stand 1 minute.
4. Using a slotted spoon, transfer an egg to each of the bowls. Repeat. If desired, drizzle with additional oil and sprinkle with more pepper.
1 SERVING: 526 cal., 24g fat (5g sat. fat), 201mg chol., 563mg sod., 58g carb. (5g sugars, 10g fiber), 21g pro.

THE SKINNY
Wheat berries are whole kernels of wheat. They cook up to a chewy texture with a hint of buttery flavor. Look for wheat berries near other whole grains at the grocery store or in the baking aisle.

TEX-MEX GRAIN BOWL

This recipe is special because it is not only healthy but also delicious. Oatmeal is one of those foods often eaten sweetened. People rarely think about using it in a savory dish—and they really should!
—*Athena Russell, Greenville, SC*

- -

Takes: **20 min.** • Makes: **4 servings**

- 4 cups water
- 2 Tbsp. reduced-sodium taco seasoning
- 2 cups old-fashioned oats or multigrain hot cereal
- 1 cup black beans, rinsed, drained and warmed
- 1 cup salsa
- ½ cup finely shredded cheddar cheese
- 1 medium ripe avocado, peeled and cubed
  Optional: Pitted ripe olives, sour cream and chopped cilantro

In a large saucepan, bring water and taco seasoning to a boil. Stir in oats; cook 5 minutes over medium heat, stirring occasionally. Remove from heat. Divide oatmeal among 4 bowls. Top with beans, salsa, cheese, avocado and toppings as desired. Serve immediately.

1 SERVING: 345 cal., 13g fat (4g sat. fat), 14mg chol., 702mg sod., 46g carb. (5g sugars, 9g fiber), 12g pro.

EARLY-RISER OVEN OMELET

Everyone will rush to the table when you serve this big, fluffy omelet. Packed with tomato, broccoli, ham and cheese, it makes a hearty brunch dish that easily serves a bunch.
—*Wendy Fawcett, Gillam, MB*

- -

Prep: **15 min.** • Bake: **35 min.**
Makes: **6 servings**

- 10 large egg whites
- 5 large eggs
- 1 cup fat-free milk
- ¼ tsp. seasoned salt
- ¼ tsp. pepper
- 1½ cups cubed fully cooked ham
- 1 cup chopped fresh broccoli
- 1 cup shredded reduced-fat cheddar cheese
- 1 medium tomato, seeded and chopped
- 3 Tbsp. finely chopped onion

In a bowl, beat the egg whites, eggs, milk, seasoned salt and pepper. Pour into a greased 10-in. cast-iron or other ovenproof skillet. Sprinkle with the ham, broccoli, cheese, tomato and onion. Bake, uncovered, at 350° until eggs are almost set, 30-35 minutes. Broil 4-6 in. from the heat until eggs are set and top is lightly browned, 1-2 minutes.

1 PIECE: 216 cal., 10g fat (4g sat. fat), 183mg chol., 805mg sod., 6g carb. (4g sugars, 1g fiber), 25g pro.
DIABETIC EXCHANGES: 3 medium-fat meat, 1 vegetable.

1. In a large nonstick skillet, saute onion in 2 tsp. oil until tender. Stir in potatoes and water. Bring to a boil. Reduce heat; cover and simmer for 15-20 minutes or until potatoes are tender. Stir in corned beef and pepper; heat through.

2. Meanwhile, in a large nonstick skillet, fry eggs in remaining oil as desired. Season with additional pepper if desired. Serve with corned beef hash.

1 EGG WITH 1 CUP HASH: 301 cal., 12g fat (3g sat. fat), 239mg chol., 652mg sod., 31g carb. (4g sugars, 4g fiber), 18g pro. **DIABETIC EXCHANGES:** 2 starch, 2 medium-fat meat, ½ fat.

TYPICAL	MAKEOVER
442 Calories	**301** Calories
30g Fat	**12g** Fat
6g Saturated Fat	**3g** Saturated Fat
895mg Sodium	**652mg** Sodium

MAKEOVER HASH & EGGS

Loaded with red potatoes and corned beef, our lightened-up version of this all-time classic delivers fresh flavors with a healthy dose of fiber.
—Taste of Home *Test Kitchen*

- -

Takes: **30 min.** • Makes: **4 servings**

- 1 large onion, chopped
- 1 Tbsp. canola oil, divided
- 6 medium red potatoes (about 1½ lbs.), cut into ½-in. cubes
- ¼ cup water
- 3 pkg. (2 oz. each) thinly sliced deli corned beef, coarsely chopped
- ¼ tsp. pepper
- 4 large eggs
  Additional pepper, optional

SLOW-COOKER FRITTATA PROVENCAL

This recipe means that a delectable brunch is always ready for lazy weekend mornings. The meatless meal also makes an impressive and tasty weeknight dinner.
—*Connie Eaton, Pittsburgh, PA*

Prep: **30 min.** • Cook: **3 hours**
Makes: **6 servings**

- ½ cup water
- 1 Tbsp. olive oil
- 1 medium Yukon Gold potato, peeled and sliced
- 1 small onion, thinly sliced
- ½ tsp. smoked paprika
- 12 large eggs
- 1 tsp. minced fresh thyme or ¼ tsp. dried thyme
- 1 tsp. hot pepper sauce
- ½ tsp. salt
- ¼ tsp. pepper
- 1 log (4 oz.) fresh goat cheese, coarsely crumbled, divided
- ½ cup chopped soft sun-dried tomatoes (not packed in oil)

1. Layer two 24-in. pieces of aluminum foil; starting with a long side, fold up foil to create a 1-in.-wide strip. Shape strip into a coil to make a rack for bottom of a 6-qt. oval slow cooker. Add water to slow cooker; set foil rack in water.
2. In a large skillet, heat oil over medium-high heat. Add potato and onion; cook and stir until potato is lightly browned, 5-7 minutes. Stir in paprika. Transfer to a greased 1½-qt. baking dish (dish must fit in slow cooker).

3. In a large bowl, whisk eggs, thyme, pepper sauce, salt and pepper; stir in 2 oz. cheese. Pour over potato mixture. Top with tomatoes and remaining goat cheese. Place dish on foil rack.
4. Cook, covered, on low until eggs are set and a knife inserted in center comes out clean, 3-4 hours.
1 WEDGE: 245 cal., 14g fat (5g sat. fat), 385mg chol., 338mg sod., 12g carb. (4g sugars, 2g fiber), 15g pro.
DIABETIC EXCHANGES: 2 medium-fat meat, 1 starch, ½ fat.

THE SKINNY
We tested this recipe with tomatoes that are ready to use without soaking. When using whole sun-dried tomatoes that are not oil-packed, cover with boiling water and let stand until soft. Drain before chopping.

RAISIN NUT OATMEAL

There's no better feeling than waking up to a hot ready-to-eat breakfast. The oats, fruit and spices in this homey meal cook together while you sleep!
—*Valerie Sauber, Adelanto, CA*

- -

Prep: **10 min.** • Cook: **7 hours**
Makes: **6 servings**

- 3½ cups fat-free milk
- 1 large apple, peeled and chopped
- ¾ cup steel-cut oats
- ¾ cup raisins
- 3 Tbsp. brown sugar
- 4½ tsp. butter, melted
- ¾ tsp. ground cinnamon
- ½ tsp. salt
- ¼ cup chopped pecans

In a 3-qt. slow cooker coated with cooking spray, combine the first 8 ingredients. Cover and cook on low for 7-8 hours or until liquid is absorbed. Spoon oatmeal into bowls; sprinkle with pecans.

¾ CUP: 289 cal., 9g fat (3g sat. fat), 10mg chol., 282mg sod., 47g carb. (28g sugars, 4g fiber), 9g pro.

MAKE IT YOUR OWN
You may substitute 1½ cups quick-cooking oats for the steel-cut oats and increase the fat-free milk to 4½ cups.

POACHED EGGS WITH TARRAGON ASPARAGUS

I adapted this recipe from a dish I had in Napa Valley. I decided to add toasted bread crumbs as a garnish. The result was a breakfast option that everyone loves. The vibrant colors are always well received.
—*Jenn Tidwell, Fair Oaks, CA*

- -

Takes: **30 min.** • Makes: **4 servings**

- 1 lb. fresh asparagus, trimmed
- 1 Tbsp. olive oil
- 1 garlic clove, minced
- 1 Tbsp. minced fresh tarragon
- ½ tsp. salt
- ¼ tsp. pepper
- 1 Tbsp. butter
- ¼ cup seasoned bread crumbs
- 4 large eggs

1. Place 3 in. of water in a large skillet with high sides; bring to a boil. Add asparagus; cook, uncovered, 2-4 minutes or until asparagus turns bright green. Remove the asparagus and immediately drop into ice water. Drain and pat dry.

2. In a separate large skillet, heat oil over medium heat. Add garlic; cook and stir 1 minute. Add asparagus, tarragon, salt and pepper; cook asparagus 2-3 minutes or until crisp-tender, turning occasionally. Remove from pan; keep warm. In same skillet, melt the butter over medium heat. Add bread crumbs; cook and stir 1-2 minutes or until toasted. Remove from heat.

3. Add 2-3 in. fresh water to skillet used to cook asparagus. Bring to a boil; adjust heat to maintain a gentle simmer. Break cold eggs, 1 at a time, into a small bowl; holding bowl close to surface of water, slip the egg into water.

4. Cook the eggs, uncovered, 3-4 minutes or until whites are completely set and yolks begin to thicken but are not hard. Using a slotted spoon, lift eggs out of water; serve over asparagus. Sprinkle with toasted bread crumbs.

1 SERVING: 170 cal., 12g fat (4g sat. fat), 194mg chol., 513mg sod., 8g carb. (2g sugars, 1g fiber), 9g pro.
DIABETIC EXCHANGES: 1½ fat, 1 vegetable, 1 medium-fat meat.

CALICO SCRAMBLED EGGS

When you're short on time and rushing to get breakfast on the table, this recipe is just what you need. It has a short ingredient list, cooking is kept to a minimum, and the green pepper and tomato make it colorful.
—Taste of Home *Test Kitchen*

- -

Takes: **15 min.** • Makes: **4 servings**

- 8 large eggs
- ¼ cup 2% milk
- ⅛ to ¼ tsp. dill weed
- ⅛ to ¼ tsp. salt
- ⅛ to ¼ tsp. pepper
- 1 Tbsp. butter
- ½ cup chopped green pepper
- ¼ cup chopped onion
- ½ cup chopped fresh tomato

1. In a bowl, whisk first 5 ingredients until blended. In a 12-in. nonstick skillet, heat butter over medium-high heat. Add green pepper and onion; cook and stir until tender. Remove from pan.

2. In same pan, pour in egg mixture; cook and stir over medium heat until eggs begin to thicken. Add tomato and pepper mixture; cook until heated through and no liquid egg remains, stirring gently.

1 CUP: 188 cal., 13g fat (5g sat. fat), 381mg chol., 248mg sod., 4g carb. (3g sugars, 1g fiber), 14g pro. **DIABETIC EXCHANGES:** 2 medium-fat meat, ½ fat.

CINNAMON FRUIT BISCUITS

Because these sweet treats are so easy, I'm almost embarrassed when people ask me for the recipe. They're a snap to make with refrigerated buttermilk biscuits, sugar, cinnamon and your favorite fruit preserves.
—*Ione Burham, Washington, IA*

Prep: **15 min.**
Bake: **15 min. + cooling**
Makes: **10 servings**

- ½ **cup sugar**
- ½ **tsp. ground cinnamon**
- 1 **tube (12 oz.) refrigerated buttermilk biscuits, separated into 10 biscuits**
- ¼ **cup butter, melted**
- 10 **tsp. strawberry preserves**

1. In a small bowl, combine sugar and cinnamon. Dip top and sides of biscuits in butter, then in the cinnamon sugar.
2. Place on ungreased baking sheets. With the end of a wooden spoon handle, make a deep indentation in the center of each biscuit; fill with 1 tsp. preserves.
3. Bake at 375° for 15-18 minutes or until golden brown. Cool biscuits for 15 minutes before serving (preserves will be hot).
1 SERVING: 178 cal., 5g fat (3g sat. fat), 12mg chol., 323mg sod., 31g carb. (14g sugars, 0 fiber), 3g pro.

TASTE OF HOME TALK
"I made these for my grandson's breakfast. They are the easiest most delicious things I've ever had for breakfast! Great job!"
LORENE0406, TASTEOFHOME.COM

MAKE IT YOUR OWN
Dress up these biscuits with:
- Different flavors of preserves
- A drizzle of melted chocolate
- Cardamom or nutmeg

BREAKFAST PARFAITS

The combination of pineapples, raspberries and bananas in these yogurt treats makes a bright and cheerful morning breakfast.
—Adell Meyer, Madison, WI

Takes: **10 min.** • Makes: **4 servings**

2 cups pineapple chunks
1 cup vanilla yogurt
1 cup fresh or frozen
  raspberries
½ cup chopped dates or raisins
1 cup sliced ripe banana
¼ cup sliced almonds

In 4 parfait glasses or serving dishes, layer pineapple, yogurt, raspberries, dates and banana. Sprinkle with almonds. Serve immediately.

1 PARFAIT: 277 cal., 4g fat (1g sat. fat), 3mg chol., 52mg sod., 60g carb. (48g sugars, 6g fiber), 5g pro.

APPLE-SAGE SAUSAGE PATTIES

Apple and sausage naturally go together. Add sage, and you've got a standout patty. They're freezer-friendly, so I make them ahead.
—Scarlett Elrod, Newnan, GA

Prep: **35 min. + chilling**
Cook: **10 min./batch**
Makes: **16 servings**

1 large apple
1 large egg, lightly beaten
½ cup chopped fresh parsley
3 to 4 Tbsp. minced fresh sage
2 garlic cloves, minced
1¼ tsp. salt
½ tsp. pepper
½ tsp. crushed red pepper flakes
1¼ lbs. lean ground turkey
6 tsp. olive oil, divided

1. Peel and coarsely shred the apple; place the apple in a colander over a plate. Let stand 15 minutes. Squeeze and blot dry with paper towels.

2. In a large bowl, combine egg, parsley, sage, garlic, seasonings and apple. Add turkey; mix lightly but thoroughly. Shape into sixteen 2-in. patties. Place the patties on waxed-paper-lined baking sheets. Refrigerate, covered, 8 hours or overnight.

3. In a large nonstick skillet, heat 2 tsp. oil over medium heat. In batches, cook patties 3-4 minutes on each side or until golden brown and a thermometer reads 165°, adding more oil as needed.

FREEZE OPTION: Place uncooked patties on waxed-paper-lined baking sheets; wrap and freeze until firm. Remove from pans and transfer to a freezer container; return to freezer. To use, cook the frozen patties as directed, increasing cook time to 4-5 minutes on each side.

1 PATTY: 79 cal., 5g fat (1g sat. fat), 36mg chol., 211mg sod., 2g carb. (1g sugars, 0 fiber), 8g pro. **DIABETIC EXCHANGES:** 1 lean meat, ½ fat.

Optional: Semisweet chocolate chips, dried cranberries, sliced ripe bananas and coarsely chopped pecans

1. In a small bowl, combine the flour, sugar, baking powder and baking soda. In another bowl, whisk the eggs, yogurt and water. Stir into dry ingredients just until moistened.
2. Pour batter by ¼ cupfuls onto a hot griddle coated with cooking spray. Sprinkle with the optional ingredients if desired. Turn when bubbles form on top; cook until the second side is golden brown.
FREEZE OPTION: Arrange cooled pancakes in a single layer on baking sheets. Freeze overnight or until frozen. Transfer to a resealable plastic freezer bag. May be frozen for up to 2 months. To use, place pancakes on a microwave-safe plate; microwave on high for 40-50 seconds or until heated through.
2 PANCAKES: 242 cal., 5g fat (2g sat. fat), 73mg chol., 432mg sod., 40g carb. (8g sugars, 1g fiber), 9g pro.
DIABETIC EXCHANGES: 2½ starch, 1 fat.

THE SKINNY
Using Greek yogurt instead of plain yogurt in this recipe will add extra protein, but it may also add a slightly tangy flavor to the pancakes.

YOGURT PANCAKES
Get your day off to a perfect start with these pancakes. Short on time? Make a batch on the weekend!
—*Cheryll Baber, Homedale, ID*

Takes: **30 min.** • Makes: **12 pancakes**

- 2 cups all-purpose flour
- 2 Tbsp. sugar
- 2 tsp. baking powder
- 1 tsp. baking soda
- 2 large eggs, room temperature, lightly beaten
- 2 cups plain yogurt
- ¼ cup water

4 cups frozen shredded hash brown potatoes, thawed
1 cup shredded reduced-fat cheddar cheese

1. Preheat oven to 350°. In a large skillet, cook bacon over medium heat until crisp, stirring occasionally. Remove with a slotted spoon; drain on paper towels. Discard drippings.
2. In same skillet, heat oil over medium-high heat. Add pepper and onion; cook and stir until tender. Remove from heat.
3. In a large bowl, whisk eggs, egg substitute, milk and seasonings until blended. Stir in potatoes, cheese, bacon and pepper mixture.
4. Transfer to a 13x9-in. baking dish coated with cooking spray. Bake until a knife inserted in the center comes out clean, 30-35 minutes.

1 PIECE: 181 cal., 8g fat (3g sat. fat), 122mg chol., 591mg sod., 11g carb. (4g sugars, 1g fiber), 16g pro.
DIABETIC EXCHANGES: 2 lean meat, 1 starch.

SUNDAY BRUNCH EGG CASSEROLE

My favorite brunch dish got a makeover with egg substitute and lower-fat cheese. The lighter version still tastes delicious, but it won't weigh you down!
—*Alice Hofmann, Sussex, WI*

Prep: **20 min.** • Bake: **30 min.**
Makes: **8 servings**

6 bacon strips, chopped
1 tsp. canola oil
1 small green pepper, chopped
1 small onion, chopped
4 large eggs
2 cartons (8 oz. each) egg substitute
1 cup fat-free milk
¾ tsp. salt
½ tsp. pepper
¼ tsp. dill weed

BAGEL WITH A VEGGIE SCHMEAR

I got this recipe from my favorite bagel shop in New York City. Now I make this every time I'm craving a quick and healthy meal. I sometimes add chopped pitted green olives to the schmear.

—Julie Merriman, Seattle, WA

Takes: **20 min.** • Makes: **4 servings**

- 4 oz. fat-free cream cheese
- 4 oz. fresh goat cheese
- ½ tsp. grated lime zest
- 1 Tbsp. lime juice
- ⅔ cup finely chopped cucumber
- ¼ cup finely chopped celery
- 3 Tbsp. finely chopped carrot
- 1 radish, finely chopped
- 2 Tbsp. finely chopped red onion
- 2 Tbsp. thinly sliced fresh basil
- 4 whole wheat bagels, split and toasted
- 8 slices tomato
  Coarsely ground pepper, optional

In a bowl, beat cheeses, lime zest and lime juice until blended. Fold in chopped vegetables and basil. Serve on bagels with tomato slices. If desired, sprinkle with pepper.

2 OPEN-FACED SANDWICHES: 341 cal., 6g fat (3g sat. fat), 22mg chol., 756mg sod., 56g carb. (15g sugars, 10g fiber), 20g pro.

A.M. RUSH ESPRESSO SMOOTHIE

Want an early morning pick-me-up that's good for you, too? Fruit and flaxseed give this sweet espresso a nutritious twist.

—Aimee Wilson, Clovis, CA

Takes: **10 min.** • Makes: **1 serving**

- ½ cup cold fat-free milk
- 1 Tbsp. vanilla flavoring syrup
- 1 cup ice cubes
- ½ medium banana, cut up
- 1 to 2 tsp. instant espresso powder
- 1 tsp. ground flaxseed
- 1 tsp. baking cocoa

In a blender, combine all ingredients; cover and process until blended, 1-2 minutes. Pour into a chilled glass; serve immediately.

1½ CUPS: 148 cal., 2g fat (0 sat. fat), 2mg chol., 54mg sod., 31g carb. (21g sugars, 3g fiber), 6g pro.

FLAXSEED OATMEAL PANCAKES

I came up with this healthy and really tasty recipe because my husband loves pancakes. They have a hearty yet pleasing texture and a delightful touch of cinnamon.
—*Sharon Hansen, Pontiac, IL*

Takes: **20 min.** • Makes: **4 pancakes**

- ⅓ cup whole wheat flour
- 3 Tbsp. quick-cooking oats
- 1 Tbsp. flaxseed
- ½ tsp. baking powder
- ¼ tsp. ground cinnamon
- ⅛ tsp. baking soda
     Dash salt
- 1 large egg, separated, room temperature
- ½ cup buttermilk
- 1 Tbsp. brown sugar
- 1 Tbsp. canola oil
- ½ tsp. vanilla extract

1. In a large bowl, combine the first 7 ingredients. In a small bowl, whisk the egg yolk, buttermilk, brown sugar, oil and vanilla; stir into dry ingredients just until moistened.
2. In a small bowl, beat egg white on medium speed until stiff peaks form. Fold into batter.
3. Pour batter by ¼ cupfuls onto a hot griddle coated with cooking spray; turn when bubbles form on top. Cook until the second side is golden brown.
2 PANCAKES: 273 cal., 13g fat (2g sat. fat), 108mg chol., 357mg sod., 31g carb. (10g sugars, 5g fiber), 10g pro. **DIABETIC EXCHANGES:** 2 starch, 2 fat.

PRESSURE-COOKER HAWAIIAN BREAKFAST HASH

Breakfast is our favorite meal, and we love a wide variety of dishes. This hash brown recipe is full of flavor and possibilities. Top with some eggs or spinach for another twist!
—*Courtney Stultz, Weir, KS*

Prep: **30 min.** • Cook: **5 min.**
Makes: **6 servings**

- 4 bacon strips, chopped
- 1 Tbsp. canola or coconut oil
- 2 large sweet potatoes (about 1½ lbs.), peeled and cut into ½-in. pieces
- 2 cups cubed fresh pineapple (½-in. cubes)
- ½ tsp. salt
- ¼ tsp. chili powder
- ¼ tsp. paprika
- ¼ tsp. pepper
- ⅛ tsp. ground cinnamon

1. Select saute or browning setting on a 6-qt. electric pressure cooker; adjust for medium heat. Add bacon; cook and stir until crisp. Remove with a slotted spoon; drain on paper towels. Discard drippings.
2. Add oil to pressure cooker. When the oil is hot, brown potatoes in batches. Remove from pressure cooker. Add 1 cup water to pressure cooker. Cook 1 minute, stirring to loosen browned bits from the pan. Press cancel. Place steamer basket in pressure cooker.
3. Stir pineapple and seasonings into potatoes; transfer to steamer basket. Lock lid; close pressure release valve. Adjust to pressure-cook on high for 2 minutes. Quick-release pressure. Sprinkle with bacon.
⅔ CUP: 194 cal., 5g fat (1g sat. fat), 6mg chol., 309mg sod., 35g carb. (17g sugars, 4g fiber), 4g pro. **DIABETIC EXCHANGES:** 2 starch, 1 fat.

QUICK CRUNCHY APPLE SALAD

This salad pairs crunchy toppings with smooth vanilla yogurt, creating a combination you'll love!
—*Kathy Armstrong, Post Falls, ID*

- -

Takes: **15 min.** • Makes: **5 servings**

6	Tbsp. vanilla yogurt
6	Tbsp. reduced-fat whipped topping
¼	tsp. plus ⅛ tsp. ground cinnamon, divided
2	medium red apples, chopped
1	large Granny Smith apple, chopped
¼	cup dried cranberries
2	Tbsp. chopped walnuts

In a large bowl, combine yogurt, whipped topping and ¼ tsp. cinnamon. Add apples and cranberries; toss to coat. Refrigerate until serving. Sprinkle with walnuts and remaining cinnamon before serving.

¾ CUP: 116 cal., 3g fat (1g sat. fat), 1mg chol., 13mg sod., 23g carb. (17g sugars, 3g fiber), 2g pro. **DIABETIC EXCHANGES:** 1 fruit, ½ starch, ½ fat.

THE SKINNY

Cinnamon comes in two types, Ceylon and cassia. Ceylon's delicate flavor is ideal for sauces. Bolder cassia (labeled simply as "cinnamon") is usually preferred for baked goods.

KALE SMOOTHIES

I enjoy drinking a kale smoothie for breakfast or even as a healthy after-school snack. The fruit and agave nectar give this healthy version a pleasant sweetness.
—*Kimberly Jackson, Marshfield, MO*

- -

Takes: **15 min.** • Makes: **4 servings**

1	small bunch kale, chopped
1	medium pear, chopped
1	cup frozen sweetened mixed berries
1	medium banana, halved
1	cup unsweetened almond milk
½	cup low-fat vanilla almond milk yogurt
3	Tbsp. agave nectar

In a large bowl, mix kale and fruits. Pour in the almond milk, yogurt and agave nectar; stir to combine. Process in batches in a blender until smooth. Serve immediately or refrigerate.

1 CUP: 184 cal., 3g fat (0 sat. fat), 0 chol., 86mg sod., 40g carb. (23g sugars, 6g fiber), 4g pro.

EGGS FLORENTINE

I wanted to impress my family with a holiday brunch but keep it healthy, too. So I pared down the hollandaise sauce in a classic egg recipe. No one could believe this tasty dish was actually light!
—*Bobbi Trautman, Burns, OR*

Takes: **30 min.** • Makes: **4 servings**

- 2 Tbsp. reduced-fat stick margarine
- 1 Tbsp. all-purpose flour
- ½ tsp. salt, divided
- 1¼ cups fat-free milk
- 1 large egg yolk
- 2 tsp. lemon juice
- ½ tsp. grated lemon zest
- ½ lb. fresh spinach
- ⅛ tsp. pepper
- 4 large eggs
- 2 English muffins, split and toasted
  Dash paprika

1. In a large saucepan, melt the margarine. Stir in flour and ¼ tsp. salt until smooth. Gradually add milk. Bring to a boil; cook and stir until thickened, 1-2 minutes. Remove from the heat.
2. Stir a small amount of sauce into egg yolk; return all to pan, stirring constantly. Bring to a gentle boil; cook and stir for 2 minutes. Remove from the heat; stir in lemon juice and zest. Set aside and keep warm.
3. Place spinach in a steamer basket. Sprinkle with pepper and remaining salt. Place in a saucepan over 1 in. of water. Bring to a boil; cover and steam until wilted and tender, 3-4 minutes.

4. Meanwhile, in a skillet or omelet pan with high sides, bring 2-3 in. of water to a boil. Reduce heat; simmer gently. Break cold eggs, 1 at a time, into a custard cup or saucer. Holding the dish close to the surface of the simmering water, gently slip the eggs, 1 at a time, into the water. Cook, uncovered, until whites are completely set and yolks begin to thicken, 3-5 minutes. Carefully lift cooked eggs out of the water with a slotted spoon.
5. Place spinach on each muffin half; top with an egg. Spoon 3 Tbsp. sauce over each egg. Sprinkle with paprika. Serve immediately.

1 SERVING: 229 cal., 10g fat (3g sat. fat), 267mg chol., 635mg sod., 21g carb. (0 sugars, 2g fiber), 14g pro.
DIABETIC EXCHANGES: 1 starch, 1 lean meat, 1 fat, ½ fat-free milk.

PARTY TIME SNACKS & BEVERAGES

BRIE CHERRY PASTRY CUPS

Golden brown and flaky, these bite-sized puff pastries with creamy Brie and sweet cherry preserves could easily double as a scrumptious dessert.
—*Marilyn McSween, Mentor, OH*

Takes: **30 min.** • Makes: **3 dozen**

- 1 **sheet frozen puff pastry, thawed**
- ½ **cup cherry preserves**
- 4 **oz. Brie cheese, cut into ½-in. cubes**
- ¼ **cup chopped pecans or walnuts**
- 2 **Tbsp. minced chives**

1. Unfold puff pastry; cut into 36 squares. Gently press squares onto the bottoms of 36 greased miniature muffin cups.
2. Bake at 375° for 10 minutes. Using the end of a wooden spoon handle, make a ½-in.-deep indentation in the center of each. Bake until golden brown, 6-8 minutes longer. With spoon handle, press squares down again.
3. Spoon ½ rounded tsp. preserves into each cup. Top with cheese; sprinkle with nuts and chives. Bake until the cheese is melted, 3-5 minutes.
1 APPETIZER: 61 cal., 3g fat (1g sat. fat), 3mg chol., 42mg sod., 7g carb. (3g sugars, 1g fiber), 1g pro.

TASTE OF HOME TALK
"Fast, easy and delicious... I absolutely love it and will make it again! I used olive tapenade for the cherry preserves in one batch and drizzled with a little olive oil. We loved the savory result!"
WAIKAHE, TASTEOFHOME.COM

BLOOMING ONIONS

Instead of being battered and deep-fried, these onions are brushed with melted butter and mustard, sprinkled with bread crumbs and seasonings, and baked. This pretty appetizer tastes as good as it looks!
—*Kendra Doss,*
Colorado Springs, CO

- -

Prep: **20 min.** • Bake: **40 min.**
Makes: **8 servings**

2   large sweet onions
1   Tbsp. butter, melted
2   tsp. Dijon mustard
3   Tbsp. dry bread crumbs
¼   tsp. salt
¼   tsp. pepper
SAUCE
¼   cup fat-free sour cream
¼   cup fat-free mayonnaise
1½   tsp. dried minced onion
¼   tsp. garlic powder
¼   tsp. dill weed

1. Preheat oven to 425°. With a sharp knife, slice ½ in. off the top of the onions; peel onions. Cut each into 16 wedges to within ½ in. of root end.
2. Place each onion on a double thickness of heavy-duty foil (about 12 in. square). Fold foil around onions and seal tightly. Place in an ungreased 11x7-in. baking dish. Bake for 20 minutes.
3. In a small bowl, combine butter and mustard. Open foil. Brush butter mixture over onions; sprinkle with bread crumbs, salt and pepper.
4. Bake onions, leaving foil open, until crisp-tender, 18-22 minutes.

Meanwhile, in a small bowl, combine the sauce ingredients. Serve with the blooming onions.
1 SERVING: 65 cal., 2g fat (1g sat. fat), 6mg chol., 205mg sod., 11g carb. (5g sugars, 1g fiber), 2g pro.
DIABETIC EXCHANGES: 1 vegetable, ½ starch.

THE SKINNY

To freeze, place the baked onion on a tray in the freezer. Once firm, put in a sealed container and keep in the freezer for up to 2-3 months. To reheat, place on a tray with a wire rack and bake at 425° until warm and crispy.

MAKEOVER CREAMY ARTICHOKE DIP

Folks are sure to gather around this ooey-gooey dip whenever it's placed on any buffet table. With mild cheese, spicy jalapenos and a hint of lemon, it's a treasured favorite.
—*Mary Spencer, Greendale, WI*

Prep: **20 min.** • Cook: **1 hour**
Makes: **5 cups**

- 2 **cans (14 oz. each) water-packed artichoke hearts, rinsed, drained and coarsely chopped**
- 1 **pkg. (8 oz.) reduced fat cream cheese, cubed**
- ¾ **cup plain yogurt**
- 1 **cup shredded part-skim mozzarella cheese**
- 1 **cup reduced-fat ricotta cheese**
- ¾ **cup shredded Parmesan cheese, divided**
- ½ **cup shredded reduced-fat Swiss cheese**
- ¼ **cup reduced-fat mayonnaise**
- 2 **Tbsp. lemon juice**
- 1 **Tbsp. chopped seeded jalapeno pepper**
- 1 **tsp. garlic powder**
- 1 **tsp. seasoned salt**
  Tortilla chips

1. In a 3-qt. slow cooker, combine the artichokes, cream cheese, yogurt, mozzarella cheese, ricotta cheese, ½ cup Parmesan cheese, Swiss cheese, mayonnaise, lemon juice, jalapeno, garlic powder and seasoned salt. Cover and cook on low 1 hour or until heated through.

2. Sprinkle with remaining Parmesan cheese. Serve with tortilla chips.
¼ CUP: 104 cal., 6g fat (3g sat. fat), 20mg chol., 348mg sod., 5g carb. (2g sugars, 0 fiber), 7g pro.

MAKE IT YOUR OWN
You can adjust the heat of this dip by either leaving out the jalapenos or by using a hotter pepper, such as a serrano.

SESAME CHICKEN DIP

I can't tell you how many times I'm asked to bring this easy dip to holidays, birthday parties or girls' weekend getaways. It's fresh and light, and the Asian flavors make it stand out. The rice crackers are a must!

—Dawn Schutte, Sheboygan, WI

Prep: **30 min. + chilling**
Makes: **36 servings**

- 2 Tbsp. reduced-sodium soy sauce
- 4 tsp. sesame oil
- 2 garlic cloves, minced
- 4 cups shredded cooked chicken breast
- 3 pkg. (8 oz. each) reduced-fat cream cheese
- 1 jar (10 oz.) sweet-and-sour sauce
- 2 cups chopped fresh baby spinach
- 1 cup thinly sliced green onions (about 8)
- ½ cup chopped salted peanuts
   Sesame rice crackers

1. Mix the soy sauce, sesame oil and garlic; toss with chicken. Refrigerate, covered, at least 1 hour.
2. Spread cream cheese onto a large serving plate; top with sweet-and-sour-sauce, spinach and chicken. Sprinkle with green onions and peanuts. Refrigerate, covered, at least 2 hours. Serve with crackers.
¼ CUP: 97 cal., 6g fat (3g sat. fat), 25mg chol., 176mg sod., 4g carb. (2g sugars, 0 fiber), 7g pro.

SLOW-COOKER CHAI TEA

A wonderful sweet and spicy aroma wafts from the slow cooker as this pleasantly flavored chai tea cooks.
—Crystal Jo Bruns, Iliff, CO

Prep: **20 min.** • Cook: **8 hours**
Makes: **12 servings (3 qt.)**

- 15 slices fresh gingerroot (about 3 oz.)
- 3 cinnamon sticks (3 in.)
- 25 whole cloves
- 15 cardamom pods, lightly crushed
- 3 whole peppercorns
- 3½ qt. water
- 8 black tea bags
- 1 can (14 oz.) sweetened condensed milk

1. Place first 5 ingredients on a double thickness of cheesecloth.

Gather corners of cloth to enclose seasonings; tie securely with string. Place spice bag and water in a 5- or 6-qt. slow cooker. Cook, covered, on low 8 hours. Discard spice bag.
2. Add tea bags; steep, covered, for 3-5 minutes according to taste. Discard tea bags. Stir in milk; heat through. Serve warm.
1 CUP: 109 cal., 3g fat (2g sat. fat), 11mg chol., 50mg sod., 19g carb. (18g sugars, 0 fiber), 3g pro.

TYPICAL	MAKEOVER
223 Calories	**109** Calories
6g Fat	**3**g Fat
39g Carbohydrates	**19**g Carbohydrates
37g Sugars	**18**g Sugars

CHICKEN SALAD PARTY SANDWICHES

My famous chicken salad arrives at the party chilled in a container. When it's time to set out the food, I stir in the pecans and assemble the sandwiches. They're a hit at buffet-style potlucks.
—*Trisha Kruse, Eagle, ID*

Takes: **25 min.** • Makes: **16 servings**

- 4 cups cubed cooked chicken breast
- 1½ cups dried cranberries
- 2 celery ribs, finely chopped
- 2 green onions, thinly sliced
- ¼ cup chopped sweet pickles
- 1 cup fat-free mayonnaise
- ½ tsp. curry powder
- ¼ tsp. coarsely ground pepper
- ½ cup chopped pecans, toasted
- 16 whole wheat dinner rolls
  Leaf lettuce

1. In a large bowl, combine first 5 ingredients. Mix mayonnaise, curry powder and pepper; stir into chicken mixture. Refrigerate until serving.
2. To serve, stir in pecans. Spoon onto lettuce-lined rolls.

1 SANDWICH: 235 cal., 6g fat (1g sat. fat), 30mg chol., 361mg sod., 33g carb. (13g sugars, 4g fiber), 14g pro.

MAKEOVER DEVILED EGGS

This updated version of a classic appetizer uses only half the egg yolks of the original recipe and calls for soft bread crumbs to help firm up the filling. We replaced the mayo with fat-free mayonnaise and reduced-fat sour cream.
—*Taste of Home Test Kitchen*

Takes: **10 min.** • Makes: **16 servings**

- 8 hard-boiled large eggs
- ¼ cup fat-free mayonnaise
- ¼ cup reduced-fat sour cream
- 2 Tbsp. soft bread crumbs
- 1 Tbsp. prepared mustard
- ¼ tsp. salt
  Dash white pepper
- 4 pimiento-stuffed olives, sliced
  Paprika, optional

Slice eggs in half lengthwise and remove yolks; refrigerate 8 yolk halves for another use. Set whites aside. In a small bowl, mash the remaining yolks. Stir in mayonnaise, sour cream, bread crumbs, mustard, salt and pepper. Stuff or pipe into egg whites. Garnish with olives. If desired, sprinkle with paprika.

1 STUFFED EGG HALF: 62 cal., 4g fat (1g sat. fat), 140mg chol., 135mg sod., 2g carb. (1g sugars, 0 fiber), 4g pro. **DIABETIC EXCHANGES:** ½ medium-fat meat.

MAKE IT YOUR OWN
If you want to give these eggs a little zip, add a favorite sauce!
- Horseradish
- Prepared salsa
- Chipotle or Sriracha sauce

BUFFALO CHICKEN MEATBALLS

I like to make these game-day appetizer meatballs with blue cheese or ranch dressing for dipping. If I'm making them for a meal, I'll skip the dressing and serve them with blue cheese polenta on the side.
—*Amber Massey, Argyle, TX*

Prep: **15 min.** • Bake: **20 min.**
Makes: **2 dozen**

- ¾ cup panko bread crumbs
- ⅓ cup plus ½ cup Louisiana-style hot sauce, divided
- ¼ cup chopped celery
- 1 large egg white
- 1 lb. lean ground chicken
  Optional: Reduced-fat ranch salad dressing or reduced-fat blue cheese salad dressing and chopped celery leaves

1. Preheat oven to 400°. In a large bowl, combine bread crumbs, ⅓ cup hot sauce, celery and egg white. Add chicken; mix lightly but thoroughly.
2. Shape into twenty-four 1-in. balls. Place on a greased rack in a shallow baking pan. Bake 20-25 minutes or until cooked through.
3. Toss meatballs with the remaining ½ cup hot sauce. If desired, drizzle with salad dressing and sprinkle with celery leaves.
1 MEATBALL: 35 cal., 1g fat (0 sat. fat), 14mg chol., 24mg sod., 2g carb. (0 sugars, 0 fiber), 4g pro.

CRANBERRY POMEGRANATE MARGARITAS

I came up with this festive twist on the traditional margarita to serve at holiday celebrations. It's light and refreshing, and it looks beautiful with sugar crystals on glass rims.
—*Mindie Hilton, Susanville, CA*

Takes: **5 min.** • Makes: **12 servings**

- 4½ cups diet lemon-lime soda, chilled
- 1½ cups tequila
- 1½ cups cranberry juice, chilled
- 1½ cups pomegranate juice, chilled
  Optional: Pomegranate seeds and frozen cranberries

In a pitcher, combine the soda, tequila and juices. Serve in chilled glasses. Garnish with pomegranate and cranberries if desired.
¾ CUP: 97 cal., 0 fat (0 sat. fat), 0 chol., 13mg sod., 8g carb. (8g sugars, 0 fiber), 0 pro.

GARLIC PUMPKIN SEEDS

What to do with all those leftover pumpkin seeds after carving your jack-o'-lantern? Try this yummy microwave-easy recipe. It works great with butternut or acorn squash seeds, too.

—*Iola Egle, Bella Vista, AR*

Takes: **25 min.** • Makes: **2 cups**

- 1 **Tbsp. canola oil**
- ½ **tsp. celery salt**
- ½ **tsp. garlic powder**
- ½ **tsp. seasoned salt**
- 2 **cups fresh pumpkin seeds**

1. In a small bowl, combine the oil, celery salt, garlic powder and seasoned salt. Add pumpkin seeds; toss to coat.

2. Spread a quarter of the seeds in a single layer on a microwave-safe plate. Microwave, uncovered, on high for 1 minute; stir.

3. Microwave 2-3 minutes longer or until seeds are crunchy and lightly browned, stirring after each minute. Repeat with remaining pumpkin seeds. Serve warm, or cool before storing in an airtight container.

¼ CUP: 87 cal., 5g fat (1g sat. fat), 0 chol., 191mg sod., 9g carb. (0 sugars, 1g fiber), 3g pro.
DIABETIC EXCHANGES: 1 fat, ½ starch.

PRESSURE-COOKER MARINATED MUSHROOMS

Here's a terrific healthy addition to any buffet. Mushrooms and pearl onions seasoned with herbs, balsamic vinegar and red wine are fantastic on their own or alongside a tenderloin roast.

—*Courtney Wilson, Fresno, CA*

Takes: **20 min.** • Makes: **5 cups**

- 2 **lbs. medium fresh mushrooms**
- 1 **pkg. (14.4 oz.) frozen pearl onions**
- 4 **garlic cloves, minced**
- ¾ **cup reduced-sodium beef broth**
- ¼ **cup dry red wine**
- 3 **Tbsp. balsamic vinegar**
- 3 **Tbsp. olive oil**
- 1 **tsp. salt**
- 1 **tsp. dried basil**
- ½ **tsp. dried thyme**
- ½ **tsp. pepper**
- ¼ **tsp. crushed red pepper flakes**

Place mushrooms, onions and garlic in a 6-qt. electric pressure cooker. In a small bowl, whisk the remaining ingredients; pour over mushrooms. Lock lid; close pressure-release valve. Adjust to pressure-cook on high for 4 minutes. Quick-release pressure.

¼ CUP: 43 cal., 2g fat (0 sat. fat), 0 chol., 138mg sod., 4g carb. (2g sugars, 0 fiber), 1g pro.

THE SKINNY

To use a slow cooker, use 2 cups broth and ½ cup wine; cook, covered, on low until mushrooms are tender, 6-8 hours.

1. Preheat air fryer to 325°. In a small skillet, cook and crumble beef over medium heat until no longer pink, 4-5 minutes. Transfer to a large bowl. In the same skillet, heat butter and olive oil over medium-high heat. Add garlic and shallot; cook for 1 minute. Stir in mushrooms and wine. Cook until mushrooms are tender, 8-10 minutes; add to beef. Stir in parsley, salt and pepper.

2. Place about 2 tsp. filling in the center of each wonton wrapper. Combine egg and water. Moisten wonton edges with egg mixture; fold opposite corners over filling and press to seal.

3. In batches, arrange the wontons in a single layer on greased tray in air-fryer basket; spritz with cooking spray. Cook until lightly browned, 4-5 minutes. Turn; spritz with cooking spray. Cook until golden brown and crisp, 4-5 minutes longer. Serve warm.

FREEZE OPTION: Cover and freeze unbaked wontons on parchment-lined baking sheets until firm. Transfer to freezer containers; return to freezer. To use, cook pastries as directed.

1 WONTON: 42 cal., 1g fat (0 sat. fat), 9mg chol., 82mg sod., 5g carb. (0 sugars, 0 fiber), 2g pro.

BEEF WELLINGTON AIR-FRIED WONTONS

These tasty appetizers scale down classic beef Wellington to an ideal party size. They feel fancy and fun!
—*Dianne Phillips, Tallapoosa, GA*

Prep: **35 min.** • Cook: **10 min./batch**
Makes: **3½ dozen**

- ½ lb. lean ground beef (90% lean)
- 1 Tbsp. butter
- 1 Tbsp. olive oil
- 2 garlic cloves, minced
- 1½ tsp. chopped shallot
- 1 cup each chopped fresh shiitake, baby portobello and white mushrooms
- ¼ cup dry red wine
- 1 Tbsp. minced fresh parsley
- ½ tsp. salt
- ¼ tsp. pepper
- 1 pkg. (12 oz.) wonton wrappers
- 1 large egg
- 1 Tbsp. water
- Cooking spray

THE SKINNY
If you don't have an air fryer, you can also make this recipe in a deep fryer, electric skillet or on the stovetop.

CLASSIC SWEDISH MEATBALLS

I'm a *Svenska flicka* (Swedish girl) from northwest Iowa, where many Swedes settled at the turn of the century. This recipe was given to me by a Swedish friend. It's obviously a 20th-century version of a 19th-century favorite, since back then they didn't have bouillon cubes or evaporated milk! These modern-day *kottbullar* are very tasty.
—*Emily Gould, Hawarden, IA*

Prep: **15 min. + chilling**
Cook: **20 min.** • Makes: **3½ dozen**

- 1⅔ cups evaporated milk, divided
- ⅔ cup chopped onion
- ¼ cup fine dry bread crumbs
- ½ tsp. salt
- ½ tsp. allspice
  Dash pepper
- 1 lb. lean ground beef (90% lean)
- 2 tsp. butter
- 2 tsp. beef bouillon granules
- 1 cup boiling water
- ½ cup cold water
- 2 Tbsp. all-purpose flour
- 1 Tbsp. lemon juice
  Canned lingonberries, optional

1. Combine ⅔ cup evaporated milk with the next 5 ingredients. Add beef; mix lightly but thoroughly. Refrigerate until chilled.
2. With wet hands, shape the meat mixture into 1-in. balls. In a large skillet, heat butter over medium heat. Brown meatballs in batches. Dissolve bouillon in boiling water. Pour over meatballs; bring to a boil. Cover; simmer 15 minutes.

3. Meanwhile, stir together cold water and flour. Remove meatballs from skillet; skim fat, reserving juices. Add the flour mixture and remaining 1 cup evaporated milk to the pan juices; cook, uncovered, over low heat, stirring until sauce thickens.

4. Return meatballs to skillet. Stir in lemon juice. If desired, top with lingonberries.
1 MEATBALL: 36 cal., 2g fat (1g sat. fat), 10mg chol., 87mg sod., 2g carb. (1g sugars, 0 fiber), 3g pro.

THE SKINNY

Don't skip seeding the cucumber. If you do, you may end up with watery salsa. To make seeding a breeze, halve cucumbers lengthwise and use a spoon to scoop out the pulpy centers. This salsa is a stellar topping for simple grilled salmon.

CRISP CUCUMBER SALSA

Here's a fantastic way to use cucumbers. You'll love the creamy and crunchy texture and super fresh summery flavors.

—*Charlene Skjerven, Hoople, ND*

Takes: **20 min.** • Makes: **2½ cups**

- 2 cups finely chopped cucumber, peeled and seeded
- ½ cup finely chopped seeded tomato
- ¼ cup chopped red onion
- 2 Tbsp. minced fresh parsley
- 1 jalapeno pepper, seeded and chopped
- 4½ tsp. minced fresh cilantro
- 1 garlic clove, minced
- ¼ cup reduced-fat sour cream
- 1½ tsp. lemon juice
- 1½ tsp. lime juice
- ¼ tsp. ground cumin
- ¼ tsp. seasoned salt
  Baked tortilla chip scoops

In a small bowl, combine the first 7 ingredients. In another bowl, combine the sour cream, lemon juice, lime juice, cumin and seasoned salt. Pour over cucumber mixture and toss gently to coat. Serve immediately with chips.

¼ CUP: 16 cal., 1g fat (0 sat. fat), 2mg chol., 44mg sod., 2g carb. (1g sugars, 0 fiber), 1g pro. **DIABETIC EXCHANGES:** 1 free food.

ROASTED EGGPLANT SPREAD

Black pepper and garlic perk up this out-of-the-ordinary spread that hits the spot on a crisp cracker or toasted bread slice.

—*Barbara McCalley, Allison Park, PA*

Prep: **20 min. + cooling**
Bake: **45 min.** • Makes: **2 cups**

- 3 Tbsp. olive oil
- 3 garlic cloves, minced
- ½ tsp. salt
- ½ tsp. pepper
- 2 large sweet red peppers, cut into 1-in. pieces
- 1 medium eggplant, cut into 1-in. pieces
- 1 medium red onion, cut into 1-in. pieces
- 1 Tbsp. tomato paste
  Toasted baguette slices or assorted crackers

1. Preheat oven to 400°. Mix the first 4 ingredients. Place vegetables in a large bowl; toss with the oil mixture. Transfer to a 15x10x1-in. pan coated with cooking spray. Roast vegetables until softened and lightly browned, 45-50 minutes, stirring once.

2. Transfer to a food processor; cool slightly. Add the tomato paste; pulse just until blended (mixture should be chunky).

3. Transfer to a bowl; let cool completely. Serve with baguette slices or crackers.

¼ CUP SPREAD: 84 cal., 5g fat (1g sat. fat), 0 chol., 153mg sod., 9g carb. (5g sugars, 3g fiber), 1g pro. **DIABETIC EXCHANGES:** 1 vegetable, 1 fat.

TEX-MEX POPCORN

Spicy southwestern seasoning makes this snackin' good popcorn ideal for any fiesta.
—*Katie Rose, Pewaukee, WI*

Takes: **15 min.** • Makes: **4 qt.**

- ½ cup popcorn kernels
- 3 Tbsp. canola oil
- ½ tsp. cumin seeds
  Refrigerated butter-flavored spray
- ¼ cup minced fresh cilantro
- 1 tsp. salt
- 1 tsp. chili powder
- ½ tsp. garlic powder
- ⅛ tsp. smoked paprika

1. In a Dutch oven over medium heat, cook the popcorn kernels, oil and cumin seeds until the oil begins to sizzle. Cover and shake for 2-3 minutes or until popcorn stops popping.

2. Transfer to a large bowl; spritz with butter-flavored spray. Add remaining ingredients and toss to coat. Continue spritzing and tossing until popcorn is coated.

1 CUP: 44 cal., 3g fat (0 sat. fat), 0 chol., 150mg sod., 5g carb. (0 sugars, 1g fiber), 1g pro. **DIABETIC EXCHANGES:** ½ starch, ½ fat.

HEALTHY PARTY SNACK MIX

Party mix has always been a tradition in our home. I lightened my mom's classic recipe, replacing margarine with heart-healthy olive oil. No one even noticed!
—*Melissa Hansen, Ellison Bay, WI*

Prep: **15 min.**
Bake: **1 hour + cooling**
Makes: **3½ qt.**

- 3 cups Corn Chex
- 3 cups Rice Chex
- 3 cups Wheat Chex
- 3 cups Multi Grain Cheerios
- 1 cup salted peanuts
- 1½ cups pretzel sticks
- ⅓ cup olive oil
- 4 tsp. Worcestershire sauce
- 1 tsp. seasoned salt
- ⅛ tsp. garlic powder

1. In a large bowl, combine the cereals, peanuts and pretzels. In a small bowl, combine the remaining ingredients; pour over cereal mixture and toss to coat.

2. Transfer to two 15x10x1-in. baking pans coated with cooking spray. Bake at 250° for 1 hour, stirring every 15 minutes. Cool completely in pans on wire racks. Store in an airtight container.

¾ CUP: 150 cal., 8g fat (1g sat. fat), 0 chol., 310mg sod., 19g carb. (3g sugars, 2g fiber), 4g pro. **DIABETIC EXCHANGES:** 1½ starch, 1½ fat.

ICED MELON MOROCCAN MINT TEA

I grow mint on my balcony, and this refreshing beverage is a wonderful way to use it. It combines two of my favorite drinks—Moroccan Mint Tea and Honeydew Agua Fresca. For extra flair, add some ginger ale.
—*Sarah Batt Throne, El Cerrito, CA*

Takes: **20 min.** • Makes: **5 servings**

- 2 **cups water**
- 12 **fresh mint leaves**
- 4 **individual green tea bags**
- ⅓ **cup sugar**
- 2½ **cups diced honeydew melon**
- 1½ **cups ice cubes**
  Additional ice cubes

1. In a large saucepan, bring water to a boil. Remove from the heat; add mint and tea bags. Cover and steep for 3-5 minutes. Discard mint and tea bags. Stir in the sugar.
2. In a blender, process honeydew until blended. Add 1½ cups ice and tea; process until blended. Serve over additional ice.
1 CUP: 81 cal., 0 fat (0 sat. fat), 0 chol., 9mg sod., 21g carb. (21g sugars, 1g fiber), 0 pro. **DIABETIC EXCHANGES:** 1 starch.

SPINACH DIP-STUFFED MUSHROOMS

I use a melon baller to hollow out the mushroom caps and make them easier to stuff. The apps fit neatly into muffin tins or a deviled egg tray for traveling.
—*Ashley Pierce, Brantford, ON*

Prep: **25 min.** • Bake: **15 min.**
Makes: **16 appetizers**

- 16 **large fresh mushrooms (about 1½ lbs.)**
- 1 **Tbsp. olive oil**
- 2 **cups fresh baby spinach, coarsely chopped**
- 2 **garlic cloves, minced**
- ½ **cup reduced-fat sour cream**
- 3 **oz. reduced-fat cream cheese**
- ⅓ **cup shredded part-skim mozzarella cheese**
- 3 **Tbsp. grated Parmesan cheese**
- ¼ **tsp. salt**
- ¼ **tsp. cayenne pepper**
- ¼ **tsp. pepper**

1. Preheat oven to 400°. Remove stems from the mushrooms and set caps aside; discard stems or save for another use. In a small skillet, heat olive oil over medium heat. Add spinach; saute until wilted. Add garlic; cook 1 minute longer.
2. Combine spinach mixture with remaining ingredients. Stuff into the mushroom caps. Place in a 15x10x1-in. baking pan coated with cooking spray. Bake, uncovered, until the mushrooms are tender, 12-15 minutes. Serve warm.
1 STUFFED MUSHROOM: 44 cal., 3g fat (2g sat. fat), 9mg chol., 100mg sod., 1g carb. (1g sugars, 0 fiber), 2g pro.

BAKED EGG ROLLS

These egg rolls are low in fat but the crispiness from baking will fool you into thinking they are fried!
—*Barbara Lierman, Lyons, NE*

Prep: **30 min.** • Bake: **10 min.**
Makes: **16 servings**

2	**cups grated carrots**
1	**can (14 oz.) bean sprouts, drained**
½	**cup chopped water chestnuts**
¼	**cup chopped green pepper**
¼	**cup chopped green onions**
1	**garlic clove, minced**
2	**cups finely diced cooked chicken**
4	**tsp. cornstarch**
1	**Tbsp. water**
1	**Tbsp. light soy sauce**
1	**tsp. canola oil**
1	**tsp. brown sugar**
	Pinch cayenne pepper
16	**egg roll wrappers**
	Cooking spray

1. Preheat oven to 425°. Heat a large skillet coated with cooking spray over medium heat. Add first 6 ingredients; cook and stir until vegetables are crisp-tender, about 3 minutes. Add chicken; heat through.
2. Combine the cornstarch, water, soy sauce, oil, brown sugar and cayenne until smooth; stir into the chicken mixture. Bring to a boil. Cook and stir for 2 minutes or until thickened; remove from heat.
3. Spoon ¼ cup chicken mixture on the bottom third of 1 egg roll wrapper; fold sides toward center and roll tightly. (Keep remaining wrappers covered with a damp paper towel until ready to use.)

Place seam side down on a baking sheet coated with cooking spray. Repeat steps.
4. Spritz tops of egg rolls with cooking spray. Bake 10-15 minutes or until lightly browned.
FREEZE OPTION: Freeze cooled egg rolls in a freezer container, separating layers with waxed paper. To use, reheat rolls on a baking sheet in a preheated 350° oven until crisp and heated through.
1 EGG ROLL: 146 cal., 2g fat (0 sat. fat), 18mg chol., 250mg sod., 22g carb. (1g sugars, 1g fiber), 9g pro.
DIABETIC EXCHANGES: 1½ starch, 1 lean meat, ½ fat.

THE SKINNY

To make a pork version of these egg rolls, thaw and chop 1 lb. frozen stir-fry vegetable blend; cook in a large skillet with 1 lb. bulk pork sausage until meat is no longer pink. Stir in 2 Tbsp. teriyaki sauce. Fill and bake the egg rolls as directed.

HEALTHY GREEK BEAN DIP

This crowd-pleasing appetizer is healthy to boot! Folks will love to eat their veggies when they can dip them in this zesty, fresh alternative to hummus.
—*Kelly Silvers, Edmond, OK*

Prep: **15 min.** • Cook: **2 hours**
Makes: **3 cups**

- 2 **cans (15 oz. each) cannellini beans, rinsed and drained**
- ¼ **cup water**
- ¼ **cup finely chopped roasted sweet red peppers**
- 2 **Tbsp. finely chopped red onion**
- 2 **Tbsp. olive oil**
- 2 **Tbsp. lemon juice**
- 1 **Tbsp. snipped fresh dill**
- 2 **garlic cloves, minced**
- ¼ **tsp. salt**
- ¼ **tsp. pepper**
- 1 **small cucumber, peeled, seeded and finely chopped**
- ½ **cup fat-free plain Greek yogurt**
  Additional snipped fresh dill
  Baked pita chips or assorted fresh vegetables

1. Process beans and water in a food processor until smooth. Transfer to a greased 1½-qt. slow cooker. Add the next 8 ingredients. Cook, covered, on low until heated through, 2-3 hours.
2. Stir in cucumber and yogurt; cool slightly. Sprinkle with additional dill. Serve warm or cold with chips or assorted fresh vegetables.

FREEZE OPTION: Omitting cucumber, yogurt and additional dill, freeze cooled dip in freezer containers. To use, thaw in refrigerator overnight. Serve cold or heat in a saucepan, stirring occasionally. Stir cucumber and yogurt into finished dip; sprinkle with additional dill.

¼ CUP: 86 cal., 3g fat (0 sat. fat), 0 chol., 260mg sod., 11g carb. (1g sugars, 3g fiber), 4g pro.
DIABETIC EXCHANGES: 1 starch, ½ fat.

WATERMELON CUPS

This lovely appetizer is almost too pretty to eat! Sweet watermelon cubes hold a refreshing topping that showcases cucumber, red onion and fresh herbs.
—Taste of Home *Test Kitchen*

- -

Takes: **25 min.**
Makes: **16 appetizers**

　16　seedless watermelon cubes
　　　 (1 in.)
　⅓　cup finely chopped cucumber
　5　tsp. finely chopped red onion
　2　tsp. minced fresh mint
　2　tsp. minced fresh cilantro
　½　to 1 tsp. lime juice

1. Using a small melon baller or measuring spoon, scoop out the center of each watermelon cube, leaving a ¼-in. shell (save centers for another use).
2. In a small bowl, combine the remaining ingredients; spoon into watermelon cubes.

1 APPETIZER: 7 cal., 0 fat (0 sat. fat), 0 chol., 1mg sod., 2g carb. (2g sugars, 0 fiber), 0 pro.

MAKE IT YOUR OWN

Try using a different melon for the shell, or other summery fillings! You can also use different herbs—try tarragon or basil instead of cilantro.
- Mango
- Peaches or nectarines
- Avocado
- Sweet onions

THE SKINNY

To make turmeric tea, combine ½ cup milk, 1 tsp. turmeric, ½ tsp. ginger (ground spice or grated fresh gingerroot), ½ tsp. cinnamon, a dash of pepper, and 1 tsp. honey in a small saucepan. Bring to a boil, then lower the heat to a simmer. Cook until the milk is a uniform golden color, about 10 minutes. Strain into a mug.

LEMON, GINGER & TURMERIC INFUSED WATER

This refreshing infused water is a fantastic pick-me-up when you feel the need for a little health boost. Turmeric is commonly used in Indian cuisines, and studies indicate it's chock-full of antioxidants.
—Taste of Home *Test Kitchen*

Prep: **5 min. + chilling**
Makes: **2 cups**

1 Tbsp. ground turmeric
4 slices fresh gingerroot
½ lemon, sliced
2 qt. water

Combine all ingredients in a large glass carafe or pitcher. Cover and refrigerate for 12–24 hours.

COMFORTING SOUPS & CHILI

LENTIL-TOMATO SOUP

Double the recipe and share this fabulous soup with friends and neighbors on cold winter nights. I like to serve it with warm cornbread for dunking.
—*Michelle Curtis, Baker City, OR*

- -

Prep: **15 min.** • Cook: **30 min.**
Makes: **6 servings**

- 4½ cups water
- 4 medium carrots, sliced
- 1 medium onion, chopped
- ⅔ cup dried brown lentils, rinsed
- 1 can (6 oz.) tomato paste
- 2 Tbsp. minced fresh parsley
- 1 Tbsp. brown sugar
- 1 Tbsp. white vinegar
- 1 tsp. garlic salt
- ½ tsp. dried thyme
- ¼ tsp. dill weed
- ¼ tsp. dried tarragon
- ¼ tsp. pepper

In a large saucepan, combine the water, carrots, onion and lentils; bring to a boil. Reduce heat; cover pan and simmer for 20-25 minutes or until the vegetables and lentils are tender. Stir in the remaining ingredients; return to a boil. Reduce heat; simmer, uncovered, for 5 minutes to allow flavors to blend.

¾ CUP: 138 cal., 0 fat (0 sat. fat), 0 chol., 351mg sod., 27g carb. (9g sugars, 9g fiber), 8g pro. **DIABETIC EXCHANGES:** 1 starch, 1 vegetable, 1 lean meat.

FOR SAUSAGE VARIATION: Stir in ½ lb. chopped fully cooked turkey sausage; heat through.

FOR KALE VARIATION: Stir in 3 cups chopped fresh kale; cook, uncovered, until kale is tender.

FOR SPICED VARIATION: Add ¾ tsp. garam masala when adding the other seasonings.

PRESSURE-COOKER CORN CHOWDER

Enjoy this chowder's rich, slow-simmered flavor in record time by using an electric pressure cooker. Corn chowder is a classic, with its hearty flavors of sweet corn, bacon, cheese and chopped parsley.
—Taste of Home *Test Kitchen*

- -

Takes: **30 min.**
Makes: **8 servings (2 qt.)**

- 4   medium red potatoes, peeled and cut into ½-in. cubes (about 2½ cups)
- 2   cans (14½ oz. each) chicken broth
- 3   cups fresh or frozen corn
- 1   medium onion, chopped
- 3   garlic cloves, minced
- ½   tsp. salt
- ½   tsp. pepper
- 2   Tbsp. cornstarch
- 1   cup half-and-half cream
- 1   cup shredded cheddar cheese
- 6   bacon strips, cooked and crumbled
     Chopped fresh parsley

1. Place the first 7 ingredients in a 6-qt. electric pressure cooker. Lock lid; close pressure-release valve. Adjust to pressure-cook on high for 15 minutes. Quick-release pressure.
2. Select saute setting and adjust for low heat. Mix the cornstarch and cream until smooth; stir into soup. Cook and stir until slightly thickened, 6-8 minutes. Stir in the cheese and bacon. Heat through until cheese is melted. Press cancel. Sprinkle servings with parsley and, if desired, additional cheese and bacon.

1 CUP: 191 cal., 9g fat (5g sat. fat), 31mg chol., 709mg sod., 21g carb. (5g sugars, 2g fiber), 7g pro.
DIABETIC EXCHANGES: 1½ starch, 1 medium-fat meat, ½ fat.

THE SKINNY

Corn chowders that have a cream base, like this version, are freezable. However, freezing cream-based soups can change the texture. So if you're planning to save your soup for later, hold off on adding the cream until the soup has defrosted.

AUTUMN BISQUE

I like cozy comfort soups that taste creamy—without the cream. This one is full of healthy good stuff like rutabagas, leeks, fresh herbs and almond milk.

—*Merry Graham, Newhall, CA*

Prep: **25 min.** • Cook: **50 min.**
Makes: **12 servings (3 qt.)**

- ¼ cup dairy-free spreadable margarine
- 2 tsp. minced fresh chives
- 2 tsp. minced fresh parsley
- ½ tsp. grated lemon zest

BISQUE

- 2 Tbsp. olive oil
- 2 large rutabagas, peeled and cubed (about 9 cups)
- 1 large celery root, peeled and cubed (about 3 cups)
- 3 medium leeks (white portion only), chopped (about 2 cups)
- 1 large carrot, cubed (about ⅔ cup)
- 3 garlic cloves, minced
- 7 cups vegetable stock
- 2 tsp. minced fresh thyme
- 1½ tsp. minced fresh rosemary
- 1 tsp. salt
- ½ tsp. coarsely ground pepper
- 2 cups almond milk
- 2 Tbsp. minced fresh chives

1. Mix first 4 ingredients. Using a melon baller or 1-tsp. measuring spoon, shape mixture into 12 balls. Freeze on a waxed paper-lined baking sheet until firm. Transfer to a freezer container; freeze up to 2 months.

2. In a 6-qt. stock pot, heat oil over medium heat; saute the rutabagas, celery root, leeks and carrot for 8 minutes. Add the garlic; cook and stir for 2 minutes. Stir in the stock, herbs, salt and pepper; bring to a boil. Reduce the heat; simmer, covered, until the vegetables are tender, 30-35 minutes.

3. Puree soup using an immersion blender. Or cool slightly and puree in batches in a blender; return to pan. Stir in milk; heat through. Remove herbed margarine from freezer 15 minutes before serving. Top servings with chives and margarine.

1 CUP: 146 cal., 7g fat (2g sat. fat), 0 chol., 672mg sod., 20g carb. (9g sugars, 5g fiber), 3g pro. **DIABETIC EXCHANGES:** 1 starch, 1 fat.

THE SKINNY
Want an extra creamy soup? Just before serving, stir in ½ to 1 cup of coconut milk.

CARROT GINGER SOUP

This light, flavorful carrot ginger soup is vegan! It's made with pantry staples and comes together in a hurry, yet always impresses. Fresh ginger makes a big difference—and what isn't used can be wrapped tightly and tossed in the freezer to use later.
—Jenna Olson, Manchester, MO

Takes: **30 min.** • Makes: **4 servings**

- 1 Tbsp. olive oil
- 1 small onion, chopped
- 1 garlic clove, minced
- 3 tsp. minced fresh gingerroot
- 4 large carrots, peeled and chopped
- 3 cups vegetable broth
- 2 tsp. grated lemon zest
- ½ tsp. salt
- ¼ tsp. ground black pepper
- 2 Tbsp. fresh lemon juice
  Additional lemon zest, optional

In a Dutch oven or stockpot, heat oil over medium heat. Add onion; cook and stir until tender, 4-5 minutes. Add garlic and ginger; cook 1 minute longer. Stir in carrots, broth, lemon zest, salt and pepper; bring to a boil. Reduce heat; simmer, covered, until carrots are tender, 10-12 minutes. Pulse mixture in a blender or with an immersion blender to desired consistency; stir in lemon juice. If desired, garnish with additional lemon zest.

FREEZE OPTION: Cool prepared soup; freeze in freezer containers. To use, partially thaw in refrigerator overnight. Heat through in a large saucepan over medium-low heat, stirring occasionally; add broth or water if necessary.

¾ CUP: 80 cal., 4g fat (1g sat. fat), 0 chol., 551mg sod., 11g carb. (5g sugars, 2g fiber), 1g pro. **DIABETIC EXCHANGES:** 2 vegetable, 1 fat.

SPICY CHICKEN TOMATO SOUP

Cumin, chili powder and cayenne pepper give my tasty slow-cooked specialty its kick. I serve bowls of it with crunchy tortilla strips that bake in no time. Leftover soup freezes well for busy nights when I don't have time to cook.
—Margaret Bailey, Coffeeville, MS

Prep: **20 min.** • Cook: **4 hours**
Makes: **8 servings**

- 2 cans (14½ oz. each) chicken broth
- 3 cups cubed cooked chicken
- 2 cups frozen corn
- 1 can (10¾ oz.) tomato puree
- 1 can (10 oz.) diced tomatoes and green chiles
- 1 large onion, finely chopped
- 2 garlic cloves, minced
- 1 bay leaf
- 1 to 2 tsp. ground cumin
- ½ tsp. salt
- ½ to 1 tsp. chili powder
- ⅛ tsp. pepper
- ⅛ tsp. cayenne pepper
- 4 white or yellow corn tortillas (6 in.), cut into ¼-in. strips

1. In a 5-qt. slow cooker, combine the first 13 ingredients. Cover and cook on low for 4 hours.

2. Place the tortilla strips on an ungreased baking sheet. Bake at 375° for 5 minutes; turn. Bake 5 minutes longer. Discard bay leaf from soup. Serve with tortilla strips.

1 SERVING: 196 cal., 5g fat (1g sat. fat), 49mg chol., 800mg sod., 19g carb. (3g sugars, 3g fiber), 19g pro.

JUMPIN' ESPRESSO BEAN CHILI

I love experimenting with chili and creating different takes on the classic hearty dish. This meatless version is low in fat but high in flavor. Everyone tries to guess the secret ingredient, but no one ever thinks it's coffee!

—Jess Apfe, Berkeley, CA

Prep: **15 min.** • Cook: **35 min.**
Makes: **7 servings**

- 3 **medium onions, chopped**
- 2 **Tbsp. olive oil**
- 2 **Tbsp. brown sugar**
- 2 **Tbsp. chili powder**
- 2 **Tbsp. ground cumin**
- 1 **Tbsp. instant espresso powder or instant coffee granules**
- 1 **Tbsp. baking cocoa**
- ¾ **tsp. salt**
- 2 **cans (14½ oz. each) no-salt-added diced tomatoes**
- 1 **can (15 oz.) black beans, rinsed and drained**
- 1 **can (15 oz.) kidney beans, rinsed and drained**
- 1 **can (15 oz.) garbanzo beans or chickpeas, rinsed and drained**
  Optional toppings: Sour cream, thinly sliced green onions, shredded cheddar cheese and pickled jalapeno slices

1. In a Dutch oven, saute the onions in oil until tender. Add the brown sugar, chili powder, cumin, espresso powder, cocoa and salt; cook and stir for 1 minute.

2. Stir in tomatoes and beans. Bring to a boil. Reduce heat; cover and simmer for 30 minutes to allow flavors to blend. If desired, serve with sour cream, onions, cheese and jalapeno slices.

1 CUP: 272 cal., 6g fat (1g sat. fat), 0 chol., 620mg sod., 45g carb. (14g sugars, 12g fiber), 12g pro. **DIABETIC EXCHANGES:** 2½ starch, 2 vegetable, 1 lean meat.

30-MINUTE CHICKEN NOODLE SOUP

This great soup is perfect for a cold, wintry day. It is my favorite thing to eat when I'm under the weather; it makes me feel so much better.

—Lacey Waadt, Payson, UT

Takes: **30 min.**
Makes: **6 servings (2¼ qt.)**

- 4 **cups water**
- 1 **can (14½ oz.) chicken broth**
- 1½ **cups cubed cooked chicken breast**
- 1 **can (10¾ oz.) condensed cream of chicken soup, undiluted**
- ¾ **cup sliced celery**
- ¾ **cup sliced carrots**
- 1 **small onion, chopped**
- 1½ **tsp. dried parsley flakes**
- 1 **tsp. reduced-sodium chicken bouillon granules**
- ¼ **tsp. pepper**
- 3 **cups uncooked egg noodles**

In a Dutch oven, combine the first 10 ingredients. Bring to a boil. Reduce heat; cover and simmer for 10 minutes or until vegetables are crisp-tender. Stir in noodles; cook 5-7 minutes longer or until noodles and vegetables are tender.

1½ CUPS: 196 cal., 5g fat (1g sat. fat), 49mg chol., 759mg sod., 22g carb. (3g sugars, 2g fiber), 15g pro. **DIABETIC EXCHANGES:** 2 lean meat, 1 starch, ½ fat.

ROASTED CAULIFLOWER & RED PEPPER SOUP

When cooler weather comes, soup is one of our favorite meals. I created this as a healthier version of all the cream-based soups out there. After a bit of trial and error, my husband and I decided this is the keeper.
—Elizabeth Bramkamp, Gig Harbor, WA

Prep: **50 min. + standing**
Cook: **25 min.**
Makes: **6 servings**

2 medium sweet red peppers, halved and seeded
1 large head cauliflower, broken into florets (about 7 cups)
4 Tbsp. olive oil, divided
1 cup chopped sweet onion
2 garlic cloves, minced
2½ tsp. minced fresh rosemary or ¾ tsp. dried rosemary, crushed
½ tsp. paprika
¼ cup all-purpose flour
4 cups chicken stock
1 cup 2% milk
½ tsp. salt
¼ tsp. pepper
⅛ to ¼ tsp. cayenne pepper
Shredded Parmesan cheese, optional

1. Preheat broiler. Place the peppers on a foil-lined baking sheet, skin side up. Broil 4 in. from heat until skins are blistered, about 5 minutes. Transfer to a bowl; let stand, covered, 20 minutes. Change oven setting to bake; preheat to 400°.
2. Toss cauliflower with 2 Tbsp. oil; spread in a 15x10x1-in. pan. Roast until tender, 25-30 minutes, stirring occasionally. Remove skin and seeds from peppers; chop peppers.
3. In a 6-qt. stockpot, heat remaining 2 Tbsp. oil over medium heat. Add onion; cook until golden and softened, 6-8 minutes, stirring occasionally. Add garlic, rosemary and paprika; cook and stir 1 minute. Stir in flour until blended; cook and stir 1 minute. Gradually stir in stock. Bring to a boil, stirring constantly; cook and stir until thickened.
4. Stir in cauliflower and peppers. Puree soup using an immersion blender. Or, cool slightly and puree soup in batches in a blender; return to pot. Stir in milk and remaining seasonings; heat through. If desired, serve with Parmesan.

FREEZE OPTION: Freeze cooled soup in freezer containers. To use, partially thaw in refrigerator overnight. Heat through in a saucepan, stirring soup occasionally; add stock or milk if necessary.

1 CUP: 193 cal., 10g fat (2g sat. fat), 3mg chol., 601mg sod., 19g carb. (8g sugars, 4g fiber), 8g pro. **DIABETIC EXCHANGES:** 2 vegetable, 2 fat, ½ starch.

THE BEST EVER TOMATO SOUP

Creamy, rich and bursting with brightness, this soup is the ultimate sidekick to a grilled cheese sandwich.
—*Josh Rink, Milwaukee, WI*

Prep: **20 minutes**
Cook: **30 minutes**
Makes: **16 servings (4 qt.)**

- 3 Tbsp. olive oil
- 3 Tbsp. butter
- ¼ to ½ tsp. crushed red pepper flakes
- 3 large carrots, peeled and chopped
- 1 large onion, chopped
- 2 garlic cloves, minced
- 2 tsp. dried basil
- 3 cans (28 oz. each) whole peeled tomatoes, undrained
- 1 container (32 oz.) chicken stock
- 2 Tbsp. tomato paste
- 3 tsp. sugar
- 1 tsp. salt
- ½ tsp. pepper
- 1 cup heavy whipping cream, optional
  Optional: Thinly sliced fresh basil leaves and grated Parmesan cheese

1. In a 6-qt. stockpot or Dutch oven, heat oil, butter and pepper flakes over medium heat until butter is melted. Add carrots and onion; cook, uncovered, over medium heat, stirring frequently, until vegetables are softened, 8-10 minutes. Add garlic and dried basil; cook and stir 1 minute longer. Stir in tomatoes, chicken stock, tomato paste, sugar, salt and pepper; mix well. Bring soup to a boil. Reduce heat; simmer, uncovered, to let flavors blend, 20-25 minutes.

2. Remove pan from heat. Using a blender, puree soup in batches until smooth. If desired, slowly stir in heavy cream, stirring continuously to incorporate; return to stove to heat through. Top servings with fresh basil and Parmesan cheese if desired.

1 CUP: 104 cal., 5g fat (2g sat. fat), 6mg chol., 572mg sod., 15g carb. (10g sugars, 2g fiber), 3g pro.
DIABETIC EXCHANGES: 1 starch, 1 fat.

THE SKINNY

You can add milk to tomato soup for a super creamy spin. However because tomatoes are acidic, the milk may curdle. To avoid this, add a half teaspoon of baking soda to the soup. The baking soda neutralizes the acidity of the tomatoes, which prevents the milk from curdling— and can improve the taste, too.

WILD RICE MUSHROOM SOUP

Mushrooms often get used only to add flavor to dishes, but I think they are delicious enough to be the main part of a meal. This recipe uses a large quantity of mushrooms and the result is wonderful. Even though this soup contains some dairy, it still freezes well.
—*Wendy Campbell,*
New Wilmington, PA

Prep: **10 min.** • Cook: **1 hour**
Makes: **8 servings (2 qt.)**

- ½ cup uncooked wild rice
- 1½ cups water
- 8 oz. smoked turkey sausage, sliced
- ⅓ cup all-purpose flour
- 1 carton (32 oz.) reduced-sodium chicken broth, divided
- 2 Tbsp. butter
- 1 large onion, chopped
- ½ lb. sliced fresh mushrooms
- 1 cup whole milk
- ¼ tsp. pepper

1. In a small saucepan, combine wild rice and water; bring to a boil. Reduce heat; simmer, covered, until rice is tender, 40-45 minutes.
2. In a large saucepan, cook and stir sausage over medium heat until lightly browned, 3-4 minutes. Remove from pan.
3. Mix flour and ½ cup broth until smooth. In same pan, heat butter over medium heat; saute onion and mushrooms until tender, about 4-5 minutes. Add remaining broth; gradually stir in flour mixture. Bring to a boil; cook and stir until slightly thickened, 2-3 minutes. Add milk,

pepper, rice and sausage; heat through, stirring occasionally.
1 CUP: 157 cal., 6g fat (3g sat. fat), 28mg chol., 644mg sod., 17g carb. (4g sugars, 1g fiber), 10g pro.
DIABETIC EXCHANGES: 1 starch, 1 lean meat, 1 fat.

SO-EASY GAZPACHO

My daughter got this recipe from a friend a few years ago. Now I serve it often as an appetizer. It certainly is the talk of any party!
—*Lorna Sirtoli, Cortland, NY*

Prep: **15 min. + chilling**
Makes: **5 servings**

- 2 cups tomato juice
- 4 medium tomatoes, peeled and finely chopped
- ½ cup chopped seeded peeled cucumber
- ⅓ cup finely chopped onion
- ¼ cup olive oil
- ¼ cup cider vinegar
- 1 tsp. sugar
- 1 garlic clove, minced
- ¼ tsp. salt
- ¼ tsp. pepper

In a bowl, combine all ingredients. Cover and refrigerate until chilled, at least 4 hours.
1 CUP: 146 cal., 11g fat (2g sat. fat), 0 chol., 387mg sod., 11g carb. (8g sugars, 2g fiber), 2g pro. **DIABETIC EXCHANGES:** 2 vegetable, 2 fat.
BLACK BEAN ZUCCHINI GAZPACHO: Substitute 2 large tomatoes for the 4 medium. Add 1 can (15 oz.) drained rinsed black beans, 2 chopped medium zucchini and ¼ tsp. cayenne.
REFRESHING GAZPACHO: Increase the tomato juice to 4½ cups. Add 2 chopped celery ribs, 1 finely chopped red onion, 1 each chopped medium sweet red pepper and green pepper, ¼ minced fresh cilantro, 2 Tbsp. lime juice, 2 tsp. sugar and 1 tsp. Worcestershire. Serve with cubed avocado if desired.

SLOW-COOKED MEXICAN BEEF SOUP

My family loves this soup, and I'm happy to make it since it's so simple! You can serve with cornbread instead of corn chips to make it an even more filling meal.
—*Angela Lively, Conroe, TX*

Prep: **15 min.** • Cook: **6 hours**
Makes: **6 servings (2 qt.)**

- 1 lb. beef stew meat (1¼-in. pieces)
- ¾ lb. potatoes (about 2 medium), cut into ¾-in. cubes
- 2 cups frozen corn (about 10 oz.), thawed
- 2 medium carrots, cut into ½-in. slices
- 1 medium onion, chopped
- 2 garlic cloves, minced
- 1½ tsp. dried oregano
- 1 tsp. ground cumin
- ½ tsp. salt
- ¼ tsp. crushed red pepper flakes
- 2 cups beef stock
- 1 can (10 oz.) diced tomatoes and green chiles, undrained
  Optional: Sour cream and tortilla chips

In a 5- or 6-qt. slow cooker, combine first 12 ingredients. Cook, covered, on low until the stew meat is tender, 6-8 hours. If desired, serve with sour cream and chips.

1⅓ CUPS: 218 cal., 6g fat (2g sat. fat), 47mg chol., 602mg sod., 24g carb. (5g sugars, 3g fiber), 19g pro.
DIABETIC EXCHANGES: 2 lean meat, 1½ starch.

VEGGIE CHOWDER

Packed with potatoes, carrots and corn, this soup is a great healthy dinner choice. It's not too heavy, so it also makes a nice light partner for a sandwich.
—*Vicki Kerr, Portland, ME*

Takes: **30 min.**
Makes: **7 servings (1¾ qt.)**

- 2 cups cubed peeled potatoes
- 2 cups reduced-sodium chicken broth
- 1 cup chopped carrots
- ½ cup chopped onion
- 1 can (14¾ oz.) cream-style corn
- 1 can (12 oz.) fat-free evaporated milk
- ¾ cup shredded reduced-fat cheddar cheese
- ½ cup sliced fresh mushrooms
- ¼ tsp. pepper
- 2 Tbsp. bacon bits

1. In a large saucepan, combine the potatoes, broth, carrots and onion; bring to a boil. Reduce heat; simmer, uncovered, 10-15 minutes or until vegetables are tender.
2. Add the corn, milk, cheddar cheese, mushrooms and pepper; cook and stir 4-6 minutes longer or until heated through. Sprinkle with the bacon bits.

1 CUP: 191 cal., 5g fat (2g sat. fat), 15mg chol., 505mg sod., 29g carb. (10g sugars, 2g fiber), 11g pro.
DIABETIC EXCHANGES: 2 starch, ½ fat.

CONTEST-WINNING NEW ENGLAND CLAM CHOWDER

This is the best New England clam chowder recipe ever! In the Pacific Northwest, we dig our own razor clams and I grind them for the chowder. Since these aren't readily available, the canned clams are perfectly acceptable.
—*Sandy Larson, Port Angeles, WA*

Prep: **20 min.** • Cook: **35 min.**
Makes: **5 servings**

- 4 **center-cut bacon strips**
- 2 **celery ribs, chopped**
- 1 **large onion, chopped**
- 1 **garlic clove, minced**
- 3 **small potatoes, peeled and cubed**
- 1 **cup water**
- 1 **bottle (8 oz.) clam juice**
- 3 **tsp. reduced-sodium chicken bouillon granules**
- ¼ **tsp. white pepper**
- ¼ **tsp. dried thyme**
- ⅓ **cup all-purpose flour**
- 2 **cups fat-free half-and-half, divided**
- 2 **cans (6½ oz. each) chopped clams, undrained**

1. In a Dutch oven, cook the bacon over medium heat until crisp. Remove to paper towels to drain; set aside. Saute the celery and onion in the drippings until tender. Add the garlic; cook 1 minute longer. Stir in the potatoes, water, clam juice, bouillon, pepper and thyme. Bring to a boil. Reduce heat; simmer, uncovered, until the potatoes are tender, 15-20 minutes.
2. In a small bowl, combine the flour and 1 cup half-and-half until smooth.

Gradually stir into soup. Bring to a boil; cook and stir until thickened, 1-2 minutes.
3. Stir in the clams and remaining half-and-half; heat through (do not boil). Crumble the cooked bacon; sprinkle over each serving.
1⅓ CUPS: 260 cal., 4g fat (1g sat. fat), 22mg chol., 788mg sod., 39g carb. (9g sugars, 3g fiber), 13g pro.
DIABETIC EXCHANGES: 2½ starch, 1 lean meat.

TYPICAL	MAKEOVER
413 Calories	**260** Calories
27g Saturated Fat	**1**g Saturated Fat
110mg Cholesterol	**22**mg Cholesterol
877mg Sodium	**788**mg Sodium

THE SKINNY

White pepper comes from fully ripened peppercorns that have had their skins removed. It has a milder flavor than black pepper and is helpful in soups and dishes like mashed potatoes where you might not want black flecks to show. You can substitute black pepper (perhaps using a bit less than called for).

CABBAGE & BEEF SOUP

When I was young, I helped my parents work the fields of their small farm. Lunchtime was always a treat when my mom picked vegetables from her garden and simmered them in her big soup pot. Now I enjoy making this soup with produce from my own garden.
—*Ethel Ledbetter, Canton, NC*

Prep: **10 min.** • Cook: **70 min.**
Makes: **12 servings (3 qt.)**

- 1 lb. lean ground beef (90% lean)
- ½ tsp. garlic salt
- ¼ tsp. garlic powder
- ¼ tsp. pepper
- 2 celery ribs, chopped
- 1 can (16 oz.) kidney beans, rinsed and drained
- ½ medium head cabbage, chopped
- 1 can (28 oz.) diced tomatoes, undrained
- 3½ cups water
- 4 tsp. beef bouillon granules
  Minced fresh parsley

1. In a Dutch oven, cook beef over medium heat until no longer pink, breaking it into crumbles; drain. Stir in the remaining ingredients except the parsley.

2. Bring to a boil. Reduce heat; cover and simmer for 1 hour. Garnish with the parsley.

1 CUP: 116 cal., 3g fat (1g sat. fat), 19mg chol., 582mg sod., 11g carb. (3g sugars, 3g fiber), 11g pro.
DIABETIC EXCHANGES: 1 starch, 1 lean meat.

TASTE OF HOME TALK

"I have now made this soup at least a dozen times. It's wonderful. I think it has become my new all-time favorite."
WENDYFITZGERALD, TASTEOFHOME.COM

PRESSURE-COOKER CHILI CON CARNE

Although multicookers can't replace every tool in the kitchen, they sure are coming close. Chili con carne is one of our favorite dishes to re-create in them. This cooks up fast but tastes as if it simmered all day!
—Taste of Home *Test Kitchen*

Takes: 30 min. • Makes: **7 cups**

- 1 can (16 oz.) pinto beans, rinsed and drained
- 1 can (14½ oz.) Mexican diced tomatoes, undrained
- 1 can (8 oz.) tomato sauce
- 1 medium green pepper, chopped
- 1 medium onion, chopped
- 1 cup beef broth
- 1 jalapeno pepper, seeded and minced
- 2 Tbsp. chili powder
- ¼ tsp. salt
- ¼ tsp. pepper
- 1½ lbs. lean ground beef (90% lean)
  Optional: Sour cream and sliced jalapeno

1. Combine the first 10 ingredients in a 6-qt. electric pressure cooker. Crumble beef over top; stir to combine. Lock lid; close pressure-release valve. Adjust to pressure-cook on high for 5 minutes.
2. Allow pressure to naturally release for 10 minutes, then quick-release any remaining pressure. Stir chili. If desired, serve with sour cream and additional jalapenos.

1 CUP: 248 cal., 9g fat (3g sat. fat), 61mg chol., 687mg sod., 18g carb. (5g sugars, 5g fiber), 24g pro.
DIABETIC EXCHANGES: 3 lean meat, 1 starch.

MAKE IT YOUR OWN
Personalize your Chili con Carne by adding a dash of one or two of the following:
- Cumin
- Fennel seed
- Oregano
- Nutmeg
- Anise seed
- Crushed red pepper flakes
- Garlic powder
- Sage

boil. Stir in pasta. Return to a boil. Reduce heat; simmer, covered, 10-12 minutes or until pasta is tender. Sprinkle with cheese.

1⅓ CUPS: 280 cal., 7g fat (3g sat. fat), 41mg chol., 572mg sod., 35g carb. (8g sugars, 4g fiber), 20g pro.
DIABETIC EXCHANGES: 2 vegetable, 2 lean meat, 1½ starch.

CHILLED MELON SOUP

Looking for something to jazz up a summer luncheon? Try this pretty, refreshing melon soup with nutmeg and a kick of cayenne pepper to get the conversation going.
—*Mary Lou Timpson, Colorado City, AZ*

Prep: **25 min. + chilling**
Makes: **6 servings**

- ¾ cup orange juice
- 1 cup plain yogurt
- 1 medium cantaloupe, peeled, seeded and cubed
- 1 Tbsp. honey
- ¼ tsp. salt
- ¼ tsp. ground nutmeg
- ⅛ tsp. cayenne pepper
- 6 mint sprigs

Place the orange juice, yogurt and cantaloupe in a blender; cover and process until pureed. Add the honey, salt, nutmeg and cayenne; cover and process until smooth. Refrigerate for at least 1 hour before serving. Garnish with mint sprigs.

⅔ CUP: 82 cal., 2g fat (1g sat. fat), 5mg chol., 126mg sod., 16g carb. (15g sugars, 1g fiber), 2g pro.
DIABETIC EXCHANGES: 1 fruit.

BEST LASAGNA SOUP

All the flavors of lasagna come together in this bowl of comfort.
—*Sheryl Olenick, Demarest, NJ*

Takes: **30 min.**
Makes: **8 servings (about 2¾ qt.)**

- 1 lb. lean ground beef (90% lean)
- 1 large green pepper, chopped
- 1 medium onion, chopped
- 2 garlic cloves, minced
- 2 cans (14½ oz. each) diced tomatoes, undrained
- 2 cans (14½ oz. each) reduced-sodium beef broth
- 1 can (8 oz.) tomato sauce
- 1 cup frozen corn
- ¼ cup tomato paste
- 2 tsp. Italian seasoning
- ¼ tsp. pepper
- 2½ cups uncooked spiral pasta
- ½ cup shredded Parmesan cheese

1. In a large saucepan, cook beef, green pepper and onion over medium heat 6-8 minutes or until meat is no longer pink, breaking up beef into crumbles. Add garlic; cook 1 minute longer. Drain.
2. Stir in tomatoes, broth, tomato sauce, corn, tomato paste, Italian seasoning and pepper. Bring to a

COUSCOUS MEATBALL SOUP

Leafy greens, homemade meatballs, pearly couscous and just-right spices are ready to simmer in less than half an hour. That makes this healthy soup our favorite go-to dinner on chilly winter nights.

—*Jonathan Pace, San Francisco, CA*

Prep: **25 min.** • Cook: **40 min.**
Makes: **10 servings (2½ qt.)**

1 **lb. lean ground beef (90% lean)**
2 **tsp. dried basil**
2 **tsp. dried oregano**
½ **tsp. salt**
1 **large onion, finely chopped**
2 **tsp. canola oil**
1 **bunch collard greens, chopped (8 cups)**
1 **bunch kale, chopped (8 cups)**
2 **cartons (32 oz. each) vegetable stock**
1 **Tbsp. white wine vinegar**
½ **tsp. crushed red pepper flakes**
¼ **tsp. pepper**
1 **pkg. (8.8 oz.) pearl (Israeli) couscous**

1. In a small bowl, combine the beef, basil, oregano and salt. Shape into ½-in. balls. In a large skillet coated with cooking spray, brown the meatballs; drain. Remove meatballs and set aside.
2. In the same skillet, brown onion in oil. Add greens and kale; cook 6-7 minutes longer or until wilted.
3. In a Dutch oven, combine the greens mixture, meatballs, stock, vinegar, pepper flakes and pepper. Bring to a boil. Reduce heat; cover and simmer for 10 minutes. Return to a boil. Stir in couscous. Reduce heat; cover and simmer, stirring once, until couscous is tender, 10-15 minutes.

1 CUP: 202 cal., 5g fat (2g sat. fat), 28mg chol., 583mg sod., 26g carb. (1g sugars, 2g fiber), 13g pro.
DIABETIC EXCHANGES: 1½ starch, 1 vegetable, 1 lean meat.

THE SKINNY
This soup is a great way to work some greens into family diets. Lighten things up even further by replacing the beef with extra-lean ground turkey.

HEARTY BEEF ENTREES

TEXAS BEEF BARBECUE

These shredded beef sandwiches are a family favorite. The beef simmers for hours in a slightly sweet sauce with plenty of spices.
—*Jennifer Bauer, Lansing, MI*

Prep: **15 min.** • Cook: **8 hours**
Makes: **16 servings**

- 1 beef sirloin tip roast (4 lbs.)
- 1 can (5½ oz.) spicy hot V8 juice
- ½ cup water
- ¼ cup white vinegar
- ¼ cup ketchup
- 2 Tbsp. Worcestershire sauce
- ½ cup packed brown sugar
- 1 tsp. salt
- 1 tsp. ground mustard
- 1 tsp. paprika
- ¼ tsp. chili powder
- ⅛ tsp. pepper
- 16 kaiser rolls, split

1. Cut roast in half; place in a 5-qt. slow cooker. Combine the V8 juice, water, vinegar, ketchup, Worcestershire sauce, brown sugar and seasonings; pour over roast. Cover and cook on low 8-10 hours or until meat is tender.

2. Remove meat and shred with 2 forks; return to slow cooker and heat through. Spoon ½ cup meat mixture onto each roll.

1 SANDWICH: 339 cal., 8g fat (2g sat. fat), 60mg chol., 606mg sod., 39g carb. (10g sugars, 1g fiber), 27g pro. **DIABETIC EXCHANGES:** 3 lean meat, 2½ starch.

WINTERTIME BRAISED BEEF STEW

This wonderful beef stew makes an easy Sunday meal. It's even better a day or two later, so we make a double batch to ensure plenty of leftovers.
—*Michaela Rosenthal, Woodland Hills, CA*

Prep: **40 min.** • Bake: **2 hours**
Makes: **8 servings (2 qt.)**

- 2   lbs. boneless beef sirloin steak or chuck roast, cut into 1-in. pieces
- 2   Tbsp. all-purpose flour
- 2   tsp. Montreal steak seasoning
- 2   Tbsp. olive oil, divided
- 1   large onion, chopped
- 2   celery ribs, chopped
- 2   medium parsnips, peeled and cut into 1½-in. pieces
- 2   medium carrots, peeled and cut into 1½-in. pieces
- 2   garlic cloves, minced
- 1   can (14½ oz.) diced tomatoes, undrained
- 1   cup dry red wine or reduced-sodium beef broth
- 2   Tbsp. red currant jelly
- 2   bay leaves
- 2   fresh oregano sprigs
- 1   can (15 oz.) cannellini beans, rinsed and drained
     Minced fresh parsley, optional

1. Preheat oven to 350°. Toss beef with flour and steak seasoning. In an ovenproof Dutch oven, heat 1 Tbsp. oil over medium heat. Brown the beef in batches; remove with a slotted spoon.

2. In same pot, heat remaining Tbsp. oil over medium heat. Add onion, celery, parsnips and carrots; cook and stir until onion is tender. Add garlic; cook 1 minute longer. Stir in tomatoes, wine, jelly, bay leaves, oregano and beef; bring to a boil.

3. Bake, covered, 1½ hours. Stir in beans; bake, covered, until the beef and vegetables are tender, 30-40 minutes longer. Remove bay leaves and oregano sprigs. If desired, sprinkle with parsley.

FREEZE OPTION: Freeze cooled stew in freezer containers. To use, partially thaw in refrigerator overnight. Heat through in a saucepan, stirring occasionally; add a little broth or water if necessary.

1 CUP: 310 cal., 9g fat (3g sat. fat), 64mg chol., 373mg sod., 26g carb. (8g sugars, 5g fiber), 25g pro.
DIABETIC EXCHANGES: 3 lean meat, 1 starch, 1 vegetable, 1 fat.

ST. PADDY'S IRISH BEEF DINNER

A variation on shepherd's pie, this hearty dish brings together saucy beef with mashed potatoes, parsnips and other vegetables. It's always the star of our March 17 meal.
—*Lorraine Caland, Shuniah, ON*

- -

Prep: **25 min.** • Cook: **35 min.**
Makes: **4 servings**

- 2 medium Yukon Gold potatoes
- 2 small parsnips
- ¾ lb. lean ground beef (90% lean)
- 1 medium onion, chopped
- 2 cups finely shredded cabbage
- 2 medium carrots, halved and sliced
- 1 tsp. dried thyme
- 1 tsp. Worcestershire sauce
- 1 Tbsp. all-purpose flour
- ¼ cup tomato paste
- 1 can (14½ oz.) reduced-sodium chicken or beef broth
- ½ cup frozen peas
- ¾ tsp. salt, divided
- ½ tsp. pepper, divided
- ¼ cup 2% milk
- 1 Tbsp. butter

1. Peel potatoes and parsnips and cut into large pieces; place in a large saucepan and cover with water. Bring to a boil. Reduce heat; cover and cook for 10-15 minutes or until tender. Drain.
2. In a large skillet, cook beef and onion over medium heat until meat is no longer pink; crumble the beef; drain. Stir in cabbage, carrots, thyme and Worcestershire sauce.
3. In a small bowl, combine flour, tomato paste and broth until smooth. Gradually stir into the meat mixture. Bring to a boil. Reduce heat; cover and simmer 15-20 minutes or until vegetables are tender. Stir in the peas, ¼ tsp. salt and ¼ tsp. pepper.
4. Drain potatoes and parsnips; mash with milk, butter and the remaining ½ tsp. salt and ¼ tsp. pepper. Serve with meat mixture.
1 SERVING: 369 cal., 11g fat (5g sat. fat), 62mg chol., 849mg sod., 46g carb. (13g sugars, 8g fiber), 24g pro.
DIABETIC EXCHANGES: 3 lean meat, 2 starch, 2 vegetable.

THE SKINNY

To keep leftovers, store the mashed potato and parsnips and the beef mixture in separate airtight containers in the refrigerator. Both components should last about 3 to 4 days when stored this way.

SLOW-COOKED HUNGARIAN GOULASH

You will love how easily this slow-cooked version of a beloved ethnic dish comes together. My son shared the recipe with me many years ago.
—Jackie Kohn, Duluth, MN

Prep: **15 min.** • Cook: **8 hours**
Makes: **8 servings**

- 2 lbs. beef top round steak, cut into 1-in. cubes
- 1 cup chopped onion
- 2 Tbsp. all-purpose flour
- 1½ tsp. paprika
- 1 tsp. garlic salt
- ½ tsp. pepper
- 1 can (14½ oz.) diced tomatoes, undrained
- 1 bay leaf
- 1 cup sour cream
  Hot cooked egg noodles
  Minced fresh parsley, optional

1. Place beef and onion in a 3-qt. slow cooker. Combine the flour, paprika, garlic salt and pepper; sprinkle over beef and stir to coat. Stir in tomatoes; add bay leaf. Cover and cook on low until meat is tender, 8-10 hours.
2. Discard bay leaf. Just before serving, stir in sour cream; heat through. Serve with noodles. Garnish with parsley if desired.
FREEZE OPTION: Before adding the sour cream, cool stew. Freeze stew in freezer containers. To use, partially thaw in refrigerator overnight. Heat through in a saucepan, stirring occasionally; add broth if necessary. Remove from heat; stir in sour cream.
1 CUP: 224 cal., 8g fat (5g sat. fat), 83mg chol., 339mg sod., 7g carb. (4g sugars, 1g fiber), 27g pro.

MEXI-MAC SKILLET

My husband loves this recipe, and I love how simple it is to put together! Because you don't need to precook the macaroni, it's a timesaving dish.
—Maurane Ramsey, Fort Wayne, IN

Takes: **30 min.** • Makes: **4 servings**

- 1 lb. extra-lean ground beef (95% lean)
- 1 large onion, chopped
- 1¼ tsp. chili powder
- 1 tsp. dried oregano
- ¼ tsp. salt
- 1 can (14½ oz.) diced tomatoes, undrained
- 1 can (8 oz.) tomato sauce
- 1 cup fresh or frozen corn
- ½ cup water
- ⅔ cup uncooked elbow macaroni
- ½ cup shredded reduced-fat cheddar cheese

1. In a large nonstick skillet, cook beef with onion over medium-high heat until the beef is no longer pink, 5-7 minutes; crumble meat.
2. Stir in chili powder, oregano, salt, tomatoes, tomato sauce, corn and water; bring to a boil. Stir in macaroni. Reduce heat; simmer, covered, until macaroni is tender, 15-20 minutes, stirring occasionally. Sprinkle with cheese.
1¼ CUPS: 318 cal., 10g fat (4g sat. fat), 75mg chol., 755mg sod., 28g carb. (9g sugars, 5g fiber), 32g pro.
DIABETIC EXCHANGES: 1 starch, 3 lean meat, 1 vegetable.

LASAGNA DELIZIOSA

Everyone loves this lasagna. It's often served as a birthday treat for guests. I've lightened it up a lot from the original, but no one can tell the difference!
—*Heather O'Neill, Troy, OH*

Prep: **45 min.**
Bake: **50 min. + standing**
Makes: **12 servings**

- 9 uncooked lasagna noodles
- 1 pkg. (19½ oz.) Italian turkey sausage links, casings removed
- ½ lb. lean ground beef (90% lean)
- 1 large onion, chopped
- 2 garlic cloves, minced
- 1 can (28 oz.) diced tomatoes, undrained
- 1 can (12 oz.) tomato paste
- ¼ cup water
- 2 tsp. sugar
- 1 tsp. dried basil
- ½ tsp. fennel seed
- ¼ tsp. pepper
- 1 large egg, lightly beaten
- 1 carton (15 oz.) reduced-fat ricotta cheese
- 1 Tbsp. minced fresh parsley
- ½ tsp. salt
- 2 cups shredded part-skim mozzarella cheese
- ¾ cup grated Parmesan cheese Torn fresh basil leaves, optional

1. Cook noodles according to package directions. Meanwhile, in a Dutch oven, cook sausage, beef and onion over medium heat until meat is no longer pink; crumble meat. Add garlic; cook 1 minute longer. Drain.

2. Stir in the tomatoes, tomato paste, water, sugar, basil, fennel and pepper. Bring to a boil. Reduce heat; cover and simmer for 15-20 minutes, stirring occasionally.

3. Meanwhile, preheat oven to 375°. In a small bowl, combine the egg, ricotta cheese, parsley and salt. Drain noodles; rinse in cold water. Spread 1 cup meat sauce into a 13x9-in. baking dish coated with cooking spray. Top with 3 noodles, 2 cups meat sauce, ⅔ cup ricotta cheese mixture, ⅔ cup mozzarella and ¼ cup Parmesan. Repeat the layers twice.

4. Cover and bake for 40 minutes. Uncover; bake 10-15 minutes longer or until bubbly. Let stand 10 minutes before cutting. If desired, top with

fresh basil leaves and sprinkle with additional Parmesan cheese.

1 PIECE: 323 cal., 12g fat (5g sat. fat), 79mg chol., 701mg sod., 28g carb. (11g sugars, 4g fiber), 25g pro.
DIABETIC EXCHANGES: 3 lean meat, 2 vegetable, 1 starch, 1 fat.

TYPICAL	MAKEOVER
503 Calories	**323** Calories
27g Fat	**12**g Fat
13g Saturated Fat	**5**g Saturated Fat
1,208mg Sodium	**701**mg Sodium

DRESSING
¼ cup lime juice
1 Tbsp. olive oil
¼ tsp. salt
¼ tsp. ground cumin
¼ tsp. pepper
⅓ cup chopped fresh cilantro

1. Rub steak with salt, cumin and pepper. Brush poblano peppers, corn and onion with oil. Grill steak, covered, over medium heat or broil 4 in. from heat 6-8 minutes on each side or until meat reaches desired doneness (for medium-rare, a thermometer should read 135°; medium, 140°; medium-well, 145°). Grill the vegetables, covered, for 8-10 minutes or until crisp-tender, turning occasionally.
2. Cook pasta according to package directions. Meanwhile, cut corn from cob; coarsely chop peppers, onion and tomatoes. Transfer vegetables to a large bowl.
3. In a small bowl, whisk lime juice, oil, salt, cumin and pepper until blended; stir in cilantro.
4. Drain pasta; add to the vegetable mixture. Drizzle with dressing; toss to coat. Cut steak into thin slices; add to salad.

2 CUPS PASTA MIXTURE WITH 2 OZ. COOKED BEEF: 456 cal., 13g fat (3g sat. fat), 34mg chol., 378mg sod., 58g carb. (15g sugars, 8g fiber), 30g pro.

GREEK SLOPPY JOES
Feta is one of my favorite kinds of cheese. It's good in a burger, but it truly shines in this Mediterranean-style sloppy joe.
—*Sonya Labbe,*
West Hollywood, CA

Takes: **25 min.** • Makes: **6 servings**

1 lb. lean ground beef (90% lean)
1 small red onion, chopped
2 garlic cloves, minced
1 can (15 oz.) tomato sauce
1 tsp. dried oregano
  Romaine leaves
6 kaiser rolls, split and toasted
½ cup crumbled feta cheese

1. In a large skillet, cook beef, onion and garlic over medium heat until meat is no longer pink, 6-8 minutes; crumble beef; drain. Stir in tomato sauce and oregano. Bring to a boil. Reduce heat; simmer, uncovered, until sauce is slightly thickened, 8-10 minutes, stirring occasionally.
2. Place romaine on roll bottoms; top with meat mixture. Sprinkle with feta cheese; replace tops.
FREEZE OPTION: Freeze cooled meat mixture in freezer containers. To use, partially thaw in refrigerator overnight. Heat through in a saucepan, stirring occasionally; add water if necessary.
1 SANDWICH: 337 cal., 10g fat (4g sat. fat), 52mg chol., 767mg sod., 36g carb. (3g sugars, 3g fiber), 24g pro.
DIABETIC EXCHANGES: 3 lean meat, 2 starch, 1 vegetable.

GRILLED SOUTHWESTERN STEAK SALAD
Pasta salad loaded with steak and veggies makes my boyfriend and me happy. We serve it warm, chilled or at room temperature.
—*Yvonne Starlin, Westmoreland, TN*

Prep: **25 min.** • Grill: **20 min.**
Makes: **4 servings**

1 beef top sirloin steak (1 in. thick and ¾ lb.)
¼ tsp. salt
¼ tsp. ground cumin
¼ tsp. pepper
3 poblano peppers, halved and seeded
2 large ears sweet corn, husks removed
1 large sweet onion, cut into ½-in. rings
1 Tbsp. olive oil
2 cups uncooked multigrain bow tie pasta
2 large tomatoes

THE SKINNY

The primary purpose of a marinade is to add flavor, so choose the soy sauce you think tastes best! Dark soy sauce (Koikuchi) offers a well-rounded flavor. Use light soy sauce (Usukuchi) sparingly due to its intense flavor. Tamari sauce can be a gluten-free option to soy sauce (check the ingredient list) and has a distinctly rich flavor.

TENDER FLANK STEAK

This mildly marinated flank steak is my son's favorite. I usually slice it thinly and serve it with twice-baked potatoes and a green salad to round out the meal. Leftovers are great for French dip sandwiches.
—*Gayle Bucknam, Greenbank, WA*

Prep: **10 min. + marinating**
Grill: **15 min.** • Makes: **4 servings**

¼	cup soy sauce
2	Tbsp. water
3	garlic cloves, thinly sliced
1	Tbsp. brown sugar
1	Tbsp. canola oil
½	tsp. ground ginger
½	tsp. pepper
1	beef flank steak (1 lb.)

1. In a shallow dish, combine the first 7 ingredients; add steak and turn to coat. Cover and refrigerate for 8 hours or overnight, turning occasionally.

2. Drain steak, discarding marinade. Grill, covered, over medium-hot heat for 6-8 minutes on each side or until meat reaches desired doneness (for medium-rare, a thermometer should read 135°; medium, 140°; medium-well, 145°).

3 OZ. COOKED BEEF: 209 cal., 11g fat, 59mg chol., 326mg sod., 3g carb., 0 fiber), 24g pro. **DIABETIC EXCHANGES:** 3 lean meat.

CHEESEBURGER MACARONI SKILLET

This is the ultimate simple, satisfying supper that uses items I typically already have in my cupboard. Plus, cleanup's a snap since I cook it all in one skillet.
—*Juli Meyers, Hinesville, GA*

Takes: **30 min.** • Makes: **6 servings**

1	lb. lean ground beef (90% lean)
8	oz. uncooked whole wheat elbow macaroni
3	cups reduced-sodium beef broth
¾	cup fat-free milk
3	Tbsp. ketchup
2	tsp. Montreal steak seasoning
1	tsp. prepared mustard
¼	tsp. onion powder
1	cup shredded reduced-fat cheddar cheese
	Minced chives

1. In a large skillet, cook beef over medium heat until no longer pink, 6-8 minutes; crumble beef; drain.

2. Stir in macaroni, broth, milk, ketchup, steak seasoning, mustard and onion powder; bring to a boil. Reduce heat; simmer, uncovered, until the macaroni is tender, 10-15 minutes.

3. Stir in the cheese until melted. Sprinkle with chives.

1 CUP: 338 cal., 11g fat (5g sat. fat), 64mg chol., 611mg sod., 32g carb. (5g sugars, 4g fiber), 27g pro.
DIABETIC EXCHANGES: 3 lean meat, 2 starch, ½ fat.

1 can (8 oz.) tomato sauce
¾ cup chopped peeled parsnips
¾ cup chopped celery
¾ cup chopped carrots
8 garlic cloves, minced
2 bay leaves
1½ tsp. dried thyme
1 tsp. chili powder
¼ cup cornstarch
¼ cup water
  Mashed potatoes

1. Sprinkle roast with salt and pepper. In a Dutch oven, brown roast in oil on all sides. Transfer to a 6-qt. slow cooker. Add mushrooms, onions, broth, wine, tomato sauce, parsnips, celery, carrots, garlic, bay leaves, thyme and chili powder. Cover and cook on low until meat is tender, 6-8 hours.

2. Remove meat and vegetables to a serving platter; keep warm. Discard bay leaves. Skim fat from cooking juices; transfer to a small saucepan. Bring liquid to a boil. Combine cornstarch and water until smooth; gradually stir into the pan. Bring to a boil; cook and stir for 2 minutes or until thickened. Serve with mashed potatoes, meat and vegetables.

4 OZ. COOKED BEEF WITH ⅔ CUP VEGETABLES AND ½ CUP GRAVY: 310 cal., 14g fat (5g sat. fat), 89mg chol., 363mg sod., 14g carb. (4g sugars, 3g fiber), 30g pro.

CONTEST-WINNING MUSHROOM POT ROAST

Everyone will love this comforting pot roast packed with wholesome veggies and tender beef. Serve with mashed potatoes to soak up every last drop of the gravy.
—*Angie Stewart, Topeka, KS*

- -

Prep: **25 min.** • Cook: **6 hours**
Makes: **10 servings**

1 boneless beef chuck roast (3 to 4 lbs.)
½ tsp. salt
¼ tsp. pepper
1 Tbsp. canola oil
1½ lbs. sliced fresh shiitake mushrooms
2½ cups thinly sliced onions
1½ cups reduced-sodium beef broth
1½ cups dry red wine or additional reduced-sodium beef broth

ARRABBIATA SAUCE WITH ZUCCHINI NOODLES

We decided to re-create one of our favorite sauces and serve it over zucchini pasta for a lighter, healthier alternative to the popular Italian dish. The results were amazing—spicy, full of flavor and naturally gluten-free.
—*Courtney Stultz, Weir, KS*

Prep: **10 min.** • Cook: **35 min.**
Makes: **4 servings**

- 1 **lb. lean ground beef (90% lean)**
- ½ **cup finely chopped onion**
- 2 **garlic cloves, minced**
- 1 **can (14½ oz.) petite diced tomatoes, undrained**
- ¼ **cup dry red wine or beef broth**
- 3 **Tbsp. tomato paste**
- 2 **tsp. honey**
- 1 **tsp. cider vinegar**
- ¾ **tsp. dried basil**
- ½ **to 1 tsp. crushed red pepper flakes**
- ½ **tsp. salt**
- ¼ **tsp. dried oregano**
- ¼ **tsp. dried thyme**

ZUCCHINI NOODLES

- 2 **large zucchini**
- 1 **Tbsp. olive oil**
- ¼ **tsp. salt**
   Chopped fresh parsley, optional

1. In a large saucepan, cook beef with onion and garlic over medium-high heat until meat is no longer pink; 5-7 minutes; crumble beef. Stir in tomatoes, wine, tomato paste, honey, vinegar and seasonings; bring to a boil. Reduce heat; simmer, uncovered, until flavors are blended, about 25 minutes; stir occasionally.

2. For noodles, trim ends of zucchini. Using a spiralizer, shave zucchini into thin strands. In a large cast-iron or other heavy skillet, heat oil over medium-high heat. Add the zucchini; cook until slightly softened, 1-2 minutes, tossing constantly with tongs (do not overcook). Sprinkle with salt. Serve with sauce. If desired, sprinkle with parsley.

FREEZE OPTION: Freeze cooled sauce in freezer containers. To use, partially thaw in refrigerator overnight. Heat through in a saucepan, stirring occasionally.

1 CUP SAUCE WITH 1 CUP ZUCCHINI NOODLES: 287 cal., 13g fat (4g sat. fat), 71mg chol., 708mg sod., 17g carb. (11g sugars, 4g fiber), 26g pro.
DIABETIC EXCHANGES: 3 lean meat, 2 vegetable, ½ starch.

THE SKINNY
If a spiralizer is not available, you can also use a vegetable peeler to cut the zucchini into ribbons. Saute as directed, increasing time as necessary.

AIR-FRYER TACO KABOBS

We typically think of the grill when making kabobs, but the air fryer does an equally good job. I will sometimes add a drop or two of liquid smoke to the marinade.
—*Dixie Terry, Goreville, IL*

Prep: **15 min. + marinating**
Cook: **10 min.** • Makes: **6 servings**

- 1 **envelope taco seasoning**
- 1 **cup tomato juice**
- 2 **Tbsp. canola oil**
- 2 **lbs. beef top sirloin steak, cut into 1-in. cubes**
- 1 **medium green pepper, cut into chunks**
- 1 **medium sweet red pepper, cut into chunks**
- 1 **large onion, cut into wedges**
- 12 **cherry tomatoes**
  Optional: Salsa con queso or sour cream

1. In a large shallow dish, combine taco seasoning, tomato juice and oil; mix well. Remove ½ cup for basting; refrigerate. Add beef to dish; turn to coat. Cover and refrigerate at least 5 hours.
2. Preheat air fryer to 400° for 10 minutes. Drain and discard the marinade from beef. On 6 metal or soaked wooden skewers, alternately thread beef, peppers, onion and tomatoes. In batches, place skewers in a single layer in greased air fryer. Cook, turning and occasionally basting with reserved marinade, until the meat reaches desired doneness, about 8-10 minutes. Serve with salsa con queso or sour cream if desired.

1 KABOB: 277 cal., 10g fat (3g sat. fat), 61mg chol., 665mg sod., 12g carb. (4g sugars, 2g fiber), 34g pro.
DIABETIC EXCHANGES: 4 lean meat, 2 vegetable, 1 fat.

FREEZER BURRITOS

I love burritos, but the frozen ones are so high in salt and chemicals, so I created these. They're great to have on hand for quick dinners or late-night snacks.
—*Laura Winemiller, Delta, PA*

Prep: **35 min.** • Cook: **15 min.**
Makes: **12 servings**

- 1¼ **lbs. lean ground beef (90% lean)**
- ¼ **cup finely chopped onion**
- 1¼ **cups salsa**
- 2 **Tbsp. reduced-sodium taco seasoning**
- 2 **cans (15 oz. each) pinto beans, rinsed and drained**
- ½ **cup water**
- 2 **cups shredded reduced-fat cheddar cheese**
- 12 **flour tortillas (8 in.), warmed**

1. In a large skillet, cook beef and onion over medium heat until meat is no longer pink, 5-7 minutes, crumbling meat; drain. Stir in salsa and taco seasoning. Bring to a boil. Reduce heat; simmer, uncovered, for 2-3 minutes. Transfer to a large bowl; set aside.
2. In a food processor, combine pinto beans and water. Cover and process until almost smooth. Add to beef mixture. Stir in cheese.
3. Spoon ½ cup beef mixture down the center of each tortilla. Fold ends and sides over filling; roll up. Wrap

each burrito in waxed paper and foil. Freeze for up to 1 month.
TO USE FROZEN BURRITOS: Remove foil and waxed paper. Place 1 burrito on a microwave-safe plate. Microwave on high 2½-2¾ minutes, until a thermometer reads 165°, turning burrito over once. Let stand for 20 seconds.

1 BURRITO: 345 cal., 11g fat (4g sat. fat), 36mg chol., 677mg sod., 40g carb. (3g sugars, 3g fiber), 22g pro.
DIABETIC EXCHANGES: 2½ starch, 2 lean meat, ½ fat.

MAKE IT YOUR OWN
Anything you like in a burrito can go in these!
- Poblano peppers
- Black beans
- Cotija cheese or queso fresco

BASIC MEAT LOAF

Because I can't have much salt, I've come up with a recipe for meat loaf that is really tasty without it.
—*Lillian Wittler, Wayne, NE*

- -

Prep: **15 min.**
Bake: **45 min. + standing**
Makes: **5 servings**

- 1 large egg, lightly beaten
- ½ cup 2% milk
- 3 slices whole wheat bread, torn into pieces
- ¼ cup finely chopped onion
- 1 tsp. Worcestershire sauce
- ¼ tsp. onion powder
- ¼ tsp. garlic powder
- ¼ tsp. ground mustard
- ¼ tsp. rubbed sage
- ¼ tsp. pepper
- 1 lb. lean ground beef (90% lean)
- 3 Tbsp. ketchup

1. Preheat oven to 350°. In a large bowl, whisk egg and milk. Add bread; let stand for 5 minutes. Stir in the onion, Worcestershire sauce and seasonings. Crumble beef over bread mixture and mix lightly but thoroughly.
2. Shape into a loaf in a greased 11x7-in. baking pan. Bake, uncovered, for 35 minutes; drain.
3. Spread ketchup over top of loaf. Bake until a thermometer reads 160°, 10-20 minutes longer. Let stand for 10 minutes before slicing.
1 PIECE: 226 cal., 10g fat (4g sat. fat), 96mg chol., 276mg sod., 12g carb. (5g sugars, 1g fiber), 22g pro.
DIABETIC EXCHANGES: 3 lean meat, 1 starch.

EASY SALISBURY STEAK

This dish can be made in 25 minutes or made ahead and reheated with the gravy in the microwave. I often double the recipe and freeze one batch of cooked steaks and gravy for an even faster meal on an especially busy night.
—*Carol Callahan, Rome, GA*

- -

Takes: **25 min.** • Makes: **4 servings**

- ⅓ cup chopped onion
- ¼ cup crushed saltines
- 1 large egg white, lightly beaten
- 2 Tbsp. 2% milk
- 1 Tbsp. prepared horseradish
- ¼ tsp. salt, optional
- ⅛ tsp. pepper
- 1 lb. lean ground beef (90% lean)
- 1 jar (12 oz.) beef gravy
- 1½ cups sliced fresh mushrooms
- 2 Tbsp. water
  Hot cooked noodles, optional

1. In a large bowl, combine the onion, saltines, egg white, milk, horseradish, salt if desired, and pepper. Crumble beef over mixture. Shape into 4 oval patties.
2. In a large skillet over medium heat, cook patties until no pink remains and a thermometer reads 160°, 5-6 minutes per side.
3. Remove patties and keep warm. Add the gravy, mushrooms and water to skillet; cook until heated through, 3-5 minutes. Serve with patties and, if desired, noodles.
1 SERVING: 253 cal., 11g fat (4g sat. fat), 78mg chol., 582mg sod., 11g carb. (2g sugars, 1g fiber), 26g pro.
DIABETIC EXCHANGES: 3 lean meat, ½ starch.

BEEF & SPINACH LO MEIN

If you like a good stir-fry, this dish will definitely satisfy. I discovered the recipe at an international luncheon, and it's now a favorite go-to meal.
—Denise Patterson, Bainbridge, OH

Takes: **30 min.** • Makes: **5 servings**

- ¼ cup hoisin sauce
- 2 Tbsp. soy sauce
- 1 Tbsp. water
- 2 tsp. sesame oil
- 2 garlic cloves, minced
- ¼ tsp. crushed red pepper flakes
- 1 lb. beef top round steak, thinly sliced
- 6 oz. uncooked spaghetti
- 4 tsp. canola oil, divided
- 1 can (8 oz.) sliced water chestnuts, drained
- 2 green onions, sliced
- 1 pkg. (10 oz.) fresh spinach, coarsely chopped
- 1 red chili pepper, seeded and thinly sliced

1. In a small bowl, mix the first 6 ingredients. Remove ¼ cup of the mixture to a large bowl; add beef and toss to coat. Marinate at room temperature for 10 minutes.
2. Cook spaghetti according to package directions. Meanwhile, in a large skillet, heat 1½ tsp. canola oil. Add half the beef mixture; stir-fry until no longer pink, 1-2 minutes. Remove from pan. Repeat with an additional 1½ tsp. oil and remaining beef mixture.
3. Stir-fry water chestnuts and green onions in the remaining 1 tsp. canola oil for 30 seconds. Stir in spinach and the remaining hoisin mixture; cook until spinach is wilted. Return beef to pan; heat through.
4. Drain spaghetti; add to the beef mixture and toss to combine. Sprinkle with chili pepper.
1⅓ CUPS: 358 cal., 10g fat (2g sat. fat), 51mg chol., 681mg sod., 40g carb. (6g sugars, 4g fiber), 28g pro.
DIABETIC EXCHANGES: 3 lean meat, 2 vegetable, 1½ starch, 1 fat.

THE SKINNY

Whole wheat or other multigrain spaghetti can be great in Asian dishes. Besides being more nutritious than regular spaghetti, they provide a more robust and toothsome texture. Buckwheat or soba noodles would also be nice, and we always love a good ramen noodle recipe!

¾ tsp. pepper
2 cups shredded part-skim mozzarella cheese, divided

1. Preheat oven to 350°. Cook mostaccioli according to package directions. Meanwhile, in a large skillet, cook beef, green pepper and onion over medium heat until the meat is no longer pink; drain. Stir in spaghetti sauce, soup, Italian seasoning and pepper.

2. Drain mostaccioli. Add the mostaccioli and 1½ cups cheese to the beef mixture. Transfer to two greased 11x7-in. baking dishes. Sprinkle evenly with the remaining ½ cup cheese.

3. Cover and bake for 20 minutes. Uncover; bake until the dish is bubbly and cheese is melted, 5-10 minutes longer.

FREEZE OPTION: Cover and freeze unbaked casseroles up to 3 months. To use, thaw in the refrigerator overnight. Remove from refrigerator 30 minutes before baking. Bake, covered, at 350° until a thermometer reads 165°, 50-60 minutes.

1 CUP: 351 cal., 12g fat (5g sat. fat), 42mg chol., 633mg sod., 39g carb. (7g sugars, 3g fiber), 22g pro.
DIABETIC EXCHANGES: 2½ starch, 2 lean meat, 1 fat.

MOSTACCIOLI

Years ago, a friend shared her cheesy baked pasta recipe with me. I love to serve it with a salad and garlic bread. It's great for entertaining.
—*Margaret McNeil, Germantown, TN*

- -

Prep: **25 min.** • Bake: **25 min.**
Makes: **2 casseroles**
(6 servings each)

1 pkg. (16 oz.) mostaccioli
1½ lbs. ground beef
1¼ cups chopped green pepper
1 cup chopped onion
1 jar (26 oz.) spaghetti sauce
1 can (10¾ oz.) condensed cheddar cheese soup, undiluted
1½ tsp. Italian seasoning

MEXICAN STUFFED PEPPERS

Stuffed peppers make a nutritious and economical meal. I top them with sour cream and serve tortilla chips and salsa on the side. Replace the ground beef with lean ground turkey if you want to cut fat.
—*Kim Coleman, Columbia, SC*

Prep: **25 min.** • Bake: **30 min.**
Makes: **8 servings**

- 1 **lb. lean ground beef (90% lean)**
- 1 **can (14½ oz.) diced tomatoes and green chiles, undrained**
- 1 **envelope (5.4 oz.) Mexican-style rice and pasta mix**
- 1½ **cups water**
- 8 **medium sweet peppers**
- 2 **cups shredded Mexican cheese blend, divided**
    Minced fresh cilantro, optional

1. Preheat oven to 375°. In a large skillet, cook and crumble beef over medium heat until no longer pink, 5-7 minutes; drain. Stir in tomatoes, rice mix and water; bring to a boil. Reduce heat; simmer, covered, until liquid is absorbed, 6-8 minutes.
2. Cut and discard tops from the peppers; remove seeds. Place peppers in a greased 13x9-in. baking dish. Place ⅓ cup beef mixture in each pepper; sprinkle each with 2 Tbsp. cheese. Top with the remaining rice mixture. Bake, covered, for 25 minutes.
3. Sprinkle with remaining 1 cup cheese. Bake, uncovered, until cheese is melted and peppers are crisp-tender, 5-10 minutes longer. If desired, top with cilantro .

1 STUFFED PEPPER: 301 cal., 14g fat (8g sat. fat), 61mg chol., 797mg sod., 23g carb. (4g sugars, 3g fiber), 20g pro.

1 medium tomato, seeded and chopped
½ cup fresh baby spinach, thinly sliced
12 Greek pitted olives, thinly sliced
½ cup shredded part-skim mozzarella cheese
¼ cup crumbled feta cheese

1. Preheat oven to 400°. Heat oil in a large nonstick skillet. Cook the beef, onion and garlic over medium heat until meat is no longer pink, 5-6 minutes; crumble meat; drain. Stir in tomato sauce and rosemary; bring to a boil. Reduce heat and simmer, uncovered, until thickened, 6-9 minutes.

2. Place pita halves, cut side up, on a baking sheet. Top with meat mixture, tomato, spinach and olives. Sprinkle with cheeses. Bake until cheeses are melted, 4-6 minutes.

1 PIZZA: 287 cal., 12g fat (5g sat. fat), 47mg chol., 783mg sod., 25g carb. (3g sugars, 4g fiber), 21g pro.
DIABETIC EXCHANGES: 2 lean meat, 1½ starch, 1 fat.

MAKE IT YOUR OWN
Pizza is infinitely adaptable! Put whatever you like on yours. Keep to the Mediterranean theme by adding artichokes or anchovies, or go for an Italian feel by using sausage and fresh mozzarella. You can also swap out the tomato sauce for a white sauce or a pesto, if you like.

MINI MEDITERRANEAN PIZZA
I was on a mini pizza kick and had already served up Mexican and Italian variations, so I opted for a Mediterranean version and came up with these.
—*Jenny Dubinsky, Inwood, WV*

Prep: **30 min.** • Bake: **5 min.**
Makes: **4 servings**

1 Tbsp. olive oil
8 oz. lean ground beef (90% lean)
¼ cup finely chopped onion
2 garlic cloves, minced
1 can (8 oz.) tomato sauce
1 tsp. minced fresh rosemary or ¼ tsp. dried rosemary, crushed
2 whole wheat pita breads (6 in.), cut in half horizontally

MEDITERRANEAN POT ROAST DINNER

I first made this recipe one cold winter day. My family (adults, kids and dogs) were having a blast playing in the snow all day, and when we came inside supper was ready!
—*Holly Battiste, Barrington, NJ*

Prep: **30 min.** • Cook: **8 hours**
Makes: **8 servings**

2 lbs. potatoes (about 6 medium), peeled and cut into 2-in. pieces
5 medium carrots (about ¾ lb.), cut into 1-in. pieces
2 Tbsp. all-purpose flour
1 boneless beef chuck roast (3 to 4 lbs.)
1 Tbsp. olive oil
8 large fresh mushrooms, quartered
2 celery ribs, chopped
1 medium onion, thinly sliced
¼ cup sliced Greek olives
½ cup minced fresh parsley, divided
1 can (14½ oz.) fire-roasted diced tomatoes, undrained
1 Tbsp. minced fresh oregano or 1 tsp. dried oregano
1 Tbsp. lemon juice
2 tsp. minced fresh rosemary or ½ tsp. dried rosemary, crushed
2 garlic cloves, minced
¾ tsp. salt
¼ tsp. pepper
¼ tsp. crushed red pepper flakes, optional

1. Place potatoes and carrots in a 6-qt. slow cooker. Sprinkle flour over all surfaces of roast. In a large skillet, heat oil over medium-high heat. Brown roast on all sides. Place over vegetables.
2. Add mushrooms, celery, onion, olives and ¼ cup parsley to slow cooker. In a small bowl, mix the remaining ingredients (excluding the remaining parsley); pour over top of the roast.
3. Cook, covered, on low until the meat and vegetables are tender, 8-10 hours. Remove beef. Stir the remaining ¼ cup parsley into the vegetables. Serve beef with the vegetables.

5 OZ. COOKED BEEF WITH 1 CUP VEGETABLES: 422 cal., 18g fat (6g sat. fat), 111mg chol., 538mg sod., 28g carb. (6g sugars, 4g fiber), 37g pro. **DIABETIC EXCHANGES:** 5 lean meat, 1½ starch, 1 vegetable, ½ fat.

PRESSURE-COOKER BEEF TIPS

These beef tips remind me of a childhood favorite. I cook them with mushrooms and serve over brown rice, noodles or mashed potatoes.
—*Amy Lents, Grand Forks, ND*

Prep: **20 min.** • Cook: **15 min.**
Makes: **4 servings**

- 3 tsp. olive oil
- 1 beef top sirloin steak (1 lb.), cubed
- ½ tsp. salt
- ¼ tsp. pepper
- ⅓ cup dry red wine or beef broth
- ½ lb. sliced baby portobello mushrooms
- 1 small onion, halved and sliced
- 2 cups beef broth
- 1 Tbsp. Worcestershire sauce
- 3 to 4 Tbsp. cornstarch
- ¼ cup cold water
  Hot cooked mashed potatoes

1. Select saute setting on a 6-qt. electric pressure cooker and adjust for medium heat. Add 2 tsp. oil. Sprinkle beef with salt and pepper. Brown meat in batches, adding the remaining oil as needed. Transfer meat to a bowl.

2. Add wine to cooker, stirring to loosen browned bits. Press cancel. Return beef to cooker; add the mushrooms, onion, broth and Worcestershire sauce. Lock lid; close the pressure-release valve. Adjust to pressure-cook on high for 15 minutes. Quick-release pressure.

3. Select saute setting and adjust for low heat; bring liquid to a boil. In a small bowl, mix cornstarch and water until smooth; gradually stir into beef mixture. Cook and stir until sauce is thickened, 1-2 minutes. Serve with mashed potatoes.

1 CUP: 235 cal., 8g fat (2g sat. fat), 46mg chol., 837mg sod., 10g carb. (2g sugars, 1g fiber), 27g pro.

ASIAN BEEF & NOODLES

This yummy, economical dish takes only 5 ingredients—all of which are easy to keep on hand. Serve with a dash of soy sauce and a side of fresh pineapple slices. You can also try it with ground turkey instead of beef!
—*Laura Shull Stenberg, Wyoming, MN*

Takes: **20 min.** • Makes: **4 servings**

- 1 **lb. lean ground beef (90% lean)**
- 2 **pkg. (3 oz. each) soy sauce ramen noodles, crumbled**
- 2½ **cups water**
- 2 **cups frozen broccoli stir-fry vegetable blend**
- ¼ **tsp. ground ginger**
- 2 **Tbsp. thinly sliced green onion**

1. In a large skillet, cook beef over medium heat until no longer pink. Crumble beef; drain. Add contents of 1 ramen noodle flavoring packet; stir until dissolved. Remove beef and set aside.

2. In the same skillet, combine the water, vegetables, ginger, noodles and contents of the remaining flavoring packet. Bring to a boil. Reduce heat; cover and simmer until the noodles are tender, 3-4 minutes, stirring occasionally. Return beef to the pan and heat through. Stir in onion.

1½ CUPS: 383 cal., 16g fat (7g sat. fat), 71mg chol., 546mg sod., 29g carb. (2g sugars, 2g fiber), 27g pro.

1. Core cabbage head. Cook cabbage, stem side down, in boiling water to cover just until outer leaves separate easily from head without tearing. Reserve 12 large leaves for rolls (refrigerate remaining cabbage for another use). Trim the thick vein from the bottom of each leaf, making a V-shaped cut.

2. In a large bowl, combine rice, onion, egg, milk, salt and pepper. Add beef; mix lightly but thoroughly. Place about ¼ of the beef mixture on each leaf. Pull together the cut edges of the leaf to overlap; fold over filling. Fold in sides and roll up.

3. Place trivet insert and ½ cup water in a 6-qt. electric pressure cooker. Set 6 rolls on the trivet, seam side down. In a bowl, mix tomato sauce, brown sugar, lemon juice and Worcestershire sauce; pour half the sauce over cabbage rolls. Top with the remaining rolls and sauce.

4. Lock lid; close pressure-release valve. Adjust to pressure-cook on high for 15 minutes. Quick-release pressure. A thermometer inserted in beef should read at least 160°.

5. Remove rolls to a serving platter; keep warm. Remove trivet. In a small bowl, mix cornstarch and remaining 2 Tbsp. water until smooth; stir into pressure cooker. Select saute setting and adjust for low heat. Simmer, stirring constantly, until thickened, 1-2 minutes. Serve with rolls.

2 CABBAGE ROLLS: 219 cal., 8g fat (3g sat. fat), 78mg chol., 446mg sod., 19g carb. (5g sugars, 2g fiber), 18g pro. **DIABETIC EXCHANGES:** 2 lean meat, 1 starch.

PRESSURE-COOKER BEEF & RICE CABBAGE ROLLS

My family can't wait for dinner when I'm serving my tasty cabbage rolls. The dish comes together in a pinch and always satisfies.
—Lynn Bowen, Geraldine, AL

Prep: **45 min.** • Cook: **20 min.**
Makes: **6 servings**

- 1 small head cabbage
- 1 cup cooked brown rice
- ¼ cup finely chopped onion
- 1 large egg, lightly beaten
- ¼ cup fat-free milk
- ½ tsp. salt
- ¼ tsp. pepper
- 1 lb. lean ground beef (90% lean)
- ½ cup plus 2 Tbsp. water, divided
- 1 can (8 oz.) tomato sauce
- 1 Tbsp. brown sugar
- 1 Tbsp. lemon juice
- 1 tsp. Worcestershire sauce
- 2 Tbsp. cornstarch

SAUCY BEEF WITH BROCCOLI

When I'm looking for a fast entree, I turn to this stir-fry. It features a tantalizing sauce made with garlic and ginger.
—*Rosa Evans, Odessa, MO*

Takes: **30 min.** • Makes: **2 servings**

1 Tbsp. cornstarch
½ cup reduced-sodium beef broth
¼ cup sherry or additional beef broth
2 Tbsp. reduced-sodium soy sauce
1 Tbsp. brown sugar
1 garlic clove, minced
1 tsp. minced fresh gingerroot

2 tsp. canola oil, divided
½ lb. beef top sirloin steak, cut into ¼-in.-thick strips
2 cups fresh small broccoli florets
8 green onions, cut into 1-in. pieces

1. Mix the first 7 ingredients. In a large nonstick skillet, heat 1 tsp. oil over medium-high heat; stir-fry beef until browned, 1-3 minutes. Remove from pan.

2. Stir-fry broccoli in remaining oil until crisp-tender, 3-5 minutes. Add green onions; cook just until tender, 1-2 minutes. Stir cornstarch mixture and add to pan. Bring to a boil; cook and stir until sauce is thickened, 2-3 minutes. Add beef; heat through.

1¼ CUPS: 313 cal., 11g fat (3g sat. fat), 68mg chol., 816mg sod., 20g carb. (11g sugars, 4g fiber), 29g pro.
DIABETIC EXCHANGES: 3 lean meat, 1 starch, 1 vegetable, 1 fat.

THE SKINNY

You can adjust this recipe by adding extra veggies like julienned red peppers or carrots, a sesame seed topping or fresh mushrooms. If you like it spicy, sprinkle in red pepper flakes.

SPAGHETTI PIE

A classic combination is remade into a creamy, family-pleasing casserole in this quick and easy dish. This recipe was given to me several years ago, and my family never gets tired of it.

—*Ellen Thompson, Springfield, OH*

Prep: **30 min.** • Bake: **25 min.**
Makes: **6 servings**

- 6 oz. uncooked spaghetti
- 1 lb. lean ground beef (90% lean)
- ½ cup finely chopped onion
- ¼ cup chopped green pepper
- 1 cup undrained canned diced tomatoes
- 1 can (6 oz.) tomato paste
- 1 tsp. dried oregano
- ¾ tsp. salt
- ½ tsp. garlic powder
- ¼ tsp. pepper
- ¼ tsp. sugar
- 2 large egg whites, lightly beaten
- 1 Tbsp. butter, melted
- ¼ cup grated Parmesan cheese
- 1 cup (8 oz.) 2% cottage cheese
- ½ cup shredded part-skim mozzarella cheese

1. Preheat oven to 350°. Cook spaghetti according to package directions for al dente; drain.
2. In a large skillet, cook beef, onion and green pepper over medium heat, until beef is no longer pink, 5-7 minutes. Crumble beef; drain. Stir in tomatoes, tomato paste, seasonings and sugar.
3. In a large bowl, whisk egg whites, melted butter and Parmesan cheese until blended. Add spaghetti and toss to coat. Press spaghetti mixture onto bottom and up the side of a greased 9-in. deep-dish pie plate, forming a crust. Spread cottage cheese onto bottom; top with the beef mixture.
4. Bake, uncovered, 20 minutes. Sprinkle with mozzarella cheese. Bake until heated through and cheese is melted, 5-10 minutes longer. Let stand for 5 minutes before serving.
1 PIECE: 348 cal., 10g fat (5g sat. fat), 52mg chol., 690mg sod., 33g carb. (9g sugars, 4g fiber), 29g pro.
DIABETIC EXCHANGES: 3 lean meat, 2 vegetable, 1½ starch, 1 fat.

SPINACH TOMATO BURGERS

Every Friday night is burger night at our house. Tomatoes add fresh flavor, and cool spinach dip brings it all together. We often skip the buns and serve these over grilled cabbage.
—*Courtney Stultz, Weir, KS*

Takes: **20 min.** • Makes: **4 servings**

- 1 large egg, lightly beaten
- 2 Tbsp. fat-free milk
- ½ cup soft bread crumbs
- 1 tsp. dried basil
- ½ tsp. salt
- ¼ tsp. pepper
- 1 lb. lean ground beef (90% lean)
- 4 whole wheat hamburger buns, split
- ¼ cup spinach dip
- ¼ cup julienned soft sun-dried tomatoes (not packed in oil) Lettuce leaves

1. Combine the first 6 ingredients. Add beef; mix lightly but thoroughly. Shape into four ½-in.-thick patties.
2. Place burgers on an oiled grill rack or in a greased 15x10x1-in. pan. Grill, covered, over medium heat or broil 4-5 in. from the heat until a thermometer reads 160°, 4-5 minutes per side. Grill buns, cut side down, over medium heat until toasted. Serve burgers on buns; top with spinach dip, tomatoes and lettuce.
1 BURGER: 389 cal., 17g fat (6g sat. fat), 125mg chol., 737mg sod., 29g carb. (7g sugars, 4g fiber), 29g pro.
DIABETIC EXCHANGES: 3 lean meat, 2 starch, 1½ fat.

THE SKINNY

Using lean ground beef instead of beef that's 80% lean saves 45 calories per 4-oz. serving of beef. Lean ground beef is also 29% lower in saturated fat.

PORK, HAM & MORE

HOISIN PORK WRAPS

For a casual get-together, set a buffet with the pork, tortillas and red cabbage slaw and have your guests make their own wraps.
—*Linda Woo, Derby, KS*

Prep: **25 min.** • Cook: **7 hours**
Makes: **15 servings**

- 1 boneless pork loin roast (3 lbs.)
- 1 cup hoisin sauce, divided
- 1 Tbsp. minced fresh gingerroot
- 6 cups shredded red cabbage
- 1½ cups shredded carrots
- ¼ cup thinly sliced green onions
- 3 Tbsp. rice vinegar
- 4½ tsp. sugar
- 15 flour tortillas (8 in.), warmed

1. Cut roast in half. Combine ⅓ cup hoisin sauce and ginger; rub over pork. Transfer to a 4 or 5-qt. slow cooker. Cover and cook on low for 7-8 hours or until pork is tender.
2. Meanwhile, in a large bowl, combine the cabbage, carrots, onions, vinegar and sugar. Chill until serving.
3. Shred meat with 2 forks and return to the slow cooker; heat through. Place 2 tsp. remaining hoisin sauce down the center of each tortilla, top with ⅓ cup shredded pork and ⅓ cup coleslaw. Roll up.
1 SERVING: 314 cal., 8g fat (2g sat. fat), 46mg chol., 564mg sod., 37g carb. (7g sugars, 1g fiber), 23g pro. **DIABETIC EXCHANGES:** 2½ starch, 2 lean meat.

THE SKINNY

Fresh gingerroot is a great way to add sharp, spicy flair with barely any extra fat or sodium. Best of all, you can wrap unused gingerroot in foil and freeze for future use.

MULTICOOKER CAJUN PORK LOIN WITH SWEET POTATO PUREE

A sauce made with sweet potatoes gives a golden look to this juicy pork roast. It will be your new fall favorite.
—*Holly Ottum, Racine, WI*

Prep: **10 min.**
Pressure-Cook: **30 min.**
Air-Fry: **10 min.**
Makes: **16 servings**

- 4   tsp. Cajun seasoning, divided
- 1   boneless pork loin roast (3½ to 4 lbs.)
- 4   cups cubed peeled sweet potatoes
- 1   medium onion, chopped
- ½   cup chicken broth
- 3   garlic cloves, minced

1. Rub 3 tsp. Cajun seasoning over roast. Add the remaining ingredients to inner pot of a large multi-cooker; top with roast. Lock pressure lid. Press pressure function; select pork setting. Set to medium cook time (30 minutes). Start.

2. Let pressure release naturally for 10 minutes; quick-release any remaining pressure. Remove roast; transfer vegetable mixture to a bowl; mash until smooth. Set aside; keep warm. Wipe inner pot clean.

3. Place roast on wire rack with handles. Use handles to lower into inner pot. Cover with air frying lid. Press air fry function; select the custom setting. Press timer; set to 10 minutes. Start. Cook until a meat thermometer reads 145°. Let stand for 5-10 minutes before slicing. Serve with sweet potato mixture.

3 OZ. COOKED PORK WITH ½ CUP VEGETABLE MIXTURE: 156 cal., 5g fat (2g sat. fat), 50mg chol., 178mg sod., 8g carb. (2g sugars, 1g fiber), 20g pro. **DIABETIC EXCHANGES:** 3 lean meat, ½ starch.

THE SKINNY
Air fryers and electric pressure cookers allow home chefs to whip up tasty meals without oil. This pork loin, for instance, offers just 5g of fat per serving.

RASPBERRY-WALNUT PORK SALAD

Raspberry, rosemary, Gorgonzola and walnuts combine to make a pork dish that's bursting with flavor.
—*Virginia C. Anthony, Jacksonville, FL*

Prep: **30 min.** • Cook: **20 min.**
Makes: **6 servings**

- 1½ **lbs. pork tenderloins, cut into 1-in. slices**
- ⅓ **cup ground walnuts**
- 2 **Tbsp. all-purpose flour**
- ½ **tsp. salt, divided**
- ½ **tsp. coarsely ground pepper, divided**
- 4½ **tsp. walnut oil**
- ⅓ **cup chopped shallot**
- 1 **medium pear, chopped**
- ¾ **cup reduced-sodium chicken broth**
- ¾ **cup seedless raspberry preserves**
- ½ **cup raspberry vinegar**
- 2 **tsp. minced fresh rosemary or ½ tsp. dried rosemary, crushed**
- 2 **tsp. minced fresh sage**
- 2 **pkg. (6 oz. each) fresh baby spinach**
- ½ **cup crumbled Gorgonzola cheese**
- ½ **cup chopped walnuts, toasted**

1. Flatten the pork slices to ½-in. thickness. In a shallow dish, combine the ground walnuts, flour, ¼ tsp. salt and ¼ tsp. pepper. Add pork, a few pieces at a time, and turn to coat.
2. In a large skillet over medium heat, cook pork in oil in batches on each side or until the meat is no longer pink, 2-3 minutes. Remove and keep warm.
3. In the same skillet, saute the shallot until tender. Add pear; cook 1 minute longer. Add the broth, preserves and vinegar. Bring to a boil; cook until slightly thickened, 6-8 minutes. Stir in the rosemary, sage and remaining ¼ tsp. salt and ¼ tsp. pepper. Remove from heat.
4. Place spinach in a large bowl. Add pear mixture; toss to coat. Divide among 6 plates; top each with pork. Sprinkle with the cheese and chopped walnuts.
1 SERVING: 398 cal., 17g fat (4g sat. fat), 71mg chol., 415mg sod., 34g carb. (25g sugars, 2g fiber), 30g pro.

BAJA PORK TACOS

This delicious recipe is my copycat version of the most excellent Mexican food we ever had. The original recipe used beef, but this pork version comes mighty close to the same taste.
—*Ariella Winn, Mesquite, TX*

Prep: **10 min.** • Cook: **8 hours**
Makes: **12 servings**

- 1 boneless pork sirloin roast (3 lbs.)
- 5 cans (4 oz. each) chopped green chiles
- 2 Tbsp. reduced-sodium taco seasoning
- 3 tsp. ground cumin
- 24 corn tortillas (6 in.), warmed
- 3 cups shredded lettuce
- 1½ cups shredded part-skim mozzarella cheese

1. Cut the roast in half; place in a 3- or 4-qt. slow cooker. Mix chiles, taco seasoning and cumin; spoon over pork. Cook, covered, on low 8-10 hours or until meat is tender.
2. Remove pork; cool slightly. Skim fat from cooking juices. Shred meat with 2 forks. Return to slow cooker; heat through. Serve in tortillas with lettuce and cheese.

FREEZE OPTION: Place cooled pork mixture in freezer containers; freeze for up to 3 months. To use, partially thaw in refrigerator overnight. Heat through in a covered saucepan, stirring gently and adding a little broth if necessary.
2 TACOS: 320 cal., 11g fat (4g sat. fat), 77mg chol., 434mg sod., 26g carb. (1g sugars, 4g fiber), 30g pro. **DIABETIC EXCHANGES:** 3 medium-fat meat, 2 starch.

AIR-FRYER STUFFED PORK CHOPS

This is one of my favorite dishes to serve to guests because I know they'll love it.
—*Lorraine Darocha, Mountain City, TN*

Prep: **40 min.** • Cook: **20 min.**
Makes: **4 servings**

- ½ tsp. olive oil
- 1 celery rib, chopped
- ¼ cup chopped onion
- 4 slices white bread, cubed
- 2 Tbsp. minced fresh parsley
- ⅛ tsp. salt
- ⅛ tsp. rubbed sage
- ⅛ tsp. white pepper
- ⅛ tsp. dried marjoram
- ⅛ tsp. dried thyme
- ⅓ cup reduced-sodium chicken broth

PORK CHOPS
- 4 pork rib chops (7 oz. each)
- ¼ tsp. salt
- ¼ tsp. pepper

1. In a large skillet, heat oil over medium-high heat. Add celery and onion; cook and stir until tender, 4-5 minutes. Remove from heat. In a large bowl, combine bread and seasonings. Add celery mixture and broth; toss to coat.
2. Cut a pocket in each pork chop by making a horizontal slice almost to the bone. Fill pork chops with the bread mixture; secure chops with toothpicks if necessary.
3. Preheat air fryer to 325°. Sprinkle chops with salt and pepper. Arrange in single layer on greased tray in air-fryer basket. Cook 10 minutes. Turn and cook until a thermometer inserted in center of stuffing reads 165° and thermometer inserted in pork reads at least 145°, 6-8 minutes longer. Let stand 5 minutes; discard toothpicks before serving.
1 PORK CHOP: 274 cal., 10g fat (4g sat. fat), 63mg chol., 457mg sod., 16g carb. (2g sugars, 1g fiber), 28g pro. **DIABETIC EXCHANGES:** 4 lean meat, 1 starch.

THE SKINNY
Using reduced-sodium taco seasoning saves about 80 mg of sodium per serving.

3 Tbsp. Worcestershire sauce
2 Tbsp. prepared mustard
½ tsp. salt
½ tsp. pepper
¼ tsp. liquid smoke, optional

1. Place ribs in an 11x7-in. baking dish coated with cooking spray. Sprinkle with liquid smoke if desired and salt. Add water to pan. Cover and bake at 350° for 1 hour.

2. Meanwhile, in a saucepan, saute onion in oil until tender. Add the remaining sauce ingredients; bring to a boil. Reduce heat; simmer, uncovered, for 15 minutes or until slightly thickened.

3. Drain ribs; top with half of the barbecue sauce. Cover and bake 1 hour longer or until meat is tender, basting every 20 minutes. Serve with remaining sauce.

FREEZE OPTION: Place cooled meat mixture in freezer containers. To use, partially thaw in refrigerator overnight. Microwave, covered, on high in a microwave-safe dish until heated through, gently stirring and adding a little water if necessary.

4 OZ.-WEIGHT: 292 cal., 14g fat (4g sat. fat), 91mg chol., 668mg sod., 14g carb. (0 sugars, 1g fiber), 28g pro.

BBQ COUNTRY RIBS

I created this sauce 45 years ago when I adapted a recipe I saw in a magazine. The original called for much more oil. I usually triple the sauce and keep some in my freezer to use on chicken, beef or pork.
—*Barbara Gerriets, Topeka, KS*

- -

Prep: **25 min.** • Bake: **2 hours**
Makes: **8 servings**

2½ lbs. boneless country-style pork ribs
2 tsp. liquid smoke, optional
½ tsp. salt
1 cup water
BARBECUE SAUCE
⅔ cup chopped onion
1 Tbsp. canola oil
¾ cup each water and ketchup
⅓ cup lemon juice
3 Tbsp. sugar

SKEWERED LAMB WITH BLACKBERRY-BALSAMIC GLAZE

This dish proves it takes only a few quality ingredients to make a classy main dish.
—*Elynor (Elly) Townsend, Summerfield, WI*

Prep: **10 min. + marinating**
Grill: **10 min.** • Makes: **6 servings**

½ cup seedless blackberry spreadable fruit
⅓ cup balsamic vinegar
1 Tbsp. minced fresh rosemary or 1 tsp. dried rosemary, crushed
1 Tbsp. Dijon mustard
1½ lbs. lean boneless lamb, cut into 1-in. cubes
¼ tsp. salt

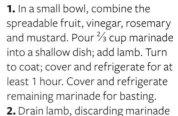

1. In a small bowl, combine the spreadable fruit, vinegar, rosemary and mustard. Pour ⅔ cup marinade into a shallow dish; add lamb. Turn to coat; cover and refrigerate for at least 1 hour. Cover and refrigerate remaining marinade for basting.

2. Drain lamb, discarding marinade in dish. Thread lamb onto 6 metal or soaked wooden skewers. Place kabobs on greased grill rack. Grill, covered, over medium heat (or broil 4 in. from the heat) until lamb reaches desired doneness (for medium-rare, a thermometer should read 135°; medium, 140°; medium-well, 145°), 10-12 minutes, turning once and basting frequently with reserved marinade. Sprinkle with salt before serving.

1 KABOB: 255 cal., 9g fat (4g sat. fat), 103mg chol., 264mg sod., 9g carb. (7g sugars, 0 fiber), 32g pro.
DIABETIC EXCHANGES: 5 lean meat, ½ starch.

CINNAMON-APPLE PORK CHOPS

When I found this recipe online a few years ago, it became a favorite. The ingredients are so easy to keep on hand, and the one-pan cleanup is a much-appreciated bonus.
—*Christina Price, Colorado Springs, CO*

- -

Takes: **25 min.** • Makes: **4 servings**

- 2 **Tbsp. reduced-fat butter, divided**
- 4 **boneless pork loin chops (4 oz. each)**
- 3 **Tbsp. brown sugar**
- 1 **tsp. ground cinnamon**
- ½ **tsp. ground nutmeg**
- ¼ **tsp. salt**
- 4 **medium tart apples, thinly sliced**
- 2 **Tbsp. chopped pecans**

1. In a large skillet, heat 1 Tbsp. butter over medium heat. Add the pork chops; cook 4-5 minutes on each side or until a thermometer reads 145°. Meanwhile, in a small bowl, mix brown sugar, cinnamon, nutmeg and salt.
2. Remove chops; keep warm. Add the apples, pecans, brown sugar mixture and remaining 1 Tbsp. butter to pan; cook and stir until apples are tender. Serve with chops.
1 PORK CHOP WITH ⅔ CUP APPLE MIXTURE: 316 cal., 12g fat (4g sat. fat), 62mg chol., 232mg sod., 31g carb. (25g sugars, 4g fiber), 22g pro.
DIABETIC EXCHANGES: 3 lean meat, 1 starch, 1 fruit, 1 fat.

HAM & SPINACH PIE

With the exception of the phyllo dough, which I always have on hand, this ham and spinach pie recipe was made entirely from my Easter dinner leftovers. One of my neighbors traded me four freshly caught trout for a slice!
—*Teena Petrus, Johnstown, PA*

- -

Prep: **30 min.**
Bake: **40 min. + cooling**
Makes: **8 servings**

- 3 **Tbsp. butter, divided**
- 1 **medium onion, halved and sliced**
- 8 **oz. sliced fresh mushrooms**
- 1 **garlic clove, minced**
- 1 **pkg. (10 oz.) frozen chopped spinach, thawed and squeezed dry**
- 6 **sheets phyllo dough (14x9 in.)**
- 2 **cups finely chopped fully cooked ham**
- 1 **cup shredded mozzarella cheese**
- 3 **large eggs, beaten**
  Optional: Salt and pepper to taste

1. Preheat oven to 350°. In a large skillet, heat 1 Tbsp. butter over medium heat. Add onion; cook and stir until transparent, 6-8 minutes. Add mushrooms and garlic; cook and stir until mushrooms are browned, about 6 minutes longer. Add the spinach and cook until heated through.
2. In a microwave, melt remaining 2 Tbsp. butter; stir until smooth. Place 1 sheet of phyllo dough on a work surface; brush with butter. Layer with 3 additional phyllo sheets, brushing each layer. Transfer to a lightly greased 11x7-in. baking dish, letting ends extend up sides. (Keep remaining phyllo covered with a damp towel to prevent it from drying out.)
3. Layer dish with ham, cheese and spinach mixture; pour eggs over filling. If desired, sprinkle with salt and pepper. Top with remaining phyllo dough. Fold dough ends over filling; pinch edges to seal. Brush with remaining butter. Cut slits in the top. Bake pie until browned, 40-45 minutes. Cool 20 minutes before cutting.
1 PIECE: 195 cal., 11g fat (6g sat. fat), 113mg chol., 633mg sod., 9g carb. (2g sugars, 2g fiber), 16g pro.
DIABETIC EXCHANGES: 2 fat, 1 lean meat, ½ starch.

1½ cups beef broth
⅓ cup all-purpose flour
⅓ cup cold water
¼ tsp. browning sauce, optional

1. Combine first 5 ingredients; rub over roast. Cover; refrigerate overnight.

2. Place carrots, potatoes and onions in a 6-qt. slow cooker; add broth. Place roast in slow cooker. Cook, covered, on low until the meat and vegetables are tender, 8-10 hours.

3. Transfer roast and vegetables to a serving platter; tent with foil. Pour cooking juices into a small saucepan. Mix flour and water until smooth; stir into pan. Bring to a boil; cook and stir until thickened, about 2 minutes. If desired, add browning sauce. Serve roast with the gravy and vegetables.

1 SERVING: 217 cal., 5g fat (2g sat. fat), 57mg chol., 230mg sod., 17g carb. (3g sugars, 2g fiber), 24g pro. **DIABETIC EXCHANGES:** 3 lean meat, 1½ starch.

MAKE IT YOUR OWN

It's easy to swap ingredients in this recipe to suit your tastes.
- Sweet potatoes for potatoes
- Rutabagas for onions
- Parsnips for carrots

SUNDAY POT ROAST

With the help of a slow cooker, you can prepare a down-home dinner any day of the week, not just on Sundays. The roast turns out tender and savory every time.
—*Brandy Schaefer, Glen Carbon, IL*

Prep: **10 min. + chilling**
Cook: **8 hours**
Makes: **14 servings**

1 tsp. dried oregano
½ tsp. onion salt
½ tsp. caraway seeds
½ tsp. pepper
¼ tsp. garlic salt
1 boneless pork loin roast (3½ to 4 lbs.), trimmed
6 medium carrots, peeled and cut into 1½-in. pieces
3 large potatoes, peeled and quartered
3 small onions, quartered

AIR-FRYER BREADED PORK CHOPS

Instant mashed potatoes and bread crumbs have a similar texture, so I wondered how the combo would be as a breading for pork chops. This is now the only way we make pork chops in our house!
—*Carrie Farias, Oak Ridge, NJ*

- -

Prep: **15 min.** • Cook: **5 min./batch**
Makes: **4 servings**

- 1   **large egg**
- 2   **Tbsp. fat-free milk**
- 2   **Tbsp. Dijon mustard**
- ¾   **cup panko bread crumbs**
- ¾   **cup mashed potato flakes**
- 2   **tsp. ground mustard**
- 2   **tsp. minced fresh sage**
- ⅓   **cup all-purpose flour**
- 8   **thin boneless pork loin chops (2 oz. each)**
- ½   **tsp. salt**
      Cooking spray

1. In a shallow bowl, whisk egg, milk and Dijon mustard. In another shallow bowl, mix bread crumbs, potato flakes, ground mustard and sage. Place flour in another shallow bowl. Sprinkle pork with salt.
2. Preheat air fryer to 400°. Dip pork in flour to coat both sides; shake off excess. Dip in egg mixture, then in bread crumb mixture, patting to help coating adhere.
3. In batches, place the chops on greased tray in air fryer basket; spritz with cooking spray. Cook until a thermometer reads at least 145°, 5-6 minutes, turning once.
2 PORK CHOPS: 297 cal., 9g fat (3g sat. fat), 101mg chol., 565mg sod., 22g carb. (1g sugars, 1g fiber), 27g pro. **DIABETIC EXCHANGES:** 3 lean meat, 1½ starch, 1 fat.

TYPICAL	MAKEOVER
405 Calories	**297** Calories
22g Fat	**9**g Fat
18g Saturated Fat	**3**g Saturated Fat
115mg Cholesterol	**101**mg Cholesterol

THE SKINNY

Keeping pork moist in the air fryer can seem tricky, but the key is to keep an eye on the meat's internal temperature. Use a digital thermometer to determine when the pork reaches 145°F, and remove the meat from the air fryer. You can also use an oil mister or even cooking spray to seal in moisture before cooking, reapplying a few times on each side of the pork.

SPICE-RUBBED LAMB CHOPS

One of my absolute favorite meals to eat anytime are lamb chops! My girls, Hanna and Amani, love watching me make my delicious chops, but they love eating them even more.
—*Nareman Dietz, Beverly Hills, MI*

Prep: **15 min. + chilling**
Bake: **5 min.**
Makes: **2 servings**

- 2 tsp. lemon juice
- 2 tsp. Worcestershire sauce
- 1½ tsp. pepper
- 1¼ tsp. ground cumin
- 1¼ tsp. curry powder
- 1 garlic clove, minced
- ½ tsp. sea salt
- ½ tsp. onion powder
- ½ tsp. crushed red pepper flakes
- 4 lamb rib chops
- 1 Tbsp. olive oil

1. Mix first 9 ingredients; spread over chops. Refrigerate chops, covered, overnight.
2. Preheat oven to 450°. In an ovenproof skillet, heat oil over medium-high heat; brown chops, about 2 minutes per side. Transfer to oven; roast until desired doneness (for medium-rare, a thermometer should read 135°; medium, 140°), 3-4 minutes.
2 LAMB CHOPS: 290 cal., 17g fat (4g sat. fat), 90mg chol., 620mg sod., 5g carb. (1g sugars, 2g fiber), 29g pro.
DIABETIC EXCHANGES: 4 lean meat, 1½ fat.

GRILLED PORK NOODLE SALAD

The only complex thing about this easy salad is the flavor! With smoky barbecued pork and a variety of fresh herbs and vegetables, this is a very comforting and tasty home-cooked meal.
—*Rosalyn Nguyen, Astoria, NY*

Prep: **40 min. + marinating**
Grill: **5 min.** • Makes: **6 servings**

- 1 jalapeno pepper, seeded and minced
- 3 Tbsp. lime juice
- 2 Tbsp. fish sauce or soy sauce
- 2 tsp. brown sugar
- 2 pork tenderloins (¾ lb. each), cut into ½-in. slices
- 1 pkg. (8.8 oz.) vermicelli-style thin rice noodles

DRESSING
- ¼ cup water
- 2 Tbsp. lime juice
- 1 Tbsp. fish sauce or soy sauce
- ½ tsp. brown sugar

SALAD
- 2 cups shredded lettuce
- 2 plum tomatoes, sliced
- 1 medium cucumber, julienned
- 2 medium carrots, julienned
- ½ cup coarsely chopped fresh cilantro
- ¼ cup loosely packed fresh mint leaves

1. In a large shallow dish, combine jalapeno, lime juice, fish sauce and brown sugar. Add the pork; turn to coat. Refrigerate, covered, 3 hours or overnight.

2. Drain the pork, discarding the marinade. On a lightly oiled grill rack, grill the pork, covered, over medium heat until a thermometer reads 145°, 1-2 minutes on each side.
3. Cook rice noodles according to package directions. Drain and rinse in cold water; drain well. In a small bowl, whisk dressing ingredients. Divide rice noodles among 6 serving bowls. Arrange vegetables, pork and herbs over noodles; drizzle with dressing and toss to combine.
1 SERVING: 315 cal., 4g fat (1g sat. fat), 64mg chol., 708mg sod., 40g carb. (3g sugars, 3g fiber), 27g pro.
DIABETIC EXCHANGES: 3 lean meat, 2 starch, 1 vegetable.

⅛ tsp. ground allspice
1 pork tenderloin (1 lb.), cut into 12 slices

1. In a small saucepan, combine the bourbon, brown sugar, vinegar, soy sauce, garlic and pepper. Bring to a boil; cook until liquid is reduced to about ½ cup, stirring occasionally.
2. Meanwhile, combine the chili powder, cinnamon, salt and allspice; rub over pork slices.
3. In a large skillet coated with cooking spray, cook pork slices over medium heat until tender, 2-4 minutes on each side. Serve with sauce.
3 OZ.-WEIGHT: 221 cal., 4g fat (1g sat. fat), 63mg chol., 581mg sod., 15g carb. (13g sugars, 0 fiber), 23g pro.
DIABETIC EXCHANGES: 3 lean meat, 1 starch.

MAKE IT YOUR OWN
Once you prepare these pork medallions, you can serve them several different ways.
- Stuff them into pitas.
- Cube them and wrap in flour tortillas.
- Slice them and toss them with fresh greens.
- Chop them up and stir into a bowl of cooked rice or orzo.

SPICED PORK MEDALLIONS WITH BOURBON SAUCE
I don't remember where I found this recipe, but it's become one of my favorite entrees to serve company. I usually prepare it with a side of roasted vegetables.
—*Kathy Kantrud, Fenton, MI*

Takes: **25 min.** • Makes: **4 servings**

½ cup bourbon or reduced-sodium chicken broth
¼ cup packed dark brown sugar
3 Tbsp. white vinegar
3 Tbsp. reduced-sodium soy sauce
2 garlic cloves, minced
½ tsp. pepper
½ tsp. chili powder
¼ tsp. ground cinnamon
⅛ tsp. salt

PORK TENDERLOIN MEDALLIONS WITH STRAWBERRY SAUCE

Pork tenderloin paired with strawberries is a heavenly match, made even more special with a tangy feta garnish. Serve with roasted spring vegetables.
—*Katherine Wollgast, Troy, MO*

Prep: **15 min.** • Cook: **20 min.**
Makes: **8 servings**

1½ cups reduced-sodium beef broth
2 cups chopped fresh strawberries, divided
½ cup white wine vinegar
¼ cup packed brown sugar
¼ cup reduced-sodium soy sauce
3 garlic cloves, minced
2 lbs. pork tenderloin, cut into ½-in. slices
1 tsp. garlic powder
½ tsp. salt
½ tsp. pepper
2 Tbsp. canola oil
2 Tbsp. cold water
2 Tbsp. cornstarch
½ cup crumbled feta cheese
½ cup chopped green onions

1. In a large saucepan, combine broth, 1 cup strawberries, vinegar, brown sugar, soy sauce and garlic; bring to a boil. Reduce heat; simmer, uncovered, 15 minutes or until slightly thickened. Strain mixture and set aside liquid, discarding any solids.

2. Sprinkle pork with garlic powder, salt and pepper. In a large skillet, heat oil over medium heat. Brown pork in batches on both sides. Remove and keep warm.

3. Add broth mixture to the pan; bring to a boil. Combine water and cornstarch until smooth and gradually stir into skillet.

4. Return pork to the pan. Bring to a boil. Reduce heat; cook and stir until sauce is thickened and pork is tender, about 2 minutes. Top servings with cheese, onions and remaining 1 cup strawberries.

1 SERVING: 244 cal., 9g fat (2g sat. fat), 68mg chol., 649mg sod., 15g carb. (9g sugars, 1g fiber), 25g pro. **DIABETIC EXCHANGES:** 3 lean meat, 1 starch, ½ fat.

HAM & CORN SOUFFLE

Breakfast is bound to be the most memorable meal of the day with this attractive souffle as its focus. The ham and corn enhance the cheesy egg flavor, and the casserole's texture is moist and light. A puffed golden top makes it look too pretty to eat...but nobody can resist!
—*Margaret Haugh Heilman, Houston, TX*

Prep: **25 min.** • Bake: **50 min.**
Makes: **4 servings**

4	**egg whites**
2	**tsp. dry bread crumbs**
1½	**cups frozen corn, thawed**
2	**green onions, thinly sliced**
⅔	**cup diced fully cooked lean ham**
¼	**cup all-purpose flour**
¼	**tsp. salt**
⅛	**tsp. cayenne pepper**
1	**cup fat-free milk**
½	**cup shredded reduced-fat sharp cheddar cheese**
2	**egg yolks**
½	**tsp. cream of tartar**

1. Place the egg whites in a large bowl; let stand at room temperature for 30 minutes. Coat a 1½-qt. baking dish with cooking spray and lightly sprinkle with the bread crumbs.

2. In a large nonstick skillet coated with cooking spray, cook corn and onions until tender. Remove from the heat; stir in ham.

3. In a small saucepan, combine the flour, salt and cayenne; gradually whisk in milk until smooth. Bring to a boil; cook and stir until thickened, about 2 minutes. Remove from the heat; stir in cheese until melted. Transfer to a large bowl; stir in corn mixture. Stir a small amount of hot mixture into egg yolks; return all to the bowl, stirring constantly. Cool slightly.

4. Add cream of tartar to egg whites; beat until stiff peaks form. With a spatula, fold a fourth of the egg whites into the milk mixture until no white streaks remain. Fold in the remaining egg whites until combined.

5. Transfer to prepared dish. Bake at 325° until top is puffed and center appears set, 50-55 minutes. Serve immediately.

1 SERVING: 248 cal., 7g fat (3g sat. fat), 123mg chol., 577mg sod., 28g carb. (0 sugars, 2g fiber), 20g pro.
DIABETIC EXCHANGES: 2 starch, 2 lean meat.

MEDITERRANEAN PORK & ORZO

On a really busy day, this meal in a bowl is one of my top picks. It's quick to put together, leaving me a lot more time to relax at the table.
—*Mary Relyea, Canastota, NY*

Takes: **30 min.** • Makes: **6 servings**

- 1½ **lbs. pork tenderloin**
- 1 **tsp. coarsely ground pepper**
- 2 **Tbsp. olive oil**
- 3 **qt. water**
- 1¼ **cups uncooked orzo pasta**
- ¼ **tsp. salt**
- 1 **pkg. (6 oz.) fresh baby spinach**
- 1 **cup grape tomatoes, halved**
- ¾ **cup crumbled feta cheese**

1. Rub pork with pepper; cut into 1-in. cubes. In a large nonstick skillet, heat oil over medium heat. Add pork; cook and stir until no longer pink, 8-10 minutes.
2. Meanwhile, in a Dutch oven, bring water to a boil. Stir in orzo and salt; cook, uncovered, 8 minutes. Stir in spinach; cook until orzo is tender and spinach is wilted, 45-60 seconds longer. Drain.
3. Add tomatoes to pork; heat through. Stir in orzo mixture and cheese.

1⅓ CUPS: 372 cal., 11g fat (4g sat. fat), 71mg chol., 306mg sod., 34g carb. (2g sugars, 3g fiber), 31g pro.
DIABETIC EXCHANGES: 3 lean meat, 2 starch, 1 vegetable, 1 fat.

FAMILY-FAVORITE POULTRY

CARIBBEAN CHICKEN STEW

I learned this recipe while living with a West Indian family. I lightened it up by leaving out the oil and sugar, removing the skin of the chicken and using chicken sausage.
—*Joanne Iovino, Kings Park, NY*

Prep: **25 min. + marinating**
Cook: **6 hours** • Makes: **8 servings**

- ¼ cup ketchup
- 3 garlic cloves, minced
- 1 Tbsp. sugar
- 1 Tbsp. hot pepper sauce
- 1 tsp. browning sauce, optional
- 1 tsp. dried basil
- 1 tsp. dried thyme
- 1 tsp. paprika
- ½ tsp. salt
- ½ tsp. dried oregano
- ½ tsp. ground allspice
- ½ tsp. pepper
- 8 bone-in chicken thighs (about 3 lbs.), skin removed
- 1 lb. fully cooked andouille chicken sausage links, sliced
- 1 medium onion, finely chopped
- 2 medium carrots, finely chopped
- 2 celery ribs, finely chopped
  Hot cooked rice, optional

1. Combine ketchup, garlic, sugar, pepper sauce and, if desired, browning sauce; stir in seasonings. Add chicken thighs, sausage and vegetables. Cover; refrigerate 8 hours or overnight.
2. Transfer chicken mixture to a 4- or 5-qt. slow cooker. Cook, covered, on low until chicken is tender, 6-8 hours. If desired, serve with rice.
1 SERVING: 309 cal., 14g fat (4g sat. fat), 131mg chol., 666mg sod., 9g carb. (6g sugars, 1g fiber), 35g pro. **DIABETIC EXCHANGES:** 5 lean meat, ½ starch.

30-MINUTE COQ AU VIN

I love being able to fix a gourmet dish in a short amount of time and still have it turn out so delicious. To reduce fat, I use chicken tenderloin pieces or skinless chicken breasts. This is really good served with rice.
—*Judy VanCoetsem, Cortland, NY*

Takes: **30 min.** • Makes: **6 servings**

- ¼ **cup all-purpose flour**
- 1 **tsp. dried thyme**
- 1 **tsp. salt, divided**
- 6 **boneless skinless chicken thighs (4 oz. each)**
- 1 **Tbsp. olive oil**
- 6 **cups quartered baby portobello mushrooms**
- 2 **cups sliced fresh carrots**
- 3 **pieces Canadian bacon, chopped**
- 1 **Tbsp. tomato paste**
- 1 **cup chicken broth**
- 1 **cup dry red wine**
  Chopped fresh thyme, optional

1. In a shallow dish, combine flour, thyme and ½ tsp. salt. Dip chicken in the flour mixture to coat both sides; shake off excess.

2. In a Dutch oven or high-sided skillet, heat oil over medium-high heat. Cook chicken until golden brown, 3-4 minutes per side. Remove from pan; keep warm.

3. In same pan, cook mushrooms, carrots, bacon, tomato paste and remaining ½ tsp. salt for 2 minutes. Add broth and wine; bring to a boil. Return chicken to the pan; reduce heat. Cook until chicken reaches 170° and carrots are just tender,

8-10 minutes. If desired, top with chopped fresh thyme.

1 SERVING: 255 cal., 11g fat (3g sat. fat), 80mg chol., 648mg sod., 9g carb. (4g sugars, 2g fiber), 26g pro.
DIABETIC EXCHANGES: 3 lean meat, ½ starch, ½ fat.

THE SKINNY

Any dry red wine will work well for this recipe. Think merlot, cabernet sauvignon or pinot noir. Coq au vin is traditionally served with a starchy side like potatoes, bread, rice or pasta, but you can also serve it with vegetables.

OVEN-FRIED CHICKEN DRUMSTICKS

This recipe uses Greek yogurt to create a marinade that makes the chicken incredibly moist. No one will guess it's been lightened up and not even fried!
—*Kimberly Wallace, Dennison, OH*

Prep: **20 min. + marinating**
Bake: **40 min.**
Makes: **4 servings**

- 1   **cup fat-free plain Greek yogurt**
- 1   **Tbsp. Dijon mustard**
- 2   **garlic cloves, minced**
- 8   **chicken drumsticks (4 oz. each), skin removed**
- ½   **cup whole wheat flour**
- 1½ **tsp. paprika**
- 1   **tsp. baking powder**
- 1   **tsp. salt**
- 1   **tsp. pepper**
      Olive oil-flavored cooking spray

1. In a large dish, combine yogurt, mustard and garlic. Add chicken and turn to coat. Cover and refrigerate 8 hours or overnight.
2. Mix flour, paprika, baking powder, salt and pepper. Remove chicken from marinade and add, 1 piece at a time, to flour mixture; toss to coat. Place on a wire rack over a baking sheet; spritz with cooking spray.
3. Bake at 425° for 40-45 minutes or until a thermometer inserted into chicken reads 170°-175°.

2 CHICKEN DRUMSTICKS: 227 cal., 7g fat (1g sat. fat), 81mg chol., 498mg sod., 9g carb. (2g sugars, 1g fiber), 31g pro. **DIABETIC EXCHANGES:** 4 lean meat, ½ starch.

TYPICAL	MAKEOVER
260 Calories	**227** Calories
16g Fat	**7g** Fat
110mg Cholesterol	**81mg** Cholesterol
860mg Sodium	**498mg** Sodium

THE SKINNY
To use an air fryer, preheat to 375°. In batches, arrange chicken in a single layer on greased tray in air-fryer basket. Cook until a thermometer reads 170°, turning halfway, about 20 minutes total. Repeat with remaining chicken. When last batch is cooked, return all chicken to basket; cook 2-3 minutes longer to heat through.

PRESSURE-COOKER
MUSHROOM CHICKEN
& PEAS

PRESSURE-COOKER MUSHROOM CHICKEN & PEAS

Amazingly fresh mushrooms from our local farmers market inspired this recipe. When you start with the best ingredients, you can't go wrong!
—*Jenn Tidwell, Fair Oaks, CA*

Takes: **20 min.** • Makes: **4 servings**

- 4 boneless skinless chicken breast halves (6 oz. each)
- 1 envelope onion mushroom soup mix
- ½ lb. baby portobello mushrooms, sliced
- 1 medium onion, chopped
- ¾ cup water
- 4 garlic cloves, minced
- 2 cups frozen peas, thawed

1. Place chicken in a 6-qt. electric pressure cooker. Sprinkle with soup mix, pressing to help seasonings adhere. Add mushrooms, onion, water and garlic. Lock lid; close pressure-release valve. Adjust to pressure-cook on high for 6 minutes.

2. Quick-release pressure. A thermometer inserted in chicken should read at least 165°. Select saute setting and adjust for low heat. Add peas; simmer, uncovered, until peas are tender, 3-5 minutes, stirring occasionally.

1 CHICKEN BREAST HALF WITH ¾ CUP VEGETABLE MIXTURE: 282 cal., 5g fat (1g sat. fat), 94mg chol., 558mg sod., 18g carb. (6g sugars, 4g fiber), 41g pro. **DIABETIC EXCHANGES:** 5 lean meat, 1 starch, 1 vegetable.

RAMEN NOODLE STIR-FRY

This mildly flavored stir-fry combines tender strips of chicken with vegetables and ramen noodles. I came up with this when I wanted a quick-fix meal for myself. Sometimes I change the vegetables or substitute ground turkey for the chicken.
—*Dawn Boothe, Lynn Haven, FL*

Takes: **15 min.** • Makes: **2 servings**

- 1 pkg. (3 oz.) ramen noodles
- 1½ cups hot water
- 8 oz. boneless skinless chicken breasts, cut into 2-in. strips
- 2 tsp. canola oil, divided
- 1 large green pepper, cubed
- ⅔ cup chopped onion
- 1 garlic clove, minced
- ½ cup reduced-sodium chicken broth
- 2 tsp. reduced-sodium soy sauce
- 1 tsp. salt-free seasoning blend
- 1 small tomato, cut into wedges

1. In a bowl, place noodles in hot water for 2 minutes; drain and set aside. Discard seasoning package or save for another use.

2. In a large nonstick skillet, stir-fry chicken in 1 tsp. oil until no longer pink. Remove and keep warm. Stir-fry green pepper, onion and garlic in the remaining 1 tsp. oil until crisp-tender. Add the chicken, broth, soy sauce, seasoning blend and noodles; toss gently. Add tomato; heat through.

2 CUPS: 410 cal., 15g fat (5g sat. fat), 63mg chol., 548mg sod., 38g carb. (6g sugars, 3g fiber), 30g pro. **DIABETIC EXCHANGES:** 3 lean meat, 2 starch, 1 vegetable, 1 fat.

THE SKINNY

The goat cheese in the burgers really stands out in this low-carb dinner. If you're not big on the earthy flavor, use feta cheese instead—it has a similar texture. If the arugula is particularly spicy or peppery, it can be a little overpowering. If so, try mixing it with spinach or other greens.

CRANBERRY TURKEY BURGERS WITH ARUGULA SALAD

These healthy burgers taste just like the holidays, all in one bite. They are a little sweet and a little savory, and they're delicious over a bed of peppery arugula.
—*Nicole Stevens, Charleston, SC*

Takes: **25 min.** • Makes: **4 servings**

- ⅓ cup dried cranberries
- ⅓ cup gluten-free soft bread crumbs
- 3 green onions, finely chopped
- 2 to 3 Tbsp. crumbled goat cheese
- 2 Tbsp. pepper jelly
- 3 garlic cloves, minced
- 1 large egg yolk
- ¼ tsp. salt
- ¼ tsp. pepper
- ¾ lb. ground turkey
- 4 cups fresh arugula
- 1 Tbsp. grapeseed oil or olive oil
- 1 Tbsp. honey

1. Preheat oven to 375°. Combine the first 9 ingredients. Add turkey and mix lightly but thoroughly. Shape into four ½-in.-thick patties; transfer to a greased baking sheet. Bake for 12 minutes. Heat broiler; broil until a thermometer inserted in the burgers reads 165°, about 5 minutes.
2. Meanwhile, toss arugula with oil. Drizzle with honey; toss to combine. Top salad with turkey burgers.
1 BURGER WITH 1 CUP SALAD: 281 cal., 12g fat (3g sat. fat), 107mg chol., 240mg sod., 26g carb. (21g sugars, 2g fiber), 19g pro.

SHEET-PAN CHICKEN CURRY DINNER

My husband loves anything curry and will even eat veggies when they have a curry sauce. This is a quick one-pan way to get a whole meal on the table with minimal fuss. Everyone loves it, and it's healthy to boot. Serve it with jasmine rice and more curry if desired.
—*Trisha Kruse, Eagle, ID*

Prep: **20 min.** • Cook: **40 min.**
Makes: **6 servings**

- 2 lbs. sweet potato, peeled and cubed
- 2 cups fresh cauliflowerets
- 1 large onion, chopped
- 3 garlic cloves, minced
- 2 Tbsp. olive oil
- 2 tsp. curry powder, divided
- 1¼ tsp. salt, divided
- 1 tsp. lemon-pepper seasoning, divided
- 6 bone-in chicken thighs (about 2¼ lbs.), skin removed
- 1 tsp. smoked paprika
- ¼ cup chicken broth

1. Preheat oven to 425°. Line a 15x10x1-in. baking pan with heavy-duty foil. Place sweet potatoes, cauliflower, onion and garlic on prepared pan. Drizzle with oil; sprinkle with 1 tsp. curry powder, ¾ tsp. salt and ½ tsp. lemon pepper; toss to coat.
2. Arrange chicken over vegetables. In a small bowl, mix paprika and the remaining 1 tsp. curry powder, ½ tsp. salt and ½ tsp. lemon pepper; sprinkle over chicken. Roast until the vegetables are almost tender, 30-35 minutes. Drizzle with chicken broth; bake until thermometer inserted in the chicken reads 170°-175° and vegetables are tender, 7-10 minutes longer.
1 SERVING: 409 cal., 14g fat (3g sat. fat), 87mg chol., 686mg sod., 42g carb. (17g sugars, 6g fiber), 28g pro.
DIABETIC EXCHANGES: 4 lean meat, 3 starch, 1 fat.

MAKE IT YOUR OWN
Try other root vegetables such as parsnips or potatoes or winter squash. You can use sweet or red onions for a different flavor or color, too.

HEALTHY CHIPOTLE CHICKEN PUMPKIN PIZZA

Think pizza and pumpkin can't go together? Think again! The sweet pumpkin paired with spicy chipotle peppers makes a delicious, balanced sauce. I love that this recipe incorporates healthy ingredients in a fun, family-friendly way.
—Julie Peterson, Crofton, MD

Prep: **20 min.** • Bake: **15 min./batch**
Makes: **2 pizzas (4 pieces each)**

2 pkg. (7½ oz. each) frozen cauliflower pizza crust or 2 prebaked 12-in. thin whole wheat pizza crusts
1 Tbsp. olive oil
¾ cup canned pumpkin
2 chipotle peppers in adobo sauce, minced
¼ tsp. salt
⅛ tsp. pepper
1½ cups cubed cooked chicken
½ cup mild chunky salsa
1½ cups shredded part-skim mozzarella cheese
¼ cup thinly sliced red onion
Minced fresh cilantro, optional

1. Preheat oven to 425°. Place crusts on ungreased baking sheets; brush with oil. Combine pumpkin, minced chipotle peppers, salt and pepper; spread over crusts. Combine chicken and salsa; spoon over pumpkin layer. Top with cheese and red onion.

2. Bake until the edges are lightly browned and the cheese is melted, 12-15 minutes. Let stand 5 minutes before cutting. If desired, sprinkle with cilantro.

1 PIECE: 225 cal., 9g fat (3g sat. fat), 37mg chol., 504mg sod., 21g carb. (4g sugars, 3g fiber), 15g pro. **DIABETIC EXCHANGES:** 2 lean meat, 1 starch, 1 vegetable, ½ fat.

PRESSURE-COOKER GARDEN CHICKEN CACCIATORE

Treat company to this perfect Italian meal. You'll have time to visit with your guests while it simmers, and it often earns me rave reviews. I like to serve it with couscous, green beans and a dry red wine. Mangia!
—*Martha Schirmacher, Sterling Heights, MI*

Takes: **25 minutes**
Makes: **12 servings**

- 12   boneless skinless chicken thighs (about 3 lbs.)
- 2   medium green peppers, chopped
- 1   can (14½ oz.) diced tomatoes with basil, oregano and garlic, undrained
- 1   can (6 oz.) tomato paste
- 1   medium onion, chopped
- ½   cup reduced-sodium chicken broth
- ¼   cup dry red wine or additional reduced-sodium chicken broth
- 3   garlic cloves, minced
- ¾   tsp. salt
- ⅛   tsp. pepper
- 2   Tbsp. cornstarch
- 2   Tbsp. cold water
  Minced fresh parsley, optional

1. Place chicken in an 6- or 8-qt. electric pressure cooker. Combine green peppers, tomatoes, tomato paste, onion, broth, wine, garlic, salt and pepper; pour over chicken. Lock lid; close pressure-release valve. Adjust to pressure-cook on high for 10 minutes.

2. Quick-release pressure. A thermometer inserted in the chicken should read at least 170°. Remove chicken to a serving patter; keep warm.

3. Mix cornstarch and water until smooth; stir into broth mixture. Select saute setting; adjust for low heat. Simmer, stirring constantly, until thickened, 1-2 minutes.

3 OZ. COOKED CHICKEN WITH ABOUT ½ CUP SAUCE: 206 cal., 8g fat (2g sat. fat), 76mg chol., 353mg sod., 8g carb. (3g sugars, 2g fiber), 23g pro. **DIABETIC EXCHANGES:** 3 lean meat, 1 vegetable.

TURKEY CABBAGE STEW

Full of ground turkey, cabbage, carrots and tomatoes, this stew delivers down-home comfort food fast!

—Susan Lasken, Woodland Hills, CA

Takes: **30 min.** • Makes: **6 servings**

- 1 lb. lean ground turkey
- 1 medium onion, chopped
- 3 garlic cloves, minced
- 4 cups chopped cabbage
- 2 medium carrots, sliced
- 1 can (28 oz.) diced tomatoes, undrained
- ¾ cup water
- 1 Tbsp. brown sugar
- 1 Tbsp. white vinegar
- 1 tsp. salt
- 1 tsp. dried oregano
- ¼ tsp. dried thyme
- ¼ tsp. pepper

1. Cook the turkey, onion and garlic in a large saucepan over medium heat until the meat is no longer pink, 5-7 minutes, breaking up turkey into crumbles; drain.

2. Add the remaining ingredients. Bring to a boil; cover and simmer until the vegetables are tender, 12-15 minutes.

FREEZE OPTION: Freeze cooled stew in freezer containers. To use, partially thaw stew in refrigerator overnight. Heat through in a saucepan, stirring occasionally; add broth if necessary to adjust consistency.

1 CUP: 180 cal., 6g fat (2g sat. fat), 52mg chol., 674mg sod., 16g carb. (10g sugars, 5g fiber), 17g pro.
DIABETIC EXCHANGES: 2 vegetable, 2 lean meat.

TURKEY BREAST WITH CRANBERRY BROWN RICE

As a single retiree, I roast a turkey breast half instead of making a whole turkey dinner. This is a perfect meal for anyone cooking for themselves, and it also leaves enough leftovers for sandwiches and tacos.

—Nancy Heishman, Las Vegas, NV

Prep: **20 min.**
Bake: **45 min. + standing**
Makes: **6 servings**

- 2 Tbsp. jellied cranberry sauce
- 2 Tbsp. chopped celery
- 2 Tbsp. minced red onion
- 1 Tbsp. olive oil
- 1½ tsp. minced fresh parsley
- ½ tsp. grated orange zest
- ⅛ tsp. garlic powder
- ½ tsp. poultry seasoning, divided
- 1 boneless skinless turkey breast half (2 lbs.)
- ½ tsp. kosher salt
- ¼ tsp. pepper
- ¼ cup orange juice

RICE

- 1⅓ cups uncooked long grain brown rice
- 2⅔ cups water
- ¼ cup chopped celery
- 3 Tbsp. minced red onion
- ¾ tsp. salt
- ¼ tsp. pepper
- ⅔ cup dried cranberries
- ⅔ cup sliced almonds, toasted
- 1 Tbsp. minced fresh parsley
- ½ tsp. grated orange zest

1. Preheat oven to 350°. Mix the first 7 ingredients and ¼ tsp. poultry seasoning.

2. Place turkey in a greased foil-lined 13x9-in. baking pan; rub with salt, pepper and remaining ¼ tsp. poultry seasoning. Spread with cranberry mixture. Roast until a thermometer reads 165°, 45-55 minutes, drizzling with orange juice halfway.

3. Meanwhile, in a saucepan, combine the first 6 rice ingredients; bring to a boil. Reduce heat; simmer, covered, until the rice is tender and liquid is absorbed, 40-45 minutes. Stir in the remaining ingredients.

4. Remove turkey from oven; tent with foil. Let stand 10 minutes before slicing. Serve with rice.

5 OZ. COOKED TURKEY WITH ⅔ CUP RICE: 465 cal., 11g fat (1g sat. fat), 86mg chol., 642mg sod., 50g carb. (13g sugars, 5g fiber), 42g pro.
DIABETIC EXCHANGES: 5 lean meat, 3 starch, 1½ fat.

CHICKEN FAJITAS FOR TWO

This is the best fajita recipe I've ever tried. It sounds complicated, but it really isn't. The servings are hearty, and it tastes so good that we never have a problem finishing it!
—*Kathleen Smith, Pittsburgh, PA*

- -

Prep: 15 min. + marinating
Cook: 15 min. • Makes: 2 servings

- 2 boneless skinless chicken breast halves (4 oz. each)
- ¼ cup lime juice plus ½ tsp. lime juice, divided
- 4 tsp. reduced-sodium soy sauce, divided
- 4 tsp. canola oil, divided
- 1 garlic clove, minced
- ½ tsp. salt
- ½ tsp. chili powder
- ½ tsp. cayenne pepper
- ¼ tsp. pepper
- ½ tsp. liquid smoke, optional
- 1 medium onion, julienned
- ½ small sweet red or green pepper, julienned
- 4 fat-free tortillas (6 in.), warmed
- Optional: Salsa, sour cream and chopped cilantro

1. Arrange chicken in a shallow dish. Combine ¼ cup lime juice, 3 tsp. soy sauce, 2 tsp. canola oil, the garlic, salt, chili powder, cayenne, pepper and, if desired, liquid smoke; pour over chicken. Refrigerate, covered, at least 2 hours.

2. Drain the chicken; discarding marinade. On a greased grill rack, grill the chicken, covered, over medium heat or broil 4 in. from heat until a thermometer reads 165°, 4-6 minutes each side.

3. In a large nonstick skillet, heat remaining 2 tsp. oil over medium-high heat. Add onion and sweet red pepper; cook and stir until tender, 5-7 minutes. Stir in the remaining ½ tsp. lime juice and remaining 1 tsp. soy sauce.

4. Cut the cooked chicken into thin slices; add to vegetables. Serve with fat-free tortillas and, if desired, salsa, sour cream and chopped cilantro.

1 SERVING: 383 cal., 12g fat (2g sat. fat), 63mg chol., 1471mg sod., 39g carb. (4g sugars, 3g fiber), 29g pro.

COCONUT CURRY CHICKEN

My husband and I love this yummy dish! It's a breeze to prepare in the slow cooker, and it tastes just like a meal you'd have at your favorite Indian or Thai restaurant.
—*Andi Kauffman, Beavercreek, OR*

Prep: **20 min.** • Cook: **5 hours**
Makes: **4 servings**

- 2 medium potatoes, peeled and cubed
- 1 small onion, chopped
- 2 tsp. canola oil
- 1 lb. boneless skinless chicken breast halves
- 1 cup light coconut milk
- 4 tsp. curry powder
- 1 garlic clove, minced
- 1 tsp. reduced-sodium chicken bouillon granules
- ¼ tsp. salt
- ¼ tsp. pepper
- 2 cups hot cooked rice
  Optional: Cilantro, shredded coconut, chopped peanuts and thinly sliced red chiles

1. Place potatoes and onion in a 3- or 4-qt. slow cooker. In a nonstick skillet, heat oil over medium heat; add chicken. Cook until lightly browned, turning once, 3-5 minutes. Transfer to slow cooker.
2. In a small bowl, combine coconut milk, curry, garlic, bouillon, salt and pepper; pour over chicken. Cover and cook on low until the meat is tender, 5-6 hours. Remove chicken to cutting board. Cut into slices.
3. Serve chicken and sauce with rice; if desired top with cilantro, coconut, peanuts and chiles.

1 SERVING: 371 cal., 10g fat (4g sat. fat), 63mg chol., 265mg sod., 42g carb. (3g sugars, 3g fiber), 27g pro. **DIABETIC EXCHANGES:** 3 starch, 3 lean meat, 1½ fat.

THE SKINNY
If you are on a low-carb diet, consider swapping cauliflower rice for the white rice in this recipe. Swap the potatoes for a root vegetable such as rutabaga or turnip, or even use sweet potatoes instead.

BLT BOW TIE PASTA SALAD

I first had this summery salad at a family reunion, and it's become one of my husband's favorite dinners. Sometimes, we leave out the chicken and serve it as a side dish instead.
—*Jennifer Madsen, Rexburg, ID*

Takes: **25 min.** • Makes: **6 servings**

- 2½ **cups uncooked bow tie pasta**
- 6 **cups torn romaine**
- 1½ **cups cubed cooked chicken breast**
- 1 **medium tomato, diced**
- 4 **bacon strips, cooked and crumbled**
- ⅓ **cup reduced-fat mayonnaise**
- ¼ **cup water**
- 1 **Tbsp. barbecue sauce**
- 1½ **tsp. white vinegar**
- ¼ **tsp. pepper**

1. Cook pasta according to package directions. Drain and rinse under cold water. In a large bowl, combine romaine, chicken, tomato, bacon and pasta.
2. In a small bowl, whisk mayonnaise, water, barbecue sauce, vinegar and pepper. Pour over salad; toss to coat. Serve immediately.
1¾ CUPS: 253 cal., 8g fat (2g sat. fat), 37mg chol., 239mg sod., 27g carb. (4g sugars, 2g fiber), 17g pro.
DIABETIC EXCHANGES: 2 lean meat, 1½ starch, 1 vegetable, 1 fat.

BARBECUED BASIL TURKEY BURGERS

After my husband built me a patio planter for growing herbs, I made an amazing turkey burger featuring fresh basil. We add toppings such as provolone, red onion and tomatoes.
—*Denise Miller, Greeley, CO*

Takes: **30 min.** • Makes: **4 servings**

- ¼ **cup chopped fresh basil**
- 3 **Tbsp. mesquite-smoke-flavored barbecue sauce**
- 2 **Tbsp. quick-cooking oats or oat bran**
- 1 **garlic clove, minced**
- ¼ **tsp. garlic salt**
- ⅛ **tsp. pepper**
- 1 **lb. lean ground turkey**
- 4 **whole wheat or multigrain hamburger buns, split**

Optional: Sliced provolone cheese, red onion slices, sliced tomato, fresh basil leaves and additional barbecue sauce

1. In a large bowl, combine basil, barbecue sauce, oats, garlic, garlic salt and pepper. Add turkey; mix lightly but thoroughly. Shape into four ½-in.-thick patties.
2. On a lightly greased grill rack, grill burgers, covered, over medium heat for 5-7 minutes on each side or until a thermometer reads 165°. Grill buns over medium heat, cut side down, for 30-60 seconds or until toasted. Serve burgers on buns with toppings of your choice.
1 BURGER: 315 cal., 11g fat (3g sat. fat), 78mg chol., 482mg sod., 29g carb. (8g sugars, 4g fiber), 27g pro.
DIABETIC EXCHANGES: 3 lean meat, 2 starch.

ASIAN CHICKEN THIGHS

A thick, tangy sauce coats golden brown chicken pieces. Serve them over long grain rice or with ramen noodle slaw.
—*Dave Farrington, Midwest City, OK*

- -

Prep: **15 min.** • Cook: **50 min.**
Makes: **5 servings**

- 5 tsp. olive oil
- 5 bone-in chicken thighs (about 1¾ lbs.), skin removed
- ⅓ cup water
- ¼ cup packed brown sugar
- 2 Tbsp. orange juice
- 2 Tbsp. reduced-sodium soy sauce
- 2 Tbsp. ketchup
- 1 Tbsp. white vinegar
- 4 garlic cloves, minced
- ½ tsp. crushed red pepper flakes
- ¼ tsp. Chinese five-spice powder
- 2 tsp. cornstarch
- 2 Tbsp. cold water
  Sliced green onions
  Hot cooked rice, optional

1. In a large skillet, heat oil over medium heat. Add chicken; cook until golden brown, 8-10 minutes on each side.
2. In a small bowl, whisk water, brown sugar, orange juice, soy sauce, ketchup, vinegar, garlic, pepper flakes and five-spice powder. Pour over chicken. Bring to a boil. Reduce heat; simmer, uncovered, until the chicken is tender, 30-35 minutes, turning occasionally.
3. In another small bowl, mix cornstarch and cold water until smooth; stir into pan. Bring to a boil; cook and stir until sauce thickens, about 1 minute. Sprinkle with green onions. If desired, serve with rice.
FREEZE OPTION: Freeze cool chicken in freezer containers. To use, partially thaw in refrigerator overnight. Heat slowly in a covered skillet until a thermometer inserted in chicken reads 165°, stirring occasionally; add water if necessary.
1 CHICKEN THIGH: 292 cal., 14g fat (3g sat. fat), 87mg chol., 396mg sod., 15g carb. (13g sugars, 0 fiber), 25g pro. **DIABETIC EXCHANGES:** 3 lean meat, 1 starch, 1 fat.

LEMON-OLIVE CHICKEN WITH ORZO

This quick skillet recipe is a healthy all-in-one meal. I just add a tossed salad to make a complete meal the entire family loves.
—*Nancy Brown, Dahinda, IL*

- -

Takes: **30 min.** • Makes: **4 servings**

- 1 Tbsp. olive oil
- 4 boneless skinless chicken thighs (about 1 lb.)
- 1 can (14½ oz.) reduced-sodium chicken broth
- ⅔ cup uncooked whole wheat orzo pasta
- ½ medium lemon, cut into 4 wedges
- ½ cup pitted Greek olives, sliced
- 1 Tbsp. lemon juice
- 1 tsp. dried oregano
- ¼ tsp. pepper

1. In a large nonstick skillet, heat oil over medium heat. Brown chicken on both sides; remove from pan.
2. Add broth to skillet; increase heat to medium-high. Cook 1-2 minutes, stirring to loosen browned bits from pan. Stir in remaining ingredients; bring to a boil. Reduce heat; simmer, uncovered, 5 minutes, stirring occasionally.
3. Return chicken to pan. Cook, covered, 5-8 minutes or until the pasta is tender and a thermometer inserted in chicken reads 170°.
1 SERVING: 345 cal., 17g fat (3g sat. fat), 76mg chol., 636mg sod., 22g carb. (1g sugars, 5g fiber), 26g pro. **DIABETIC EXCHANGES:** 3 lean meat, 2 fat, 1 starch.

BLUEBERRY-DIJON CHICKEN

Blueberries and chicken may seem like a strange combination, but prepare to be dazzled. I add a sprinkling of minced fresh basil as the finishing touch.
—*Susan Marshall,*
Colorado Springs, CO

Takes: **30 min.** • Makes: **4 servings**

- 4 **boneless skinless chicken breast halves (6 oz. each)**
- ¼ **tsp. salt**
- ¼ **tsp. pepper**
- 1 **Tbsp. butter**
- ½ **cup blueberry preserves**
- ⅓ **cup raspberry vinegar**
- ¼ **cup fresh or frozen blueberries**
- 3 **Tbsp. Dijon mustard**
  Minced fresh basil or tarragon, optional

1. Sprinkle chicken with salt and pepper. In a large skillet, cook chicken in butter over medium heat until a thermometer reads 165°, 6-8 minutes on each side. Remove and keep warm.

2. In the same skillet, combine the preserves, vinegar, blueberries and mustard, stirring to loosen any browned bits from pan. Bring to a boil; cook and stir until thickened. Serve with chicken. Sprinkle with basil if desired.

1 CHICKEN BREAST WITH 2 TBSP. SAUCE: 325 cal., 7g fat (3g sat. fat), 102mg chol., 522mg sod., 27g carb. (25g sugars, 0 fiber), 34g pro.

AIR-FRYER MEDITERRANEAN TURKEY POTPIES

Your family and friends are sure to love these wonderful potpies with a little Mediterranean flair. If you don't have turkey, cooked chicken works just as well.
—*Marie Rizzio, Interlochen, MI*

Prep: **30 min.** • Cook: **15 min.**
Makes: **6 servings**

- 2 medium onions, thinly sliced
- 2 tsp. olive oil
- 3 garlic cloves, minced
- 3 Tbsp. all-purpose flour
- 1¼ cups reduced-sodium chicken broth
- 1 can (14½ oz.) no-salt-added diced tomatoes, undrained
- 2½ cups cubed cooked turkey breast
- 1 can (14 oz.) water-packed artichoke hearts, rinsed, drained and sliced
- ½ cup pitted ripe olives, halved
- ¼ cup sliced pepperoncini
- 1 Tbsp. minced fresh oregano or 1 tsp. dried oregano
- ¼ tsp. pepper

CRUST

- 1 loaf (1 lb.) frozen pizza dough, thawed
- 1 large egg white
- 1 tsp. minced fresh oregano or ¼ tsp. dried oregano

1. In a Dutch oven, saute onions in oil until tender. Add garlic; cook 2 minutes longer. In a small bowl, whisk flour and broth until smooth; gradually stir into onion mixture. Stir in the tomatoes. Bring to a boil; cook and stir for 2 minutes or until thickened.

2. Remove from the heat. Add turkey breast, artichokes, olives, pepperoncini, oregano and pepper; stir gently. Divide turkey mixture among six 10-oz. ramekins.

3. Preheat air fryer to 375°. Roll out 2 oz. of dough to fit each ramekin (reserve remaining dough for another use). Cut slits in dough; place over filling. Press to seal edges. Combine egg white and oregano; brush over dough.

4. Place ramekins on tray in air-fryer basket. Cook until crusts are golden brown, 15-20 minutes.

1 POTPIE: 323 cal., 6g fat (1g sat. fat), 47mg chol., 578mg sod., 39g carb. (4g sugars, 3g fiber), 26g pro. **DIABETIC EXCHANGES:** 2 starch, 2 vegetable, 2 lean meat, ½ fat.

CHICKEN FLORENTINE MEATBALLS

Served over spaghetti squash and a chunky mushroom-tomato sauce, these tender meatballs are tops when it comes to fantastic flavor.
—*Diane Nemitz, Ludington, MI*

Prep: **40 min.** • Cook: **20 min.**
Makes: **6 servings**

- 2 **large eggs, lightly beaten**
- 1 **pkg. (10 oz.) frozen chopped spinach, thawed and squeezed dry**
- ½ **cup dry bread crumbs**
- ¼ **cup grated Parmesan cheese**
- 1 **Tbsp. dried minced onion**
- 1 **garlic clove, minced**
- ¼ **tsp. salt**
- ⅛ **tsp. pepper**
- 1 **lb. ground chicken**
- 1 **medium spaghetti squash**

SAUCE
- ½ **lb. sliced fresh mushrooms**
- 2 **tsp. olive oil**
- 1 **can (14½ oz.) diced tomatoes, undrained**
- 1 **can (8 oz.) tomato sauce**
- 2 **Tbsp. minced fresh parsley**
- 1 **garlic clove, minced**
- 1 **tsp. dried oregano**
- 1 **tsp. dried basil**

1. Preheat oven to 400°. In a large bowl, combine first 8 ingredients. Crumble chicken over mixture; mix lightly but thoroughly. Shape into 1½-in. balls.

2. Place meatballs on a rack in a shallow baking pan. Bake, uncovered, until no longer pink, 20-25 minutes.

3. Meanwhile, cut squash in half lengthwise; discard seeds.

Place squash cut side down on a microwave-safe plate. Microwave, uncovered, on high until tender, 15-18 minutes.

4. In a large nonstick skillet, saute mushrooms in oil until tender. Stir in remaining ingredients. Bring to a boil. Reduce heat; simmer, until slightly thickened, 8-10 minutes. Add meatballs and heat through.

5. When squash is cool enough to handle, use a fork to separate strands. Serve with meatballs and sauce.

FREEZE OPTION: Place individual portions of cooled meatballs and squash in freezer containers. To use, partially thaw in refrigerator overnight. Microwave, covered, on high in a microwave-safe dish until heated through, gently stirring and adding a little water if necessary.

1 SERVING: 303 cal., 12g fat (3g sat. fat), 123mg chol., 617mg sod., 31g carb. (4g sugars, 7g fiber), 22g pro.
DIABETIC EXCHANGES: 3 lean meat, 2 starch, ½ fat.

AIR-FRYER COCONUT-CRUSTED TURKEY STRIPS

My granddaughter first shared these turkey strips with me. With a plum dipping sauce, they're just the thing for a light supper.
—*Agnes Ward, Stratford, ON*

- -

Prep: **20 min.** • Cook: **10 min./batch**
Makes: **6 servings**

- 2 **large egg whites**
- 2 **tsp. sesame oil**
- ½ **cup sweetened shredded coconut, lightly toasted**
- ½ **cup dry bread crumbs**
- 2 **Tbsp. sesame seeds, toasted**
- ½ **tsp. salt**
- 1½ **lbs. turkey breast tenderloins, cut into ½-in. strips**
  Cooking spray

DIPPING SAUCE
- ½ **cup plum sauce**
- ⅓ **cup unsweetened pineapple juice**
- 1½ **tsp. prepared mustard**
- 1 **tsp. cornstarch**
  Optional: Grated lime zest and lime wedges

1. Preheat air fryer to 400°. In a shallow bowl, whisk egg whites and oil. In another shallow bowl, mix coconut, bread crumbs, sesame seeds and salt. Dip turkey in egg mixture, then in coconut mixture, patting to help coating adhere.
2. Working in batches, place turkey in a single layer on greased tray in air-fryer basket; spritz with cooking spray. Cook until golden brown, 3-4 minutes. Turn; spritz again. Cook until golden brown and turkey is no longer pink, 3-4 minutes longer.

3. Meanwhile, in a small saucepan, mix the sauce ingredients. Bring to a boil; cook and stir until thickened, 1-2 minutes. Serve turkey with sauce. If desired, top turkey strips with grated lime zest and serve with lime wedges.

3 OZ. COOKED TURKEY WITH 2 TBSP. SAUCE: 292 cal., 9g fat (3g sat. fat), 45mg chol., 517mg sod., 24g carb. (5g sugars, 1g fiber), 31g pro.

THE SKINNY

If you don't have an air fryer, you can make this recipe in the oven instead. Bake at 425° for 10-12 minutes, turning once.

CURRIED CHICKEN & PEACH SALAD

This is a very healthy and simple salad to make; even my non-cooking husband can whip it together in just a few minutes. We've served this to friends over the years, and they always ask for the recipe.
—*Radelle Knappenberger, Oviedo, FL*

Takes: **10 min.** • Makes: **4 servings**

- ½ cup fat-free mayonnaise
- 1 tsp. curry powder
- 2 cups cubed cooked chicken breasts
- ½ cup chopped walnuts
- ¼ cup raisins
- 2 medium peaches, sliced
- 1 pkg. (5 oz.) spring mix salad greens

Mix mayonnaise and curry powder; toss gently with chicken, walnuts and raisins. Serve chicken mixture and peaches over greens.

1 SERVING: 286 cal., 12g fat (2g sat. fat), 54mg chol., 315mg sod., 23g carb. (14g sugars, 4g fiber), 24g pro.
DIABETIC EXCHANGES: 3 lean meat, 1½ fat, 1 vegetable, 1 fruit.

EASY MEDITERRANEAN CHICKEN

Friends and family love this special chicken recipe. I've changed a few things to make it healthier, but it still tastes just as good.
—*Kara Zilis, Oak Forest, IL*

Takes: **30 min.** • Makes: **4 servings**

- 4 boneless skinless chicken breast halves (4 oz. each)
- 1 Tbsp. olive oil
- 1 can (14½ oz.) no-salt-added stewed tomatoes
- 1 cup water
- 1 tsp. dried oregano
- ¼ tsp. garlic powder
- 1½ cups instant brown rice
- 1 pkg. (12 oz.) frozen cut green beans
- 12 pitted Greek olives, halved
- ½ cup crumbled feta cheese

1. In a large nonstick skillet, brown chicken in oil on each side. Stir in the tomatoes, water, oregano and garlic powder. Bring to a boil; reduce heat. Cover and simmer 10 minutes.
2. Stir in rice and green beans. Return to a boil. Cover and simmer until a thermometer reads 165° and rice is tender, 8-10 minutes longer. Stir in olives; sprinkle with cheese.

1 SERVING: 417 cal., 12g fat (3g sat. fat), 70mg chol., 386mg sod., 44g carb. (6g sugars, 6g fiber), 31g pro.
DIABETIC EXCHANGES: 3 lean meat, 2 starch, 2 vegetable, 1 fat.

sauce; rub over chicken. Place in a 5-qt. slow cooker; add broth. Cover and cook on low until chicken is tender, 4-5 hours.

1 CHICKEN BREAST HALF: 211 cal., 7g fat (2g sat. fat), 91mg chol., 392mg sod., 1g carb. (0 sugars, 0 fiber), 33g pro. **DIABETIC EXCHANGES:** 5 lean meat, 1 fat.

THE SKINNY

Slow cookers are designed to cook raw meats. The direct heat from the pot, lengthy cooking time and steam created from the tightly covered container destroy bacteria, making slow cooking a safe method.

We recommend putting a small amount of liquid (such as broth, water or tomatoes) into your slow cooker. It will help prevent burning and its steam cooks the chicken while keeping it from drying out.

HERBED SLOW-COOKER CHICKEN

I use my slow cooker to prepare these well-seasoned chicken breasts that cook up moist and tender. My daughter, who has two young sons to keep up with, shared this recipe with me several years ago. I've since made it repeatedly.
—*Sundra Hauck, Bogalusa, LA*

Prep: **5 min.** • Cook: **4 hours**
Makes: **4 servings**

1 Tbsp. olive oil
1 tsp. paprika
½ tsp. garlic powder
½ tsp. seasoned salt
½ tsp. dried thyme
½ tsp. dried basil
½ tsp. pepper
½ tsp. browning sauce, optional
4 bone-in chicken breast halves (8 oz. each)
½ cup chicken broth

In a small bowl, combine the first 7 ingredients and, if desired, browning

CONTEST-WINNING CHICKEN CACCIATORE

My husband and I own and operate a busy farm. There are days when no time is left for cooking! It's really nice to be able to come into the house at night and smell this wonderful dinner already simmering.

—Aggie Arnold-Norman, Liberty, PA

Prep: **15 min.** • Cook: **6 hours**
Makes: **6 servings**

- 2 **medium onions, thinly sliced**
- 1 **broiler/fryer chicken (3 to 4 lbs.), cut up and skin removed**
- 2 **garlic cloves, minced**
- 1 **to 2 tsp. dried oregano**
- 1 **tsp. salt**
- ½ **tsp. dried basil**
- ¼ **tsp. pepper**
- 1 **bay leaf**
- 1 **can (14½ oz.) diced tomatoes, undrained**
- 1 **can (8 oz.) tomato sauce**
- 1 **can (4 oz.) mushroom stems and pieces, drained, or 1 cup sliced fresh mushrooms**
- ¼ **cup white wine or water**
  Hot cooked pasta

1. Place onions in a 5-qt. slow cooker. Add chicken, seasonings, tomatoes, tomato sauce, mushrooms and wine.

2. Cook, covered, on low until the chicken is tender, 6-8 hours. Discard bay leaf. Serve chicken with sauce over pasta.

1 SERVING: 207 cal., 6g fat (2g sat. fat), 73mg chol., 787mg sod., 11g carb. (6g sugars, 3g fiber), 27g pro. **DIABETIC EXCHANGES:** 4 lean meat, 2 vegetable.

AIR-FRYER SWEET-POTATO-CRUSTED CHICKEN NUGGETS

I was looking for ways to spice up chicken nuggets and came up with this recipe. The chips add crunchy texture while the meat stays tender.
—*Kristina Segarra, Yonkers, NY*

Prep: **15 min.** • Cook: **10 min./batch**
Makes: **4 servings**

- 1 cup sweet potato chips
- ¼ cup all-purpose flour
- 1 tsp. salt, divided
- ½ tsp. coarsely ground pepper
- ¼ tsp. baking powder
- 1 Tbsp. cornstarch
- 1 lb. chicken tenderloins, cut into 1½-in. pieces
  Cooking spray

1. Preheat air fryer to 400°. Place chips, flour, ½ tsp. salt, pepper and baking powder in a food processor; pulse until ground. Transfer to a shallow dish.
2. Mix cornstarch and remaining ½ tsp. salt; toss with chicken. Toss chicken with potato chip mixture, pressing to coat.
3. In batches, arrange chicken in a single layer on greased tray in air-fryer basket; spritz with cooking spray. Cook until golden brown, 3-4 minutes. Turn; spritz with cooking spray. Cook until golden brown and chicken is no longer pink, 3-4 minutes longer.

3 OZ. COOKED CHICKEN: 190 cal., 4g fat (0 sat. fat), 56mg chol., 690mg sod., 13g carb. (1g sugars, 1g fiber), 28g pro. **DIABETIC EXCHANGES:** 3 lean meat, 1 starch.

LIME CHICKEN TACOS

Our fun, simple recipe is perfect for taco Tuesdays or a relaxing dinner with friends. If we have any leftover filling, I toss it into a garden-fresh taco salad.
—*Tracy Gunter, Boise, ID*

Prep: **10 min.** • Cook: **5½ hours**
Makes: **6 servings**

- 1½ **lbs. boneless skinless chicken breast halves**
- 3 **Tbsp. lime juice**
- 1 **Tbsp. chili powder**
- 1 **cup frozen corn, thawed**
- 1 **cup chunky salsa**
- 12 **fat-free flour tortillas (6 in.), warmed**
  Optional: Sour cream, pickled onions, shredded lettuce and shredded cheddar or Cotija cheese

1. Place chicken in a 3-qt. slow cooker. Combine lime juice and chili powder; pour over chicken. Cook, covered, on low until chicken is tender, 5-6 hours.
2. Remove chicken. When cool enough to handle, shred meat with 2 forks; return to slow cooker. Stir in corn and salsa. Cook, covered, on low until heated through, about 30 minutes.
3. Place filling on tortillas; if desired, serve with sour cream, pickled onions, lettuce and cheese.
2 TACOS: 291 cal., 3g fat (1g sat. fat), 63mg chol., 674mg sod., 37g carb. (2g sugars, 2g fiber), 28g pro.
DIABETIC EXCHANGES: 3 lean meat, 2½ starch.

TASTE OF HOME TALK

"This was so good and so easy to put together. We topped the tacos with sautéed red and green pepper strips and onions, which is a favorite. I doubled the recipe, and had plenty of the chicken mixture to freeze for a later meal when grandkids stop over."
GRAMMA AMY, TASTEOFHOME.COM

COUNTRY CHICKEN WITH GRAVY

Here's a lightened-up take on classic southern comfort food. It's been a hit at our house since the first time we tried it!

—*Ruth Helmuth, Abbeville, SC*

Takes: **30 min.** • Makes: **4 servings**

- ¾ cup crushed cornflakes
- ½ tsp. poultry seasoning
- ½ tsp. paprika
- ¼ tsp. salt
- ¼ tsp. dried thyme
- ¼ tsp. pepper
- 2 Tbsp. fat-free evaporated milk
- 4 boneless skinless chicken breast halves (4 oz. each)
- 2 tsp. canola oil

GRAVY

- 1 Tbsp. butter
- 1 Tbsp. all-purpose flour
- ¼ tsp. pepper
- ⅛ tsp. salt
- ½ cup fat-free evaporated milk
- ¼ cup condensed chicken broth, undiluted
- 1 tsp. sherry or additional condensed chicken broth
- 2 Tbsp. minced chives

1. In a shallow bowl, combine the first 6 ingredients. Place milk in another shallow bowl. Dip chicken in milk, then roll in cornflake mixture.
2. In a large nonstick skillet, cook chicken in oil over medium heat until a thermometer reads 170°, 6-8 minutes on each side.
3. Meanwhile, for the gravy, in a small saucepan, melt butter. Stir in flour, pepper and salt until smooth.

Gradually stir in the milk, broth and sherry. Bring to a boil; cook and stir until thickened, 1-2 minutes. Stir in chives. Serve with chicken.

1 CHICKEN BREAST HALF WITH 2 TBSP. GRAVY: 274 cal., 8g fat (3g sat. fat), 72mg chol., 569mg sod., 20g carb. (6g sugars, 0 fiber), 28g pro. **DIABETIC EXCHANGES:** 3 lean meat, 1 starch, ½ fat.

THE SKINNY

Feel free to play with this recipe! Create your own blend for the coating using seasonings such as dried basil, crushed dried rosemary, celery seed, cumin, garlic powder, onion powder or seasoned salt. This recipe calls for chicken breast; you can also use thighs, which will yield a juicier, more tender final result.

POMEGRANATE, CHICKEN & FARRO SALAD

This salad recipe is special—simple, yet sophisticated—and never fails to win raves. I use quick-cooking farro, which takes only 10 minutes on the stovetop. Many stores now carry packaged pomegranate seeds in the refrigerated produce section year-round.

—David Dahlman, Chatsworth, CA

Prep: **15 min.**
Cook: **25 min. + cooling**
Makes: **8 servings**

- 1½ **cups uncooked farro, rinsed, or wheat berries**
- 2 **medium ripe avocados, peeled, pitted and chopped**
- 3 **cups shredded rotisserie chicken**
- ¾ **cup chopped dried apricots**
- ½ **cup thinly sliced green onions**
- ½ **cup chopped walnuts, toasted**
- 1 **Tbsp. chopped seeded jalapeno pepper, optional**
- ¾ **cup pomegranate seeds**

DRESSING

- ⅓ **cup olive oil**
- ¼ **cup orange juice**
- 3 **Tbsp. white wine vinegar**
- 1 **Tbsp. Dijon mustard**
- ½ **tsp. salt**
- ½ **tsp. pepper**

1. Place farro in large saucepan; add water to cover. Bring to a boil. Reduce heat; cook, covered, until farro is tender, 25-30 minutes. Drain and cool.

2. Arrange farro, avocados, chicken, apricots, green onions, walnuts and, if desired, jalapeno on a platter.

Sprinkle with pomegranate seeds.

3. For dressing, in a small bowl, whisk remaining ingredients until blended. Serve with salad.

1 SERVING: 482 cal., 24g fat (3g sat. fat), 47mg chol., 251mg sod., 44g carb. (9g sugars, 9g fiber), 23g pro.

MAKE IT YOUR OWN
Play with this salad by adding different dried and fresh fruits
- Dates, dried figs, currants
- Chopped nectarines

PRESSURE-COOKER CHICKEN THIGHS IN WINE SAUCE

I adore this recipe—it has amazing flavor, and everyone who has tried it loves it! For an easy meal, pair it with mashed potatoes and peas.
—*Heike Annucci, Hudson, NC*

Prep: **15 min.**
Cook: **20 min. + releasing**
Makes: **4 servings**

- 2 **Tbsp. butter, divided**
- 1 **cup sliced fresh mushrooms**
- 6 **bone-in chicken thighs, skin removed (about 2¼ lbs.)**
- ¼ **tsp. salt**
- ¼ **tsp. pepper**
- ¼ **tsp. Italian seasoning**
- ¼ **tsp. paprika**
- ⅓ **cup all-purpose flour**
- ½ **cup chicken broth**
- ½ **cup white wine or additional chicken broth**
- 3 **green onions, thinly sliced**

1. Select the saute setting on a 6-qt. electric pressure cooker and adjust for medium heat; add 1 Tbsp. butter. When hot, add mushrooms; cook until tender, 3-4 minutes. Remove.
2. Sprinkle chicken with salt, pepper, Italian seasoning and paprika. Place flour in a shallow bowl. Add chicken, a few pieces at a time, and toss to coat with flour; shake off excess.
3. Heat remaining 1 Tbsp. butter in pressure cooker; brown chicken on both sides. Remove. Add the broth and wine to pressure cooker. Cook 2-3 minutes, stirring to loosen browned bits. Press cancel.

4. Return chicken and mushrooms to cooker; add green onions. Lock lid and close pressure-release valve. Adjust to pressure-cook on high for 10 minutes. Let pressure naturally release 10 minutes; quick-release any remaining pressure. (A thermometer inserted in chicken should read at least 165°.)

1 SERVING: 243 cal., 13g fat (5g sat. fat), 97mg chol., 284mg sod., 3g carb. (1g sugars, 0 fiber), 25g pro.
DIABETIC EXCHANGES: 3 lean meat, 1½ fat.

THE SKINNY

For a slow-cooked option, place browned chicken and mushrooms in slow cooker; add the remaining ingredients and cook on low until chicken is tender, 3-4 hours.

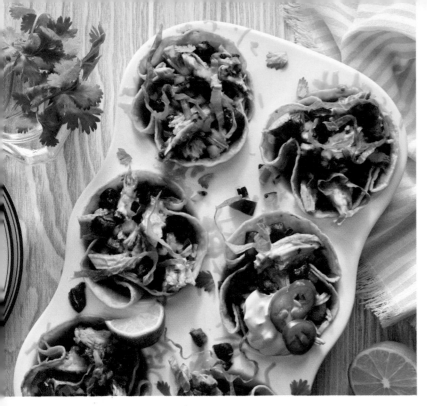

CHICKEN TOSTADA CUPS

Years ago, I tried a version of these cups at a restaurant in Santa Fe, and I wanted to make my own spin. They're perfect for party fare because it's easy to let everyone add their own favorite toppings.
—*Marla Clark, Moriarty, NM*

Prep: **25 min.** • Bake: **15 min.**
Makes: **6 servings**

- 12 **corn tortillas (6 in.), warmed**
  Cooking spray
- 2 **cups shredded rotisserie chicken**
- 1 **cup salsa**
- 1 **can (16 oz.) refried beans**
- 1 **cup shredded reduced-fat Mexican cheese blend**
  Optional: Shredded lettuce, reduced-fat sour cream, chopped cilantro, diced avocado, sliced jalapeno, lime wedges, sliced ripe olives, sliced green onions, sliced radishes, and pico de gallo or additional salsa

1. Preheat oven to 425°. Press warm tortillas into 12 muffin cups coated with cooking spray, pleating sides as needed. Spritz tortillas with additional cooking spray. Bake until lightly browned, 5-7 minutes.
2. Toss chicken with salsa. Layer each cup with beans, chicken mixture and cheese. Bake until heated through, 9-11 minutes longer. Serve cups with the toppings as desired.

2 TOSTADA CUPS: 338 cal., 11g fat (4g sat. fat), 52mg chol., 629mg sod., 35g carb. (2g sugars, 6g fiber), 25g pro. **DIABETIC EXCHANGES:** 3 lean meat, 2 starch, 1 fat.

THAI CHICKEN PASTA

I try to buy fresh chicken when it's on sale. I cook a big batch in the slow cooker, then cut it up and package it in small amounts suitable for recipes like this. When I want it, I just need to be pull it out of the freezer and let it thaw.
—*Jeni Pittard, Statham, GA*

- -

Takes: **25 min.** • Makes: **2 servings**

3	oz. uncooked whole wheat linguine
½	cup salsa
2	Tbsp. reduced-fat creamy peanut butter
1	Tbsp. orange juice
1½	tsp. honey
1	tsp. reduced-sodium soy sauce
1	cup cubed cooked chicken breast
1	Tbsp. chopped unsalted peanuts
1	Tbsp. minced fresh cilantro

1. Cook linguine according to package directions.
2. Meanwhile, in a microwave-safe dish, combine salsa, peanut butter, orange juice, honey and soy sauce. Cover and microwave on high for 1 minute; stir. Add the chicken; heat through.
3. Drain linguine. Serve with chicken mixture. Garnish with peanuts and fresh cilantro.
1 SERVING: 409 cal., 10g fat (2g sat. fat), 54mg chol., 474mg sod., 46g carb. (10g sugars, 6g fiber), 33g pro.

SLOW-COOKED CHICKEN A LA KING

When I know I'll be having a busy day with little time to prepare a meal, I use my slow cooker to make this chicken a la king. It smells so good while it's cooking!
—*Eleanor Mielke, Snohomish, WA*

Prep: **10 min.** • Cook: **7½ hours**
Makes: **6 servings**

- 1 can (10¾ oz.) reduced-fat reduced-sodium condensed cream of chicken soup, undiluted
- 3 Tbsp. all-purpose flour
- ¼ tsp. pepper
  Dash cayenne pepper
- 1 lb. boneless skinless chicken breasts, cubed
- 1 celery rib, chopped
- ½ cup chopped green pepper
- ¼ cup chopped onion
- 1 pkg. (10 oz.) frozen peas, thawed
- 2 Tbsp. diced pimientos, drained
  Hot cooked rice

1. In a 3-qt. slow cooker, combine soup, flour, pepper and cayenne until smooth. Stir in chicken, celery, green pepper and onion.
2. Cook, covered, on low 7-8 hours or until meat is no longer pink. Stir in the peas and pimientos. Cook for 30 minutes longer or until heated through. Serve with rice.
1 CUP CHICKEN MIXTURE: 174 cal., 3g fat (1g sat. fat), 44mg chol., 268mg sod., 16g carb. (6g sugars, 3g fiber), 19g pro. **DIABETIC EXCHANGES:** 2 lean meat, 1 starch.

BOW TIES WITH SAUSAGE & ASPARAGUS

We love asparagus, so I look for ways to go green. This pasta dish comes together fast on hectic nights and makes wonderful leftovers.
—*Carol Suto, Liverpool, NY*

Takes: **30 min.** • Makes: **6 servings**

- 3 cups uncooked whole wheat bow tie pasta (about 8 oz.)
- 1 lb. fresh asparagus, trimmed and cut into 1½-in. pieces
- 1 pkg. (19½ oz.) Italian turkey sausage links, casings removed
- 1 medium onion, chopped
- 3 garlic cloves, minced
- ¼ cup shredded Parmesan cheese
  Additional shredded Parmesan cheese, optional

1. In a 6-qt. stockpot, cook pasta according to package directions, adding asparagus during the last 2-3 minutes of cooking. Drain, reserving ½ cup pasta water; return pasta and asparagus to pot.
2. Meanwhile, in a large skillet, cook sausage, onion and garlic over medium heat until no longer pink, 6-8 minutes, breaking sausage into large crumbles. Add to stockpot. Stir in ¼ cup cheese and reserved pasta water as desired. Serve with additional cheese if desired.
1⅓ CUPS: 247 cal., 7g fat (2g sat. fat), 36mg chol., 441mg sod., 28g carb. (2g sugars, 4g fiber), 17g pro. **DIABETIC EXCHANGES:** 2 lean meat, 1½ starch, 1 vegetable.

1 CUP CHICKEN MIXTURE: 279 cal., 8g fat (2g sat. fat), 84mg chol., 856mg sod., 13g carb. (5g sugars, 2g fiber), 32g pro. **DIABETIC EXCHANGES:** 4 lean meat, 1 starch, 1 fat.

GREEK FETA CHICKEN

Feta cheese takes this chicken-and-potato dinner over the top. Serve with a side salad tossed with pepperoncinis, black olives and low-fat vinaigrette for a fresh and healthy meal.
—Taste of Home *Test Kitchen*

Prep: **15 min.** • Bake: **50 min.**
Makes: **6 servings**

- 7 **medium red potatoes, cut into 1-in. cubes**
- 6 **boneless skinless chicken thighs (about 1½ lbs.)**
- ½ **cup reduced-fat sun-dried tomato salad dressing**
- 2 **tsp. Greek seasoning**
- 1 **tsp. dried basil**
- ½ **cup crumbled reduced-fat feta cheese**

1. Preheat oven to 400°. In a large bowl, combine first 5 ingredients. Transfer to a 13x9-in. baking dish coated with cooking spray.
2. Cover and bake for 40 minutes. Sprinkle with cheese. Bake, uncovered, until chicken juices run clear and potatoes are tender, 10-15 minutes longer.
1 SERVING: 316 cal., 12g fat (3g sat. fat), 79mg chol., 767mg sod., 25g carb. (3g sugars, 2g fiber), 26g pro. **DIABETIC EXCHANGES:** 3 lean meat, 1½ starch, 1 fat.

PRESSURE-COOKER CHICKEN TIKKA MASALA

The flavors of this Indian-style entree keep me coming back for more. It isn't fancy, and it's simply spiced—but it's simply amazing.
—*Jaclyn Bell, Logan, UT*

Prep: **20 min.** • Cook: **20 min.**
Makes: **8 servings**

- 2 **Tbsp. olive oil**
- ½ **large onion, finely chopped**
- 4½ **tsp. minced fresh gingerroot**
- 4 **garlic cloves, minced**
- 1 **Tbsp. garam masala**
- 2½ **tsp. salt**
- 1½ **tsp. ground cumin**
- 1 **tsp. paprika**
- ¾ **tsp. pepper**
- ½ **tsp. cayenne pepper**
- ¼ **tsp. ground cinnamon**
- 2½ **lbs. boneless skinless chicken breasts, cut into 1½-in. cubes**
- 1 **can (29 oz.) tomato puree**
- ⅓ **cup water**
- 1 **jalapeno pepper, halved and seeded**
- 1 **bay leaf**
- 1 **Tbsp. cornstarch**
- 1½ **cups plain yogurt**
  Hot cooked basmati rice
  Chopped fresh cilantro, optional

1. Select saute setting on a 6-qt. electric pressure cooker and adjust for medium heat; add oil. When oil is hot, cook onion until tender. Add ginger and garlic; cook 1 minute. Stir in seasonings and cook 30 seconds. Press cancel. Add chicken, tomato puree, water, jalapeno and bay leaf.
2. Lock lid; close pressure-release valve. Adjust to pressure-cook on high; cook for 10 minutes. Quick-release pressure. Discard jalapeno and bay leaf.
3. Select saute setting and adjust for medium heat; bring mixture to a boil. In a small bowl, mix cornstarch and yogurt until smooth; gradually stir into sauce. Cook and stir until sauce is thickened, about 3 minutes. Serve with rice. If desired, sprinkle with cilantro.

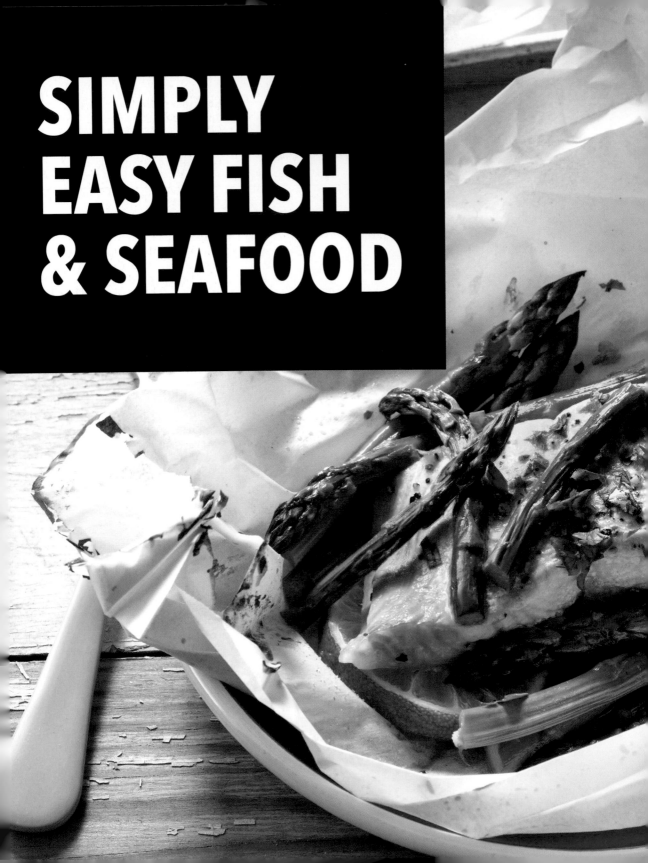

SIMPLY EASY FISH & SEAFOOD

CITRUS SALMON EN PAPILLOTE

This salmon dish is so easy to make yet so delicious, elegant and impressive.
—*Dahlia Abrams, Detroit, MI*

Prep: **20 min.** • Bake: **15 min.**
Makes: **6 servings**

- 6 orange slices
- 6 lime slices
- 6 salmon fillets (4 oz. each)
- 1 lb. fresh asparagus, trimmed and halved
- Olive oil-flavored cooking spray
- ½ tsp. salt
- ¼ tsp. pepper
- 2 Tbsp. minced fresh parsley
- 3 Tbsp. lemon juice

1. Preheat oven to 425°. Cut parchment or heavy-duty foil into six 15x10-in. pieces; fold in half. Arrange citrus slices on 1 side of each piece. Top with fish and asparagus. Spritz with cooking spray. Sprinkle with salt, pepper and minced parsley. Drizzle with the lemon juice.
2. Fold parchment over fish; draw edges together and crimp with fingers to form tightly sealed packets. Place in baking pans.
3. Bake until fish flakes easily with a fork, 12-15 minutes. Open packets carefully to allow steam to escape.
1 PACKET: 224 cal., 13g fat (2g sat. fat), 57mg chol., 261mg sod., 6g carb. (3g sugars, 1g fiber), 20g pro. **DIABETIC EXCHANGES:** 3 lean meat, 1 vegetable.

MODERN TUNA CASSEROLE

I loved tuna casserole as a kid and found myself craving it as an adult. However, the traditional recipe has massive amounts of fat and salt, and it just doesn't taste as good as I remembered. I've reconfigured the recipe to include more vegetables and the result is delicious.
—*Rebecca Blanton, St. Helena, CA*

Prep: **20 min.** • Cook: **20 min.**
Makes: **6 servings**

- 3 Tbsp. butter, divided
- 4 medium carrots, chopped
- 1 medium onion, chopped
- 1 medium sweet red pepper, chopped
- 1 cup sliced baby portobello mushrooms
- 2 cans (5 oz. each) albacore white tuna in water, drained and flaked
- 2 cups fresh baby spinach
- 1 cup frozen peas
- 3 cups uncooked spiral pasta
- 1 Tbsp. all-purpose flour
- ⅔ cup reduced-sodium chicken broth
- ⅓ cup half-and-half cream
- ½ cup shredded Parmesan cheese
- ¾ tsp. salt
- ¼ tsp. pepper

1. In a large skillet, heat 1 Tbsp. butter over medium-high heat. Add the carrots, onion, red pepper and mushrooms. Cook and stir until tender, 8-10 minutes. Add the tuna, spinach and peas; cook until spinach is just wilted, 2-3 minutes.

2. Meanwhile, cook pasta according to package directions for al dente.

Drain pasta, reserving 1 cup pasta water. In a large bowl, place pasta and tuna mixture; toss to combine. Wipe skillet clean.

3. In the same skillet, melt remaining butter over medium heat. Stir in flour until smooth; gradually whisk in broth and cream. Bring to a boil, stirring constantly; cook and stir

until thickened, 1-2 minutes, adding reserved pasta water if needed. Stir in cheese, salt and pepper. Pour over pasta; toss to coat.

1¾ CUPS: 372 cal., 11g fat (6g sat. fat), 47mg chol., 767mg sod., 44g carb. (7g sugars, 5g fiber), 23g pro.
DIABETIC EXCHANGES: 3 lean meat, 2½ starch, 1½ fat, 1 vegetable.

SHEET-PAN SHRIMP FAJITAS

I love easy weeknight dinners like this. This meal comes together so quickly and is customizable with your favorite toppings.
—Carla Hubl, Hastings, NE

- -

Prep: **30 min.** • Cook: **15 min./batch**
Makes: **6 servings**

- 1½ lbs. uncooked shrimp (31-40 per lb.), peeled and deveined
- 1 each medium green, sweet red and yellow peppers, cut into ½-in. strips
- 1 sweet onion, cut into ½-in. strips
- 2 garlic cloves, minced
- 2 Tbsp. olive oil
- 2 tsp. chili powder
- 1 tsp. ground cumin
- ¾ tsp. salt
- 12 corn tortillas (6 in.), warmed
  Optional: Lime wedges, crema, fresh cilantro and sliced avocado

1. Preheat oven to 425°. In a large bowl, combine shrimp, peppers, onion and garlic. Drizzle with oil; sprinkle with chili powder, cumin and salt. Toss to coat. Spread evenly between 2 greased 15x10x1-in. baking pans.
2. Roast 10 minutes, rotating pans halfway through cooking. Remove pans from oven; preheat broiler.
3. Broil the shrimp mixture, 1 pan at a time, 3-4 in. from heat until vegetables are lightly browned and shrimp turn pink, 4-5 minutes. Serve in tortillas with toppings as desired.

2 FAJITAS: 280 cal., 8g fat (1g sat. fat), 138mg chol., 484mg sod., 31g carb. (5g sugars, 5g fiber), 22g pro.
DIABETIC EXCHANGES: 3 lean meat, 1½ starch, 1 vegetable, 1 fat.

THE SKINNY
There are so many ways to dress up fajitas without a lot of extra fat. Add sliced jalapenos, grilled corn, beans, tomato wedges or sliced mushrooms. Top the fajitas off with a little salsa, fat-free sour cream or even light ranch salad dressing.

SALMON SPINACH SALAD

I have always loved the combination of salmon and orange, but you can create variations of this salad to suit your own taste. If you don't have goat cheese, try feta.
—*Stephanie Matthews, Tempe, AZ*

Prep: **25 min.** • Grill: **10 min.**
Makes: **4 servings**

- 4 salmon fillets (4 oz. each)
- 6 Tbsp. thawed orange juice concentrate, divided
- ½ tsp. salt, divided
- ½ tsp. paprika
- ¼ tsp. pepper
- 5 cups fresh baby spinach
- 1 medium navel orange, peeled and cut into ½-in. pieces
- 2 green onions, thinly sliced
- ¼ cup chopped walnuts, toasted
- 4½ tsp. balsamic vinegar
- 1 Tbsp. olive oil

- 1 garlic clove, minced
- ¼ cup crumbled goat cheese

1. Brush the salmon with 4 Tbsp. orange juice concentrate. Sprinkle with ¼ tsp. salt, paprika and pepper. Grill salmon, covered, over medium heat on a greased rack or broil 4 in. from the heat until the fish flakes easily with a fork, 8-10 minutes.
2. Meanwhile, in a large bowl, combine the spinach, orange, green onions and walnuts. In a small bowl, whisk the vinegar, oil, garlic, and the remaining orange juice concentrate and salt. Drizzle over the salad; toss to coat.
3. Divide among plates; sprinkle with cheese. Top with salmon.
1 SERVING: 350 cal., 21g fat (4g sat. fat), 66mg chol., 420mg sod., 19g carb. (14g sugars, 3g fiber), 24g pro.
DIABETIC EXCHANGES: 3 lean meat, 2½ fat, 1 starch.

HOMEMADE FISH STICKS

I am a nutritionist and needed a healthy fish fix. Moist inside and crunchy outside, these are great with oven fries or roasted veggies and low-fat homemade tartar sauce.
—*Jennifer Rowland, Elizabethtown, KY*

Takes: **25 min.** • Makes: **2 servings**

- ½ cup dry bread crumbs
- ½ tsp. salt
- ½ tsp. paprika
- ½ tsp. lemon-pepper seasoning
- ½ cup all-purpose flour
- 1 large egg, beaten
- ¾ lb. cod fillets, cut into 1-in. strips
  Butter-flavored cooking spray

1. Preheat oven to 400°. In a shallow bowl, mix the bread crumbs and seasonings. Place flour and egg in separate shallow bowls. Dip fish in flour to coat both sides; shake off excess. Dip in egg, then in crumb mixture, patting to help coating adhere.
2. Place on a baking sheet coated with cooking spray; spritz fish with butter-flavored cooking spray. Bake 10-12 minutes or until fish just begins to flake easily with a fork, turning once.
1 SERVING: 278 cal., 4g fat (1g sat. fat), 129mg chol., 718mg sod., 25g carb. (2g sugars, 1g fiber), 33g pro.
DIABETIC EXCHANGES: 4 lean meat, 1½ starch.

PRESSURE-COOKER CLAM SAUCE

I serve this bright and fresh clam sauce often, usually with pasta. But it's also delectable as a hot dip.
—*Frances Pietsch,*
Flower Mound, TX

- -

Prep: **10 min.** • Cook: **5 min.**
Makes: **4 cups**

4   Tbsp. butter
2   Tbsp. olive oil
½   cup finely chopped onion
8   oz. fresh mushrooms, chopped
2   garlic cloves, minced
2   cans (10 oz. each) whole baby clams
½   cup water
¼   cup sherry
2   tsp. lemon juice
1   bay leaf
¾   tsp. dried oregano
½   tsp. garlic salt
¼   tsp. white pepper
¼   tsp. Italian seasoning
¼   tsp. pepper
2   Tbsp. chopped fresh parsley
    Hot cooked pasta
    Grated Parmesan cheese, optional

1. Select saute setting on a 6-qt. electric pressure cooker. Adjust for medium heat; heat butter and oil. Add onion; cook and stir 2 minutes. Add mushrooms and garlic; cook 1 minute longer. Press cancel.
2. Drain clams, reserving liquid; coarsely chop. Add the clams, reserved clam juice and the next 9 ingredients to pressure cooker. Lock lid; close pressure-release valve. Adjust to pressure-cook on high for 2 minutes. Quick-release pressure.
3. Discard bay leaf; stir in parsley. Serve with pasta. If desired, serve with grated Parmesan cheese and additional lemon juice and parsley.
½ CUP: 138 cal., 10g fat (4g sat. fat), 40mg chol., 580mg sod., 5g carb. (1g sugars, 0 fiber), 7g pro.

MAKE IT YOUR OWN
Take your clam sauce to a new level by adding...
- Capers
- Asiago cheese

BROILED PARMESAN TILAPIA

Even picky eaters will find a way to love fish when you plate up this toasty Parmesan-coated entree. I serve it with mashed cauliflower and a green salad for a low-calorie meal everyone can enjoy.
—*Trisha Kruse, Eagle, ID*

Takes: **20 min.** • Makes: **6 servings**

- 6 tilapia fillets (6 oz. each)
- ¼ cup grated Parmesan cheese
- ¼ cup reduced-fat mayonnaise
- 2 Tbsp. lemon juice
- 1 Tbsp. butter, softened
- 1 garlic clove, minced
- 1 tsp. minced fresh basil or
  ¼ tsp. dried basil
- ½ tsp. seafood seasoning

1. Place fillets on a broiler pan coated with cooking spray. In a small bowl, combine remaining ingredients; spread over fillets.
2. Broil 3-4 in. from the heat for 10-12 minutes or until fish flakes easily with a fork.
1 FILLET: 207 cal., 8g fat (3g sat. fat), 94mg chol., 260mg sod., 2g carb. (1g sugars, 0 fiber), 33g pro. **DIABETIC EXCHANGES:** 5 lean meat, 1 fat.

AIR-FRYER CRUMB-TOPPED SOLE

Looking for a low-carb supper that's ready in a flash? These buttery sole fillets are covered with a rich sauce and topped with toasty bread crumbs. They're super speedy thanks to your air fryer.
—*Taste of Home Test Kitchen*

Prep: **10 min.**
Cook: **10 min./batch**
Makes: **4 servings**

- 3 Tbsp. reduced-fat mayonnaise
- 3 Tbsp. grated Parmesan cheese, divided
- 2 tsp. mustard seed
- ¼ tsp. pepper
- 4 sole fillets (6 oz. each)
- 1 cup soft bread crumbs
- 1 green onion, finely chopped
- ½ tsp. ground mustard
- 2 tsp. butter, melted
  Cooking spray

1. Preheat air fryer to 375°. Combine mayonnaise, 2 Tbsp. cheese, mustard seed and pepper; spread over tops of fillets.
2. In batches, place fish in a single layer on greased tray in air-fryer basket. Cook until fish flakes easily with a fork, 3-5 minutes.
3. Meanwhile, in a small bowl, combine bread crumbs, onion, mustard and remaining 1 Tbsp. cheese; stir in butter. Spoon over fillets, patting gently to adhere; spritz topping with cooking spray. Cook 2-3 minutes longer or until golden brown. If desired, sprinkle with additional green onions.
1 FILLET: 233 cal., 11g fat (3g sat. fat), 89mg chol., 714mg sod., 8g carb. (1g sugars, 1g fiber), 24g pro.

THE SKINNY

If you don't have an air fryer, you can easily make this recipe in an oven. Broil 4 in. from the heat until fish flakes easily with a fork, 3-5 minutes.

CILANTRO LIME SHRIMP

A quick garlicky lime marinade works magic on these juicy shrimp. They come off the grill with huge flavors perfect for your next cookout.
—*Melissa Rodriguez, Van Nuys, CA*

- -

Takes: **30 min.** • Makes: **4 servings**

- ⅓ **cup chopped fresh cilantro**
- 1½ **tsp. grated lime zest**
- ⅓ **cup lime juice**
- 1 **jalapeno pepper, seeded and minced**
- 2 **Tbsp. olive oil**
- 3 **garlic cloves, minced**
- ¼ **tsp. salt**
- ¼ **tsp. ground cumin**
- ¼ **tsp. pepper**
- 1 **lb. uncooked shrimp (16-20 per lb.), peeled and deveined Lime slices**

1. Mix the first 9 ingredients; toss with shrimp. Let stand 15 minutes.
2. Thread shrimp and lime slices onto 4 metal or soaked wooden skewers. Grill, covered, over medium heat until shrimp turn pink, 2-4 minutes per side.
1 KABOB: 167 cal., 8g fat (1g sat. fat), 138mg chol., 284mg sod., 4g carb. (1g sugars, 0 fiber), 19g pro.
DIABETIC EXCHANGES: 3 lean meat, 1½ fat.

HALIBUT SOFT TACOS

I sometimes serve the fish wrapped in lettuce instead of tortillas. Either way, the mango salsa tastes amazing with grilled halibut. This warm-weather favorite is quick, colorful and full of nutrients.
—*Kristin Kossak, Bozeman, MT*

- -

Takes: **30 min.** • Makes: **4 servings**

- 1 **medium mango, peeled and cubed**
- ½ **cup cubed avocado**
- ¼ **cup chopped red onion**
- 2 **Tbsp. chopped seeded jalapeno pepper**
- 1 **Tbsp. minced fresh cilantro**
- 3 **tsp. olive oil, divided**
- 1 **tsp. lemon juice**
- 1 **tsp. honey**
- 1 **lb. halibut steaks (¾ in. thick)**
- ½ **tsp. salt**
- ¼ **tsp. pepper**

- 4 **Bibb lettuce leaves**
- 4 **flour tortillas (6 in.), warmed**
- 4 **tsp. sweet Thai chili sauce**

1. In a small bowl, combine the mango, avocado, onion, jalapeno, cilantro, 2 tsp. oil, lemon juice and honey; set aside. Brush halibut with remaining oil; sprinkle with the salt and pepper.
2. Grill the halibut on a greased rack, covered, over high heat or broil 3-4 in. from the heat until fish flakes easily with a fork, 3-5 minutes on each side.
3. Place lettuce leaves on tortillas; top with fish and mango mixture. Drizzle with chili sauce.
1 TACO WITH ⅓ CUP MANGO MIXTURE: 330 cal., 12g fat (1g sat. fat), 36mg chol., 648mg sod., 28g carb. (12g sugars, 2g fiber), 28g pro.
DIABETIC EXCHANGES: 3 lean meat, 2 starch, 1 fat.

2 Tbsp. extra virgin olive oil
1 Tbsp. minced fresh gingerroot
2 garlic cloves, minced
SALAD
1 pkg. (5 oz.) fresh baby spinach
1 medium sweet yellow pepper, cut into 1-in. pieces
8 cherry tomatoes, halved

1. Thread tuna chunks onto 4 metal or soaked wooden skewers. Thread the pepper and onion pieces onto 4 more skewers. Place skewers in a 13x9-in. baking dish.

2. Whisk together marinade ingredients. Reserve half of mixture for salad dressing. Pour remaining marinade over skewers; refrigerate, covered, 30 minutes.

3. Grill kabobs, covered, on a greased grill rack over medium heat, turning occasionally, until tuna is slightly pink in center for medium-rare (2-3 minutes per side) and vegetables are crisp-tender (10-12 minutes). Remove tuna kabobs from direct heat and keep warm while vegetables finish grilling.

4. For salad, toss spinach, yellow pepper and cherry tomatoes with reserved dressing. For each portion, serve a tuna kabob and vegetable kabob over salad.

1 TUNA KABOB AND 1 VEGETABLE KABOB: 389 cal., 16g fat (2g sat. fat), 66mg chol., 444mg sod., 15g carb. (9g sugars, 4g fiber), 45g pro.
DIABETIC EXCHANGES: 5 lean meat, 2 vegetable, 2 fat.

TUNA TERIYAKI KABOBS

I love to barbecue but don't always want a heavy dinner. These tasty tuna and veggie kabobs are the perfect light meal, and you'll have room for dessert!
—*Holly Battiste, Barrington, NJ*

- -

Prep: **25 min. + marinating**
Grill: **15 min.** • Makes: **8 kabobs**

1½ lbs. tuna steaks, cut into 1½-in. chunks
2 medium sweet red peppers, cut into 1-in. pieces
1 large sweet onion, cut into 1-in. pieces
MARINADE/DRESSING
¼ cup minced fresh cilantro
¼ cup sesame oil
3 Tbsp. lime juice
2 Tbsp. soy sauce

CALIFORNIA ROLL IN A JAR

I'm a big sushi fan but don't always have time to make those intricate rolls at home. This jar is layered with my favorite California roll ingredients, for all the flavor without the fuss.
—*James Schend,*
Pleasant Prairie, WI

Prep: **20 min.**
Cook: **15 min. + standing**
Makes: **4 servings**

- 1 **cup uncooked sushi rice**
- 1 **cup water**
- ½ **tsp. salt**
- 1 **Tbsp. rice vinegar**
- 1 **Tbsp. sugar**
- 2 **medium ripe avocados, peeled and cubed**
- 1 **cup lump crabmeat, drained**
- 1 **cup chopped cucumber**
- 2 **nori sheets, thinly sliced**
  Optional toppings: Pickled ginger slices, soy sauce and toasted sesame seeds

1. Wash rice in a colander until water runs clear. Combine rice, 1 cup water and salt in a large saucepan; bring to a boil. Reduce heat; cover. Simmer until water is absorbed and the rice is tender, 15-20 minutes. Remove from heat. Let stand 10 minutes. Combine rice vinegar and sugar, stirring until sugar is dissolved. Stir into rice.
2. Place ⅓ cup rice into each of four 1-pint wide-mouth canning jars; layer with half of the avocados, crabmeat, cucumber and nori. Top with remaining rice and repeat layers. Cover jars and refrigerate until serving. Transfer into bowls;

toss to combine. Serve with toppings as desired.
1 SERVING: 349 cal., 11g fat (2g sat. fat), 33mg chol., 562mg sod., 52g carb. (6g sugars, 7g fiber), 11g pro.

THE SKINNY
Imitation crabmeat is a very acceptable substitution for the more costly lump crabmeat. Tuna fish, smoked salmon or smoked trout are also good replacements for the crab.

EASY CITRUS SEAFOOD SALAD

This super simple, deceptively delicious recipe was inspired by a seafood salad I had in the Bahamas that featured conch. I substituted crab and shrimp for the conch and liked it even more!
—*Cindy Heyd, Edmond, OK*

Takes: **15 min.** • Makes: **4 servings**

- 1 medium orange
- 1 medium lemon
- 1 medium lime
- ½ lb. peeled and deveined cooked shrimp, coarsely chopped
- ½ lb. refrigerated fresh or imitation crabmeat, coarsely chopped
- 2 Tbsp. finely chopped sweet onion
- 2 Tbsp. finely chopped sweet red pepper
  Shredded lettuce
  Assorted crackers

Finely grate zest from orange. Cut orange crosswise in half; squeeze juice from orange. Transfer zest and juice to a large bowl. Repeat with lemon and lime. Add shrimp, crab, onion and pepper; toss to coat. Serve on lettuce with crackers.
¾ CUP: 128 cal., 2g fat (0 sat. fat), 141mg chol., 309mg sod., 6g carb. (3g sugars, 1g fiber), 22g pro.
DIABETIC EXCHANGES: 3 lean meat.

BLOCK ISLAND LITTLENECKS WITH CHORIZO

Every summer my family digs clams on the shores of Block Island, Rhode Island. This dish highlights the fresh sweet and salty clam flavor and the chorizo adds a little kick. Fresh Swiss chard greens from our garden, corn, and cannellini beans round out the flavor profile. For me, the best part is dipping crusty bread into the delicious broth! Quick and easy to put together, it's the perfect dinner on a hot summer night!
—*Pamela Gelsomini, Wrentham, MA*

Prep: **20 min.** • Cook: **25 min.**
Makes: **8 servings (4 qt.)**

- 3 lbs. fresh littleneck clams
- 1 bunch Swiss chard, stems removed and chopped (about 4 cups)
- ½ lb. fully cooked Spanish chorizo links, chopped
- 1 can (15 oz.) cannellini beans, rinsed and drained
- 1 medium onion, chopped
- 1 cup fresh or frozen corn
- 4 garlic cloves, minced
- 1 tsp. salt
- 1 tsp. pepper
- 1 bottle (12 oz.) beer
- ⅓ cup olive oil
  Grilled French bread baguette slices

1. Place clams in a stockpot; top with the next 8 ingredients. Add beer and oil; bring to a boil. Reduce heat; simmer, covered, for 10 minutes.
2. Stir; cook, covered, until clams open, 5-7 minutes longer. Discard any unopened clams. Ladle into bowls; serve with grilled bread.
2 CUPS: 265 cal., 17g fat (4g sat. fat), 28mg chol., 729mg sod., 16g carb. (3g sugars, 4g fiber), 12g pro.

THE SKINNY

Clams that have been frozen in their shell can be used in place of fresh. Thaw and clean completely before proceeding with recipe.

AIR-FRYER COCONUT SHRIMP WITH APRICOT SAUCE

Coconut and panko crumbs give this spicy air-fryer shrimp its crunch. It's perfect for an appetizer or for your main meal.
—*Debi Mitchell, Flower Mound, TX*

Takes: **30 min.** • Makes: **2 servings**

- ½ lb. uncooked large shrimp
- ½ cup sweetened shredded coconut
- 3 Tbsp. panko bread crumbs
- 2 large egg whites
- ⅛ tsp. salt
  Dash pepper
  Dash Louisiana-style hot sauce
- 3 Tbsp. all-purpose flour

SAUCE
- ⅓ cup apricot preserves
- ½ tsp. cider vinegar
  Dash crushed red pepper flakes

1. Preheat air fryer to 375°. Peel and devein shrimp, leaving tails on.
2. In a shallow bowl, toss coconut with bread crumbs. In another shallow bowl, whisk egg whites, salt, pepper and hot sauce. Place flour in a third shallow bowl.
3. Dip shrimp in flour to coat lightly; shake off excess. Dip in egg white mixture, then in coconut mixture, patting to help coating adhere.
4. Place shrimp in a single layer on greased tray in air-fryer basket. Cook 4 minutes; turn shrimp and continue cooking until coconut is lightly browned and shrimp turn pink, about 4 minutes longer.
5. Meanwhile, combine the sauce ingredients in a small saucepan; cook and stir over medium-low heat until the preserves are melted. Serve shrimp immediately with sauce.
6 SHRIMP WITH 2 TBSP. SAUCE: 423 cal., 10g fat (8g sat. fat), 138mg chol., 440mg sod., 59g carb. (34g sugars, 2g fiber), 25g pro.

TILAPIA WITH JASMINE RICE

This tender, full-flavored tilapia with fragrant jasmine rice is absolutely to die for. Your family will love this healthy and delicious dish!
—*Shirl Parsons, Cape Carteret, NC*

Takes: **25 min.** • Makes: **2 servings**

- ¾ cup water
- ½ cup uncooked jasmine rice
- 1½ tsp. butter
- ¼ tsp. ground cumin
- ¼ tsp. seafood seasoning
- ¼ tsp. pepper
- ⅛ tsp. salt
- 2 tilapia fillets (6 oz. each)
- ¼ cup Italian salad dressing

1. In a small saucepan, combine water, rice and butter; bring to a boil. Reduce heat; simmer, covered, until liquid is absorbed and rice is tender, 15-20 minutes.
2. Meanwhile, mix the seasonings; sprinkle over tilapia. In a large skillet, heat salad dressing over medium heat until hot. Add fillets; cook until fish just begins to flake easily with a fork, 3-4 minutes per side. Serve with rice.
1 FILLET WITH ¾ CUP RICE: 412 cal., 9g fat (3g sat. fat), 90mg chol., 615mg sod., 42g carb. (2g sugars, 1g fiber), 36g pro.

sides; shake off excess. Dip in egg mixture, then in cornflake mixture, patting to help coating adhere.

4. Remove fries from basket; keep warm. Place fish in a single layer on tray in air-fryer basket. Cook until fish is lightly browned and just beginning to flake easily with a fork, 8-10 minutes, turning halfway through cooking. Do not overcook. Return fries to basket to heat through. Serve immediately. If desired, serve with tartar sauce.

1 SERVING: 312 cal., 9g fat (2g sat. fat), 85mg chol., 503mg sod., 35g carb. (3g sugars, 1g fiber), 23g pro. **DIABETIC EXCHANGES:** 3 lean meat, 2 starch, 2 fat.

TYPICAL	MAKEOVER
28g Fat	**9**g Fat
4g Saturated Fat	**2**g Saturated Fat
1,060mg Sodium	**503**mg Sodium

THE SKINNY

Cook times can vary dramatically among brands of air fryers. As a result, we have given wider than normal ranges on suggested cook times. Begin checking at the first time listed and adjust as needed.

AIR-FRYER FISH & FRIES

Looking for easy air-fryer recipes? Try these simple fish and chips. The fish fillets have a fuss-free coating that's healthier but just as crunchy and golden as the deep-fried kind. Simply seasoned, the crispy fries are perfect on the side.
—*Janice Mitchell, Aurora, CO*

- -

Prep: **15 min.** • Cook: **25 min.**
Makes: **4 servings**

- 1 lb. potatoes (about 2 medium)
- 2 Tbsp. olive oil
- ¼ tsp. pepper
- ¼ tsp. salt

FISH

- ⅓ cup all-purpose flour
- ¼ tsp. pepper
- 1 large egg
- 2 Tbsp. water
- ⅔ cup crushed cornflakes
- 1 Tbsp. grated Parmesan cheese
- ⅛ tsp. cayenne pepper
- 1 lb. haddock or cod fillets
- ¼ tsp. salt
   Tartar sauce, optional

1. Preheat air fryer to 400°. Peel and cut potatoes lengthwise into ½-in.-thick slices; cut slices into ½-in.-thick sticks.

2. In a large bowl, toss the potatoes with oil, pepper and salt. Working in batches, place potatoes in a single layer on tray in air-fryer basket; cook 5-10 minutes or until just tender. Toss the potatoes to redistribute; cook until lightly browned and crisp, 5-10 minutes longer.

3. Meanwhile, in a shallow bowl, mix flour and pepper. In another shallow bowl, whisk egg with water. In a third bowl, toss cornflakes with cheese and cayenne. Sprinkle fish with salt. Dip into flour mixture to coat both

MEATLESS MAIN DISHES

LEMONY GARBANZO SALAD

Everybody goes for this super fresh salad with the cumin-coriander dressing, especially on warm days.
—*Sonya Labbe, West Hollywood, CA*

Takes: **15 min.** • Makes: **4 servings**

- ¼ cup olive oil
- 3 Tbsp. lemon juice
- ¾ tsp. ground cumin
- ¼ tsp. salt
- ¼ tsp. ground coriander
- ¼ tsp. pepper
- 2 cans (15 oz. each) garbanzo beans or chickpeas, rinsed and drained
- 3 green onions, chopped
- ½ cup plain yogurt
- 1 Tbsp. minced fresh parsley
- 1 Tbsp. orange marmalade
- 4 cups spring mix salad greens

1. In a large bowl, whisk together first 6 ingredients; stir in beans and green onions. In another bowl, mix yogurt, parsley and marmalade.

2. To serve, divide salad greens among 4 plates; top with bean mixture. Serve with yogurt sauce.

1 SERVING: 363 cal., 19g fat (3g sat. fat), 4mg chol., 478mg sod., 41g carb. (10g sugars, 10g fiber), 11g pro.

THE SKINNY

The garbanzo beans in this hearty salad are responsible for most of the dish's 10 g fiber. They also add iron, vitamin B6, folate, manganese and phosphorous.

CUMIN-SPICED LENTIL BURGERS

A few years ago, my son married his lovely Turkish bride. She has shared with our family many Turkish recipes that we enjoy but our favorite is her recipe for lentil logs, which is an appetizer served at various events in Turkey. It is typically eaten in log form, wrapped in a lettuce leaf and served with a lemon wedge. I have transformed the recipe into vegan burgers; for a spicier version of burger, hot chili powder or crushed red chili peppers may be added.
—*Sheila Joan Suhan, Scottdale, PA*

Prep: **30 min.**
Cook: **10 min./batch**
Makes: **8 servings**

2¼ cups water, divided
 1 cup dried red lentils, rinsed
 1 cup bulgur (fine grind)
1½ tsp. salt, divided
 6 Tbsp. canola oil, divided
 1 large onion, chopped
 1 Tbsp. ground cumin
 1 Tbsp. chili powder
 1 large egg, lightly beaten
 6 green onions, sliced
 3 Tbsp. chopped fresh parsley
 8 flatbread wraps
 8 Tbsp. Sriracha mayonnaise
   Optional toppings: Lettuce leaves, sliced tomato and sliced onions

1. Place 2 cups water and lentils in a large saucepan. Bring to a boil. Reduce the heat and simmer, uncovered, until lentils are tender, 15-20 minutes, stirring occasionally. Remove from heat; stir in bulgur and 1 tsp. salt. Cover and let stand until bulgur is tender and liquid is absorbed, 15-20 minutes.

2. Meanwhile, in a large nonstick skillet, heat 2 Tbsp. oil over medium-high heat. Add onion; cook and stir until tender, 5-7 minutes. Add cumin and chili powder; cook 1 minute longer. Remove from heat. Add onion mixture to lentil mixture. Stir in egg, green onions, parsley and remaining ½ tsp. salt, mixing lightly but thoroughly. If needed, add remaining ¼ cup water, 1 Tbsp. at a time, to help mixture stay together when squeezed; shape into eight ½-in.-thick patties.

3. In the same skillet, heat remaining 4 Tbsp. oil over medium heat. Add the burgers in batches; cook until golden brown, 3-5 minutes on each side. Serve in wraps with Sriracha mayonnaise and, if desired, toppings of your choice.

1 BURGER: 434 cal., 23g fat (2g sat. fat), 1mg chol., 780mg sod., 54g carb. (2g sugars, 16g fiber), 16g pro.

THE SKINNY
If the lentil burger mixture is too dry and does not stick together, mix in 1 or 2 tablespoons of water to soften things up a little bit.

INDIAN SPICED CHICKPEA WRAPS

Raita, an Indian condiment made with yogurt, elevates this vegetarian dish into a satisfying gourmet wrap. I sometimes substitute diced mango or cucumber for the pineapple and add fresh herbs like cilantro or mint.
—*Jennifer Beckman, Falls Church, VA*

Takes: **30 min.** • Makes: **4 servings**

- 1 **cup reduced-fat plain yogurt**
- ½ **cup unsweetened pineapple tidbits**
- ¼ **tsp. salt**
- ¼ **tsp. ground cumin**

WRAPS
- 2 **tsp. canola oil**
- 1 **small onion, chopped**
- 1 **Tbsp. minced fresh gingerroot**
- 2 **garlic cloves, minced**
- ½ **tsp. curry powder**
- ¼ **tsp. salt**
- ¼ **tsp. ground coriander**
- ¼ **tsp. ground cumin**
- ¼ **tsp. cayenne pepper, optional**
- 1 **can (15 oz.) chickpeas or garbanzo beans, rinsed and drained**
- 1 **cup canned crushed tomatoes**
- 3 **cups fresh baby spinach**
- 4 **whole wheat tortillas (8 in.), warmed**

1. For pineapple raita, mix first 4 ingredients.
2. For wraps, in a large nonstick skillet, heat oil over medium-high heat; saute onion until tender. Add ginger, garlic and seasonings; cook and stir until fragrant, about 1 minute. Stir in chickpeas and tomatoes; bring to a boil. Reduce heat; simmer, uncovered, until slightly thickened, 5-8 minutes, stirring occasionally.
3. To serve, place spinach and chickpea mixture on tortillas. Top with raita and roll up.
1 WRAP: 321 cal., 7g fat (1g sat. fat), 3mg chol., 734mg sod., 55g carb. (15g sugars, 10g fiber), 13g pro.

THE SKINNY

This handheld has it all—fruit, vegetables, whole grains, reduced-fat dairy and pro-packed pulses. And it tastes amazing, as well!

SPINACH BURRITOS

I made up this recipe a couple of years ago after trying a similar dish in a restaurant. Our oldest son tells me these burritos are awesome! Plus, they're easy and inexpensive.
—*Dolores Zornow, Poynette, WI*

Prep: **20 min.** • Bake: **20 min.**
Makes: **6 servings**

- ½ cup chopped onion
- 2 garlic cloves, minced
- 2 tsp. butter
- 1 pkg. (10 oz.) frozen chopped spinach, thawed and squeezed dry
- ⅛ tsp. pepper
- 6 flour tortillas (10 in.), warmed
- ¾ cup picante sauce, divided
- 2 cups shredded reduced-fat cheddar cheese, divided

1. In a large skillet, saute onion and garlic in butter until tender. Add spinach and pepper; cook until heated through, 2-3 minutes.
2. Place about 3 Tbsp. of mixture off-center on each tortilla; top with 1 Tbsp. picante sauce and 2 Tbsp. cheese. Fold sides and ends over filling and roll up.
3. Place seam side down in a 13x9-in. baking dish coated with cooking spray. Top with remaining picante sauce and cheese. Bake, uncovered, at 350° for 20-25 minutes or until the sauce is bubbly and cheese is melted.

1 BURRITO: 382 cal., 15g fat (8g sat. fat), 30mg chol., 1049mg sod., 42g carb. (5g sugars, 4g fiber), 19g pro.

BETTER THAN EGG SALAD

Tofu takes on the taste and texture of egg salad in this tasty sandwich. It makes a great quick-to-fix lunch.
—*Lisa Renshaw, Kansas City, MO*

Takes: **20 min.** • Makes: **4 servings**

- ¼ cup reduced-fat mayonnaise
- ¼ cup chopped celery
- 2 green onions, chopped
- 2 Tbsp. sweet pickle relish
- 1 Tbsp. Dijon mustard
- ¼ tsp. ground turmeric
- ¼ tsp. salt
- ⅛ tsp. cayenne pepper
- 1 pkg. (12.3 oz.) silken firm tofu, cubed
- 8 slices whole wheat bread
- 4 lettuce leaves
  Coarsely ground pepper, optional

Mix first 8 ingredients; stir in tofu. Line 4 slices of bread with lettuce. Top with tofu mixture. If desired, sprinkle with pepper; close the sandwiches.

1 SANDWICH: 266 cal., 9g fat (2g sat. fat), 5mg chol., 692mg sod., 31g carb. (7g sugars, 4g fiber), 14g pro.
DIABETIC EXCHANGES: 2 starch, 1 lean meat, 1 fat.

ROASTED RED PEPPER MOCK EGG SALAD: Omit the green onion, sweet pickle relish, turmeric and cayenne. To the mayonnaise mixture, add 2 Tbsp. diced roasted sweet red pepper, 1 Tbsp. minced fresh parsley, ½ tsp. dried oregano and ⅛ tsp. pepper. Proceed as directed.

GNOCCHI WITH WHITE BEANS

Here's one of those no-fuss recipes you can toss together and cook in one skillet. Ideal for a busy weeknight, it's also good with crumbled Italian chicken sausage if you need to please meat lovers.
—*Juli Meyers, Hinesville, GA*

Takes: **30 min.** • Makes: **6 servings**

- 1 Tbsp. olive oil
- 1 medium onion, chopped
- 2 garlic cloves, minced
- 1 pkg. (16 oz.) potato gnocchi
- 1 can (15 oz.) cannellini beans, rinsed and drained
- 1 can (14½ oz.) Italian diced tomatoes, undrained
- 1 pkg. (6 oz.) fresh baby spinach
- ¼ tsp. pepper
- ½ cup shredded part-skim mozzarella cheese
- 3 Tbsp. grated Parmesan cheese

1. In a large skillet, heat oil over medium-high heat. Add onion; cook and stir until tender. Add garlic; cook 1 minute longer. Add gnocchi; cook and stir 5-6 minutes or until golden brown. Stir in beans, tomatoes, spinach and pepper; heat through.
2. Sprinkle with cheeses; cover and remove from heat. Let stand 3-4 minutes or until cheese is melted.
1 CUP: 307 cal., 6g fat (2g sat. fat), 13mg chol., 789mg sod., 50g carb. (10g sugars, 6g fiber), 13g pro.

VEG JAMBALAYA

The flavorful entree won't leave you hungry since it uses convenient canned beans in place of the meat.
—*Crystal Jo Bruns, Iliff, CO*

Prep: **10 min.** • Cook: **30 min.**
Makes: **6 servings**

- 1 Tbsp. canola oil
- 1 medium green pepper, chopped
- 1 medium onion, chopped
- 1 celery rib, chopped
- 3 garlic cloves, minced
- 2 cups water
- 1 can (14½ oz.) diced tomatoes, undrained
- 1 can (8 oz.) tomato sauce
- ½ tsp. Italian seasoning
- ¼ tsp. salt
- ¼ tsp. crushed red pepper flakes
- ⅛ tsp. fennel seed, crushed
- 1 cup uncooked long grain rice
- 1 can (16 oz.) butter beans, rinsed and drained
- 1 can (16 oz.) red beans, rinsed and drained

1. In a Dutch oven, heat oil over medium-high heat. Add the green pepper, onion and celery; cook and stir until tender. Add garlic; cook 1 minute longer.
2. Add the water, tomatoes, tomato sauce and seasonings. Bring to a boil; stir in rice. Reduce heat; cover and simmer for 15-18 minutes or until liquid is absorbed and rice is tender. Stir in beans; heat through.
1⅓ CUPS: 281 cal., 3g fat (0 sat. fat), 0 chol., 796mg sod., 56g carb. (6g sugars, 9g fiber), 11g pro.

VEGGIE NICOISE SALAD

More and more people in my workplace are becoming vegetarians. When we cook or eat together, the focus is on fresh produce. This salad combines some of our favorite ingredients in one dish—and with the hard-cooked eggs and kidney beans, it delivers enough protein to satisfy those who are skeptical of vegetarian fare.
—*Elizabeth Kelley, Chicago, IL*

Prep: **40 min.** • Cook: **25 min.**
Makes: **8 servings**

- ⅓ cup olive oil
- ¼ cup lemon juice
- 2 tsp. minced fresh oregano
- 2 tsp. minced fresh thyme
- 1 tsp. Dijon mustard
- 1 garlic clove, minced
- ¼ tsp. coarsely ground pepper
- ⅛ tsp. salt
- 1 can (16 oz.) kidney beans, rinsed and drained
- 1 small red onion, halved and thinly sliced
- 1 lb. small red potatoes (about 9), halved
- 1 lb. fresh asparagus, trimmed
- ½ lb. fresh green beans, trimmed
- 12 cups torn romaine (about 2 small bunches)
- 6 hard-boiled large eggs, quartered
- 1 jar (6½ oz.) marinated quartered artichoke hearts, drained
- ½ cup Nicoise or kalamata olives

1. For vinaigrette, whisk together first 8 ingredients. In another bowl, toss kidney beans and onion with 1 Tbsp. vinaigrette. Set aside bean mixture and remaining vinaigrette.

2. Place potatoes in a saucepan and cover with water. Bring to a boil. Reduce heat; simmer, covered, until tender, 10-15 minutes. Drain. While potatoes are warm, toss with 1 Tbsp. vinaigrette; set aside.

3. In a pot of boiling water, cook asparagus just until crisp-tender, 2-4 minutes. Remove with tongs and immediately drop into ice water. Drain and pat dry. In same pot of boiling water, cook green beans until crisp-tender, 3-4 minutes. Remove beans; place in ice water. Drain and pat dry.

4. To serve, toss the asparagus with 1 Tbsp. vinaigrette; toss green beans with 2 tsp. vinaigrette. Toss romaine with remaining vinaigrette; place on a platter. Arrange vegetables, kidney bean mixture, eggs, artichoke hearts and olives over top.

1 SERVING: 329 cal., 19g fat (4g sat. fat), 140mg chol., 422mg sod., 28g carb. (6g sugars, 7g fiber), 12g pro. **DIABETIC EXCHANGES:** 3 fat, 2 vegetable, 2 medium-fat meat, 1½ starch.

FRESH CORN & TOMATO FETTUCCINE

This recipe combines delicious whole wheat pasta with the best of fresh garden produce. It's tossed with heart-healthy olive oil, and a little feta cheese gives it bite.
—*Angela Spengler, Niceville, FL*

Takes: **30 min.** • Makes: **4 servings**

8 oz. uncooked whole wheat fettuccine
2 medium ears sweet corn, husked
2 tsp. plus 2 Tbsp. olive oil, divided
½ cup chopped sweet red pepper
4 green onions, chopped
2 medium tomatoes, chopped
½ tsp. salt
½ tsp. pepper
1 cup crumbled feta cheese
2 Tbsp. minced fresh parsley

1. In a Dutch oven, cook fettuccine according to package directions, adding sweet corn during the last 8 minutes of cooking.
2. Meanwhile, in a small skillet, heat 2 tsp. oil over medium-high heat. Add red pepper and green onions; cook and stir until tender.
3. Drain pasta and corn; transfer pasta to a large bowl. Cool corn slightly; cut corn from cob and add to pasta. Add tomatoes, salt, pepper, remaining oil and the pepper mixture; toss to combine. Sprinkle with cheese and parsley.
2 CUPS: 527 cal., 17g fat (5g sat. fat), 84mg chol., 1051mg sod., 75g carb. (7g sugars, 9g fiber), 21g pro.

AIR-FRIED BUTTERNUT SQUASH TACOS

Butternut squash tossed with southwestern spices makes a wonderful base for vegetarian tacos. I'm always looking for easy and healthy dinners for my family, and this dish is delicious!
—*Elisabeth Larsen, Pleasant Grove, UT*

Prep: **10 min.** • Cook: **15 min./batch**
Makes: **6 servings**

2 Tbsp. canola oil
1 Tbsp. chili powder
½ tsp. ground cumin
½ tsp. ground coriander
½ tsp. salt
¼ tsp. cayenne pepper
1 medium butternut squash (3 to 4 lbs.), peeled and cut into ½-in. pieces
12 corn tortillas (6 in.), warmed
1 cup crumbled queso fresco or feta cheese
1 medium ripe avocado, peeled and sliced thin
¼ cup diced red onion
   Pico de gallo, optional

1. Preheat the air fryer to 400°. Combine the first 6 ingredients. Add squash pieces; toss to coat. In batches, arrange squash in a single layer on a greased tray in air-fryer basket. Cook until tender, 15-20 minutes.
2. Divide squash evenly among tortillas. Top with queso fresco, avocado and red onion. If desired, serve with pico de gallo.
2 TACOS: 353 cal., 13g fat (3g sat. fat), 13mg chol., 322mg sod., 54g carb. (7g sugars, 13g fiber), 11g pro.

THE SKINNY
This mac and cheese is extremely creamy but feel free to cut back the half-and-half down to 1 cup.

½ cup shredded reduced-fat cheddar cheese
OPTIONAL GARNISH
   sliced cherry tomatoes and minced chives

1. Preheat oven to 350°. Cook macaroni according to package directions; drain.
2. Meanwhile, in small bowl, whisk flour, seasonings and half-and-half until smooth. In a large saucepan, melt butter over medium heat. Stir in half-and-half mixture. Add milk. Bring to a gentle boil, stirring constantly; remove from heat. Add cheese; stir until melted. Stir in macaroni. Transfer to a 13x9-in. baking dish coated with cooking spray.
3. For optional topping, in a large skillet, heat butter over medium-high heat. Add the onion; cook and stir until tender. Add bread crumbs; cook and stir 2 minutes longer. Sprinkle over macaroni mixture; top with cheese.
4. Bake, uncovered, until heated through, 25-30 minutes. Garnish as desired.
1 CUP: 343 cal., 11g fat (6g sat. fat), 31mg chol., 354mg sod., 45g carb. (8g sugars, 2g fiber), 18g pro.

MAKEOVER CREAMY MAC & CHEESE
Macaroni and cheese just may be king of the comfort foods. This sensational version is bubbling with creamy goodness—but is lighter on calories.
—*April Taylor, Holcomb, KS*

Prep: **30 min.** • Bake: **25 min.**
Makes: **10 servings**

1   **pkg. (16 oz.) elbow macaroni**
⅓   **cup all-purpose flour**
½   **tsp. garlic powder**
½   **tsp. pepper**
¼   **tsp. salt**
2   **cups fat-free half-and-half**
2   **Tbsp. butter**
2   **cups fat-free milk**
3   **cups shredded reduced-fat sharp cheddar cheese**
OPTIONAL TOPPING
2   **Tbsp. butter**
1   **medium onion, chopped**
3   **cups soft bread crumbs**

TYPICAL	MAKEOVER
653 Calories	**343** Calories
46g Fat	**11**g Fat
30g Saturated Fat	**6**g Saturated Fat
1,141mg Sodium	**354**mg Sodium

AIR-FRYER CHICKPEA & RED ONION BURGERS

When chilly days arrive and we retire the grill to the garage, I bake a batch of these air-fryer chickpea burgers. Even my die-hard meat eaters can't resist them.
—*Lily Julow, Lawrenceville, GA*

Takes: **30 min.** • Makes: **6 servings**

- 1 large red onion, thinly sliced
- ¼ cup fat-free red wine vinaigrette
- 2 cans (15 oz. each) chickpeas or garbanzo beans, rinsed and drained
- ⅓ cup chopped walnuts
- ¼ cup toasted wheat germ or dry bread crumbs
- ¼ cup packed fresh parsley
- 2 large eggs
- 1 tsp. curry powder
- ½ tsp. pepper
   Cooking spray
- ⅓ cup fat-free mayonnaise
- 2 tsp. Dijon mustard
- 6 sesame seed hamburger buns, split and toasted
- 6 lettuce leaves
- 3 Tbsp. thinly sliced fresh basil leaves

1. Preheat air fryer to 375°. In a small bowl, mix the onion and vinaigrette; set aside. Place the chickpeas, walnuts, wheat germ and parsley in a food processor; pulse until blended. Add eggs, curry and pepper; process until smooth.
2. Shape into 6 patties. In batches, place patties in a single layer on greased tray in air-fryer basket, spray with cooking spray. Cook until a thermometer reads 160°, 8-10 minutes, flipping halfway through.
3. In a small bowl, mix mayonnaise and mustard; spread over cut sides of buns. Serve patties on buns with lettuce, basil and onion mixture.

1 BURGER: 381 cal., 13g fat (2g sat. fat), 62mg chol., 697mg sod., 54g carb. (10g sugars, 9g fiber), 16g pro.

THE SKINNY
Cut calories by omitting the bun and serving the patties as lettuce wraps.

PROVOLONE ZITI BAKE

Instead of waiting for water to boil, I throw the makings for a meatless ziti into one baking dish. After a long day, I'm more than happy to make the oven do the work.
—Vicky Palmer, Albuquerque, NM

Prep: **20 min.** • Bake: **65 min.**
Makes: **8 servings**

- 1 Tbsp. olive oil
- 1 medium onion, chopped
- 3 garlic cloves, minced
- 2 cans (28 oz. each) Italian crushed tomatoes
- 1½ cups water
- ½ cup dry red wine or reduced-sodium chicken broth
- 1 Tbsp. sugar
- 1 tsp. dried basil
- 1 pkg. (16 oz.) ziti or small tube pasta
- 8 slices provolone cheese

1. Preheat oven to 350°. In a 6-qt. stockpot, heat oil over medium-high heat. Add chopped onion; cook and stir 2-3 minutes or until tender. Add garlic; cook 1 minute longer. Stir in tomatoes, water, wine, sugar and basil. Bring to a boil; remove from heat. Stir in uncooked ziti.
2. Transfer to a 13x9-in. baking dish coated with cooking spray. Bake, covered, 1 hour. Top with cheese. Bake, uncovered, 5-10 minutes longer or until ziti is tender and cheese is melted.
1½ CUPS: 381 cal., 8g fat (4g sat. fat), 15mg chol., 763mg sod., 60g carb. (13g sugars, 4g fiber), 16g pro.

AIR-FRYER BLACK BEAN CHIMICHANGAS

These chimichangas get a little love from the air fryer, so they're much healthier than their deep-fried counterparts. Black beans provide protein, and the recipe is a smart way to use up leftover rice.
—Kimberly Hammond, Kingwood, TX

Prep: **20 min.** • Cook: **5 min./batch**
Makes: **6 servings**

- 2 cans (15 oz. each) black beans, rinsed and drained
- 1 pkg. (8.8 oz.) ready-to-serve brown rice
- ⅔ cup frozen corn
- ⅔ cup minced fresh cilantro
- ⅔ cup chopped green onions
- ½ tsp. salt
- 6 whole wheat tortillas (8 in.), warmed if necessary
- 4 tsp. olive oil
  Optional: Guacamole and salsa

1. Preheat air fryer to 400°. In a large microwave-safe bowl, mix beans, rice and corn; microwave, covered, until heated through, 4-5 minutes, stirring halfway. Stir in cilantro, green onions and salt.
2. To assemble, spoon ¾ cup bean mixture across the center of each tortilla. Fold bottom and sides of tortilla over filling and roll up. Brush with olive oil.
3. In batches, place seam side down on greased tray in air-fryer basket. Cook until golden brown and crispy, 2-3 minutes. If desired, serve with guacamole and salsa.
1 CHIMICHANGA: 337 cal., 5g fat (0 sat. fat), 0 chol., 602mg sod., 58g carb. (2g sugars, 10g fiber), 13g pro.

1   **prebaked 12-in. thin pizza crust**
2   **cups chopped fresh spinach**
2   **Tbsp. minced fresh cilantro**
    Hot pepper sauce to taste
½   **cup shredded reduced-fat cheddar cheese**
½   **cup shredded pepper jack cheese**

1. In a small bowl, mash black beans. Stir in onion, yellow pepper, chili powder and cumin. In another bowl, combine the tomatoes, jalapeno and garlic.
2. Place crust on an ungreased 12-in. pizza pan; spread with bean mixture. Top with the tomato mixture and spinach. Sprinkle with cilantro, pepper sauce and cheeses.
3. Bake at 400° for 12-15 minutes or until cheese is melted.
1 PIECE: 295 cal., 8g fat (3g sat. fat), 17mg chol., 581mg sod., 40g carb. (5g sugars, 6g fiber), 15g pro.
DIABETIC EXCHANGES: 2.5 starch, 1 lean meat, 1 vegetable.

THE SKINNY

Spread some salsa or fat-free refried beans over the crust for an extra boost of flavor.

LOADED MEXICAN PIZZA

My husband is a picky eater, but this healthy pizza has lots of flavor, and he actually looks forward to eating it. Leftovers are no problem, because this meal tastes better the next day.
—*Mary Barker, Knoxville, TN*

- -

Takes: **30 min.** • Makes: **6 servings**

1   **can (15 oz.) black beans, rinsed and drained**
1   **medium red onion, chopped**
1   **small sweet yellow pepper, chopped**
3   **tsp. chili powder**
¾   **tsp. ground cumin**
3   **medium tomatoes, chopped**
1   **jalapeno pepper, seeded and finely chopped**
1   **garlic clove, minced**

SIDES, SALADS & BREADS

PRESSURE-COOKER GREEN BEANS

Free up room on your stovetop when you're cooking for company and make this easy green bean recipe in the all-in-one cooker. Mix and match with your favorite herbs and spices. It really does only take 1 minute to get perfectly crisp-tender green beans. The recipe easily cuts in half to serve four on busy weeknights.
—*Peggy Woodward, Shullsburg, WI*

- -

Takes: **15 min.** • Makes: **10 servings**

- 2 **lbs. fresh green beans, trimmed**
- ¼ **cup chopped fresh parsley**
- 3 **Tbsp. butter, melted**
- 2 **Tbsp. minced chives**
- 2 **Tbsp. lemon juice**
- 1 **tsp. salt**
- ¼ **tsp. pepper**
  Chopped toasted walnuts, optional

1. Place the steamer basket and 1 cup water in a 6-qt. electric pressure cooker. Set green beans in basket. Lock lid; close pressure-release valve. Adjust to pressure-cook on high for 1 minute. Quick-release pressure; drain.

2. Return beans to pressure cooker. Add parsley, butter, chives, lemon juice, salt and pepper; toss to coat. If desired, sprinkle with nuts.

¾ CUP: 60 cal., 4g fat (2g sat. fat), 9mg chol., 270mg sod., 7g carb. (2g sugars, 3g fiber), 2g pro. **DIABETIC EXCHANGES:** 1 vegetable, 1 fat.

NEVER-FAIL SCALLOPED POTATOES

Take the chill off any blustery day with something special to accompany meaty entrees. These creamy homemade scalloped potatoes do the trick nicely and are sure to be a favorite.
—*Agnes Ward, Stratford, ON*

Prep: **25 min.** • Bake: **1 hour**
Makes: **6 servings**

- 2 Tbsp. butter
- 3 Tbsp. all-purpose flour
- 1 tsp. salt
- ¼ tsp. pepper
- 1½ cups fat-free milk
- ½ cup shredded reduced-fat cheddar cheese
- 2 lbs. red potatoes, peeled and thinly sliced (about 4 cups)
- 1 cup thinly sliced onions, divided

1. Preheat oven to 350°. In a small saucepan, melt butter; stir in the flour, salt and pepper until smooth. Gradually whisk in milk. Bring to a boil, stirring constantly; cook and stir until thickened, about 2 minutes. Remove from heat; stir in cheese until melted.

2. Coat an 8-in. square baking dish with cooking spray. Place half of the potatoes in dish; layer with ½ cup onion and half of the cheese sauce. Repeat layers.

3. Bake, covered, 50 minutes. Uncover; bake until bubbly and the potatoes are tender, 10-15 minutes longer.

¾ CUP: 215 cal., 6g fat (4g sat. fat), 18mg chol., 523mg sod., 32g carb. (5g sugars, 3g fiber), 8g pro.
DIABETIC EXCHANGES: 2 starch, 1 fat.

THE SKINNY

To thicken scalloped potatoes, just keep cooking the sauce a minute or so longer than directed before adding the cheese. This will create a rich, extra-thick sauce. You can also use whole or 2% milk in place of the fat-free milk.

GRILLED VEGETABLE PLATTER

Here's the best of summer in one dish! These pretty marinated veggies are perfect for entertaining. Grilling brings out their natural sweetness.
—*Heidi Hall, North St. Paul, MN*

Prep: **20 min. + marinating**
Grill: **10 min.** • Makes: **6 servings**

- ¼ cup olive oil
- 2 Tbsp. honey
- 4 tsp. balsamic vinegar
- 1 tsp. dried oregano
- ½ tsp. garlic powder
- ⅛ tsp. pepper
  Dash salt
- 1 lb. fresh asparagus, trimmed
- 3 small carrots, cut in half lengthwise
- 1 large sweet red pepper, cut into 1-in. strips
- 1 medium yellow summer squash, cut into ½-in. slices
- 1 medium red onion, cut into wedges

1. In a small bowl, whisk the first 7 ingredients. Place 3 Tbsp. marinade in a large bowl. Add vegetables; turn to coat. Cover; marinate 1½ hours at room temperature.

2. Transfer vegetables to a grilling grid; place grid on grill rack. Grill vegetables, covered, over medium heat until crisp-tender, 8-12 minutes, turning occasionally.

3. Place the vegetables on a large serving plate. Drizzle with the remaining marinade.

NOTE: If you do not have a grilling grid, use a disposable foil pan. Poke holes in the bottom of the pan with a meat fork to allow liquid to drain.

1 SERVING: 144 cal., 9g fat (1g sat. fat), 0 chol., 50mg sod., 15g carb. (11g sugars, 3g fiber), 2g pro.
DIABETIC EXCHANGES: 2 vegetable, 2 fat.

THE SKINNY
Common olive oil works better for cooking at very high heat than virgin or extra-virgin oil. These higher grades have ideal flavor for colder foods.

GRILLED POTATOES & PEPPERS

My husband, Matt, grills this recipe for both breakfast and dinner gatherings. Besides our company, his potatoes are one of the best parts of the meal!
—*Susan Nordin, Warren, PA*

Prep: **20 min.** • Grill: **40 min.**
Makes: **10 servings**

- 8 medium red potatoes, cut into wedges
- 2 medium green peppers, sliced
- 1 medium onion, cut into thin wedges
- 2 Tbsp. olive oil
- 5 garlic cloves, thinly sliced
- 1 tsp. paprika
- 1 tsp. steak seasoning
- 1 tsp. Italian seasoning
- ¼ tsp. salt
- ¼ tsp. pepper

1. In a large bowl, combine all of the ingredients. Divide between 2 pieces of heavy-duty foil (about 18 in. square). Fold foil around potato mixture and crimp edges to seal.
2. Grill, covered, over medium heat until potatoes are tender, 40-45 minutes. Open foil carefully to allow steam to escape.
¾ CUP: 103 cal., 3g fat (0 sat. fat), 0 chol., 134mg sod., 18g carb. (2g sugars, 2g fiber), 2g pro. **DIABETIC EXCHANGES:** 1 starch, ½ fat.

DILL & CHIVE PEAS

Growing my own vegetables and herbs helps keep things fresh in the kitchen. This side is a breeze to prepare.
—*Tanna Richard, Cedar Rapids, IA*

Takes: **10 min.** • Makes: **4 servings**

- 1 pkg. (16 oz.) frozen peas
- ¼ cup snipped fresh dill
- 2 Tbsp. minced fresh chives
- 1 Tbsp. butter
- 1 tsp. lemon-pepper seasoning
- ¼ tsp. kosher salt

Cook peas according to package directions. Stir in remaining ingredients; serve immediately.
¾ CUP: 113 cal., 3g fat (2g sat. fat), 8mg chol., 346mg sod., 16g carb. (6g sugars, 5g fiber), 6g pro. **DIABETIC EXCHANGES:** 1 starch, ½ fat.

CRUNCHY BROCCOLI SALAD

I never liked broccoli when I was younger, but now I'm hooked on this salad's light, sweet taste. It gives broccoli a whole new look and taste, in my opinion.
—*Jessica Conrey, Cedar Rapids, IA*

Takes: **25 min.** • Makes: **10 servings**

- 8 cups fresh broccoli florets (about 1 lb.)
- 1 bunch green onions, thinly sliced
- ½ cup dried cranberries
- 3 Tbsp. canola oil
- 3 Tbsp. seasoned rice vinegar
- 2 Tbsp. sugar
- ¼ cup sunflower kernels
- 3 bacon strips, cooked and crumbled

In a large bowl, combine broccoli, green onions and cranberries. In a small bowl, whisk oil, vinegar and sugar until blended; drizzle over broccoli mixture and toss to coat. Refrigerate until serving. Sprinkle with sunflower kernels and bacon before serving.

¾ CUP: 121 cal., 7g fat (1g sat. fat), 2mg chol., 233mg sod., 14g carb. (10g sugars, 3g fiber), 3g pro.
DIABETIC EXCHANGES: 1 vegetable, 1 fat, ½ starch.

CRUNCHY CAULIFLOWER-BROCCOLI SALAD: Substitute 4 cups fresh cauliflowerets for 4 cups of the broccoli florets.

MAKE IT YOUR OWN
Experiment with the salad's ingredients for something new!
- Add pecan halves
- Stir in dried apricots
- Use sesame oil
- Consider turkey bacon

AIR-FRYER LATKES

Hot, crispy potato latkes is such a treat but who wants to deal with all the oil and grease? I tried making them in an air fryer and they came out just as good without all the clean up.
—*Nancy Salinas, Grand Rapids, MN*

Prep: **20 min.**
Cook: **15 min./batch**
Makes: **3 servings**

- 2 medium potatoes, peeled
- 1 large egg
- ⅓ cup chopped onion
- 1 Tbsp. all-purpose flour
- ½ tsp. salt
- ¼ tsp. pepper
- ¼ tsp. garlic powder
  Cooking spray

1. Finely grate potatoes; firmly squeeze and drain any liquid. Place potatoes in a large bowl. Add egg, onion, flour, salt, pepper and garlic powder; mix well.
2. Preheat air fryer to 375°. In batches, drop batter by ¼ cupfuls onto greased tray in air-fryer basket; press lightly to flatten. Spritz with cooking spray. Cook until golden brown, 12-17 minutes. Serve the latkes immediately.
2 LATKES: 134 cal., 3g fat (1g sat. fat), 62mg chol., 421mg sod., 24g carb. (2g sugars, 2g fiber), 4g pro.
DIABETIC EXCHANGES: 1½ starch.

FLAKY WHOLE WHEAT BISCUITS

Whole wheat flour gives these biscuits a nutty flavor. Ever since I started making these, white flour biscuits just don't taste as good! Pair them with soup or slather them with whipped cream and sweetened berries for a dessert treat.
—*Trisha Kruse, Eagle, ID*

Takes: **25 min.** • Makes: **10 biscuits**

- 1 cup all-purpose flour
- 1 cup whole wheat flour
- 3 tsp. baking powder
- 1 Tbsp. brown sugar
- 1 tsp. baking soda
- ½ tsp. salt
- ¼ cup cold butter
- 1 cup 2% milk

1. In a large bowl, combine the first 6 ingredients. Cut in butter until mixture resembles coarse crumbs. Stir in milk just until moistened. Turn onto a lightly floured surface; knead 8-10 times.
2. Pat or roll out to ½-in. thickness; cut with a floured 2½-in. biscuit cutter. Place 2 in. apart on an ungreased baking sheet.
3. Bake at 425° for 8-10 minutes or until golden brown.
1 BISCUIT: 144 cal., 6g fat (3g sat. fat), 14mg chol., 417mg sod., 21g carb. (3g sugars, 2g fiber), 4g pro.
DIABETIC EXCHANGES: 1½ starch, 1 fat.

TYPICAL	MAKEOVER
208 Calories	**144** Calories
11g Fat	**6g** Fat
23mg Cholesterol	**14mg** Cholesterol

THE SKINNY

This air-fryer latkes recipe calls for peeled potatoes, but leaving the peels on before grating will not have a negative impact on these crispy potato pancakes. The latkes will appear a little darker when fried and the color may be a bit uneven. But the peels have some extra nutrition.

SMOKY CAULIFLOWER

The smoked Spanish paprika gives a simple side of cauliflower more depth of flavor. We are fans of roasted veggies of any kind, and this one is a definite winner.
—*Juliette Mulholland, Corvallis, OR*

Takes: **30 min.** • Makes: **8 servings**

- 1 large head cauliflower, broken into 1-in. florets (about 9 cups)
- 2 Tbsp. olive oil
- 1 tsp. smoked paprika
- ¾ tsp. salt
- 2 garlic cloves, minced
- 2 Tbsp. minced fresh parsley

1. Place cauliflower in a large bowl. Combine the oil, paprika and salt. Drizzle over cauliflower; toss to coat. Transfer to a 15x10x1-in. baking pan. Bake, uncovered, at 450° for 10 minutes.

2. Stir in garlic. Bake 10-15 minutes longer or until the cauliflower is tender and lightly browned, stirring occasionally. Sprinkle with parsley.

¾ CUP: 58 cal., 4g fat (0 sat. fat), 0 chol., 254mg sod., 6g carb. (3g sugars, 3g fiber), 2g pro. **DIABETIC EXCHANGES:** 1 vegetable, ½ fat.

PUMPKIN PAN ROLLS

Serve these spicy-sweet pumpkin rolls for dinner—or any time of day—and get ready to hear a chorus of "yums" in your kitchen!
—*Linnea Rein, Topeka, KS*

Prep: **20 min. + rising** • Bake: **20 min.**
Makes: **20 rolls**

- ¾ cup 2% milk
- ⅓ cup packed brown sugar
- 5 Tbsp. butter, divided
- 1 tsp. salt
- 2 pkg. (¼ oz. each) active dry yeast
- ½ cup warm water (110° to 115°)
- 2 to 2½ cups all-purpose flour
- 1½ cups whole wheat flour
- ½ cup canned pumpkin
- ½ tsp. ground cinnamon
- ¼ tsp. ground ginger
- ¼ tsp. ground nutmeg

1. In a small saucepan, heat the milk, brown sugar, 4 Tbsp. butter and salt to 110°-115°; set aside.

2. In a large bowl, dissolve the yeast in warm water. Stir in milk mixture. Add 1½ cups all-purpose flour, whole wheat flour, pumpkin, cinnamon, ginger and nutmeg. Beat until smooth. Add enough of the remaining all-purpose flour to form a soft dough.

3. Turn onto a floured surface; knead until smooth and elastic, 6-8 minutes. Place in a greased bowl, turning once to grease top. Cover and let rise in a warm place until doubled, about 1 hour.

4. Punch the dough down. Divide into 20 pieces; shape into balls. Place in a greased 13x9-in. baking pan. Cover and let rise for 30 minutes or until doubled.

5. Preheat oven to 375°. Melt the remaining butter; brush over dough. Bake 20-25 minutes or until golden brown. Remove from pan to a wire rack. Serve warm.

1 ROLL: 124 cal., 3g fat (2g sat. fat), 9mg chol., 154mg sod., 21g carb. (5g sugars, 2g fiber), 3g pro. **DIABETIC EXCHANGES:** 1½ starch, ½ fat.

1. Preheat oven to 400°. Place the asparagus, tomatoes and pine nuts on a foil-lined 15x10x1-in. baking pan. Mix 2 Tbsp. oil, garlic, salt and pepper; add to asparagus and toss to coat.

2. Bake 15-20 minutes or just until asparagus is tender. Drizzle with remaining oil and the lemon juice; sprinkle with cheese and lemon zest. Toss to combine.

1 SERVING: 95 cal., 8g fat (2g sat. fat), 3mg chol., 294mg sod., 4g carb. (2g sugars, 1g fiber), 3g pro. **DIABETIC EXCHANGES:** 1½ fat, 1 vegetable.

THE SKINNY

For the ultimate flavor, use fresh produce when it's in season. In spring, that means asparagus, peas, artichokes and fennel. In summer, eggplant, arugula, summer squash and tomatoes shine. Fall's finest? Butternut squash, Brussels sprouts and carrots, to name a few.

TUSCAN-STYLE ROASTED ASPARAGUS

This is especially wonderful when locally grown asparagus is in season and so easy for celebrations because you can serve it hot or cold.
—*Jannine Fisk, Malden, MA*

Prep: **20 min.** • Bake: **15 min.**
Makes: **8 servings**

1½ lbs. fresh asparagus, trimmed
1½ cups grape tomatoes, halved
3 Tbsp. pine nuts
3 Tbsp. olive oil, divided
2 garlic cloves, minced
1 tsp. kosher salt
½ tsp. pepper
1 Tbsp. lemon juice
⅓ cup grated Parmesan cheese
1 tsp. grated lemon zest

PRESSURE-COOKER CHICKPEA TAGINE

While traveling through Morocco, my wife and I fell in love with the complex flavors of the many tagines we tried, so we came up with this no-fuss dish. It's fantastic alongside grilled fish, or add shredded cooked chicken in the last 10 minutes for a change-of-pace entree.
—*Raymond Wyatt, West St. Paul, MN*

Prep: **30 min.** • Cook: **5 min.**
Makes: **12 servings**

- 2 **Tbsp. olive oil**
- 2 **garlic cloves, minced**
- 2 **tsp. paprika**
- 1 **tsp. ground ginger**
- 1 **tsp. ground cumin**
- ½ **tsp. salt**
- ¼ **tsp. pepper**
- ¼ **tsp. ground cinnamon**
- 1 **small butternut squash (about 2 lbs.), peeled and cut into ½-in. cubes**
- 2 **medium zucchini, cut into ½-in. pieces**
- 1 **can (15 oz.) chickpeas or garbanzo beans, rinsed and drained**
- 1 **medium sweet red pepper, coarsely chopped**
- 1 **medium onion, coarsely chopped**
- 12 **dried apricots, halved**
- ½ **cup water**
- 2 **to 3 tsp. harissa chili paste**
- 2 **tsp. honey**
- 1 **can (14.5 oz.) crushed tomatoes, undrained**
- ¼ **cup chopped fresh mint leaves Plain Greek yogurt, optional**

1. Select saute setting on a 6-qt. electric pressure cooker. Adjust for medium heat; add oil. When oil is hot, add garlic, paprika, ginger, cumin, salt, pepper and cinnamon; cook and stir until fragrant, about 1 minute. Press cancel.

2. Add the squash, zucchini, chickpeas, red pepper, onion, apricots, water, harissa and honey. Lock lid; close pressure-release valve. Adjust to pressure-cook on high for 3 minutes. Quick-release pressure. Press cancel. Gently stir in tomatoes and mint; heat through.

3. If desired, top with yogurt and additional mint, olive oil and honey.

¾ CUP: 127 cal., 3g fat (0 sat. fat), 0 chol., 224mg sod., 23g carb. (9g sugars, 6g fiber), 4g pro. **DIABETIC EXCHANGES:** 1½ starch, ½ fat.

PRESSURE-COOKER SMOKY WHITE BEANS & HAM

I had never made or even eaten this dish before meeting my husband. Now I make it at least once a week. I serve it with homemade cornbread.
—*Christine Duffy, Sturgis, KY*

Prep: **15 min.**
Cook: **30 min. + releasing**
Makes: **10 servings**

- 1 **lb. dried great northern beans**
- 3 **smoked ham hocks (about 1½ lbs.)**
- 3 **cans (14½ oz. each) reduced-sodium chicken or beef broth**
- 2 **cups water**
- 1 **large onion, chopped**
- 1 **Tbsp. onion powder**
- 1 **Tbsp. garlic powder**
- 2 **tsp. pepper**
  Thinly sliced green onions, optional

1. Rinse and sort beans. Transfer to a 6-qt. electric pressure cooker. Add ham hocks. Stir in broth, water, onion and seasonings. Lock lid; close pressure-release valve. Adjust to pressure-cook on high for 30 minutes. Let pressure release naturally for 10 minutes; quick-release any remaining pressure.
2. When cool enough to handle, remove meat from bones; cut ham into small pieces and return to pressure cooker. Serve with a slotted spoon. Sprinkle with green onions if desired.
⅔ CUP: 196 cal., 2g fat (0 sat. fat), 8mg chol., 594mg sod., 32g carb. (2g sugars, 10g fiber), 15g pro. **DIABETIC EXCHANGES:** 2 starch, 2 lean meat.

FLAVORFUL MASHED POTATOES

Earthy herbs bring a full chorus of flavor to creamy red potatoes, making this side dish anything but ordinary. Save it for special occasions or simply serve as a dressy accompaniment to a weeknight meal.
—*Mary Relyea, Canastota, NY*

Prep: **20 min.** • Cook: **15 min.**
Makes: **12 servings**

- 4 **lbs. red potatoes (about 12 medium), quartered**
- 6 **garlic cloves, peeled and thinly sliced**
- 1 **cup fat-free milk**
- ½ **cup reduced-fat sour cream**
- 2 **Tbsp. butter, melted**
- 2 **Tbsp. minced fresh parsley**
- 1 **to 2 Tbsp. minced fresh thyme**
- 2 **to 3 tsp. minced fresh rosemary**
- 1¼ **tsp. salt**

1. Place potatoes and garlic in a Dutch oven; add water to cover. Bring to a boil. Reduce heat; cook, uncovered, 15-20 minutes or until potatoes are tender.
2. Drain; return to pan. Mash potatoes, gradually adding remaining ingredients.
¾ CUP: 146 cal., 3g fat (2g sat. fat), 7mg chol., 286mg sod., 26g carb. (3g sugars, 3g fiber), 4g pro. **DIABETIC EXCHANGES:** 2 starch, ½ fat.

	TYPICAL	MAKEOVER
Calories	341	146
Fat	24g	3g
Saturated Fat	15g	2g
Cholesterol	76mg	7mg

TARRAGON ASPARAGUS

I grow purple asparagus, so I'm always looking for new ways to prepare it. Recently, my husband and I discovered how wonderful any color of asparagus tastes when it is grilled.
—*Sue Gronholz, Beaver Dam, WI*

Takes: **15 min.** • Makes: **8 servings**

- 2 **lbs. fresh asparagus, trimmed**
- 2 **Tbsp. olive oil**
- 1 **tsp. salt**
- ½ **tsp. pepper**
- ¼ **cup honey**
- 2 **to 4 Tbsp. minced fresh tarragon**

QUINOA WITH PEAS & ONION

Even picky eaters will love this protein-packed dish. If you have freshly shelled peas on hand, substitute them for the frozen.
—*Lori Panarella, Phoenixville, PA*

Prep: **30 min.** • Cook: **10 min.** Makes: **6 servings**

- 2 **cups water**
- 1 **cup quinoa, rinsed**
- 1 **small onion, chopped**
- 1 **Tbsp. olive oil**
- 1½ **cups frozen peas**
- ½ **tsp. salt**
- ¼ **tsp. pepper**
- 2 **Tbsp. chopped walnuts**

1. In a large saucepan, bring water to a boil. Add quinoa. Reduce heat; cover and simmer until water is absorbed, 12-15 minutes. Remove from the heat; fluff with a fork.

2. Meanwhile, in a large cast-iron or other heavy skillet, saute onion in oil until tender, 2-3 minutes. Add peas; cook and stir until heated through. Stir in the cooked quinoa, salt and pepper. Sprinkle with walnuts.
⅔ CUP: 174 cal., 6g fat (1g sat. fat), 0 chol., 244mg sod., 26g carb. (2g sugars, 4g fiber), 6g pro. **DIABETIC EXCHANGES:** 1½ starch, 1 fat.
HOT AND ZESTY QUINOA: Omit the peas, salt, pepper and walnuts. Prepare quinoa as directed. Saute the onion in oil until tender. Add 3 minced garlic cloves; cook for 1 minute. Add 2 cans (10 oz. each) tomatoes and green chiles. Bring to a boil over medium heat. Reduce heat; simmer, uncovered, 10 minutes. Stir in the quinoa and ¼ cup chopped marinated quartered artichoke hearts; heat through. Sprinkle with 2 Tbsp. grated Parmesan.

On a large plate, toss asparagus with oil, salt and pepper. Grill, covered, over medium heat 6-8 minutes or until crisp-tender, turning occasionally and basting frequently with honey during last 3 minutes. Sprinkle with tarragon.
1 SERVING: 76 cal., 4g fat (1g sat. fat), 0 chol., 302mg sod., 11g carb. (10g sugars, 1g fiber), 2g pro. **DIABETIC EXCHANGES:** 1 vegetable, ½ starch, ½ fat.

MAKEOVER FLUFFY LIME SALAD

Loaded with crunchy walnuts, tangy pineapple and lip-smacking lime flavor, this delicious salad could even double as dessert!
—Taste of Home *Test Kitchen*

Prep: **15 min. + chilling**
Makes: **8 servings**

- 1 can (8 oz.) unsweetened crushed pineapple, undrained
- 1 pkg. (.3 oz.) sugar-free lime gelatin
- 3 Tbsp. water
- 6 oz. reduced-fat cream cheese
- 1 cup miniature marshmallows
- ½ cup chopped walnuts
- 1 carton (8 oz.) frozen reduced-fat whipped topping, thawed

1. Drain pineapple, reserving juice; set pineapple aside. In a small saucepan, combine the gelatin, water and reserved juice. Cook and stir over low heat until gelatin is dissolved. Refrigerate until syrupy, about 30 minutes.
2. In a small bowl, beat cream cheese until fluffy. Stir in gelatin mixture, marshmallows, walnuts and pineapple. Fold in whipped topping.
3. Transfer mixture to a serving bowl. Cover and refrigerate for 2 hours or until set.
¾ CUP: 206 cal., 12g fat (7g sat. fat), 15mg chol., 125mg sod., 21g carb. (11g sugars, 1g fiber), 4g pro.

MACARONI COLESLAW

My friend Peggy brought this coleslaw to one of our picnics, and everyone liked it so much, we all had to have the recipe.
—Sandra Matteson, Westhope, ND

Prep: **25 min. + chilling**
Makes: **16 servings**

- 1 pkg. (7 oz.) ring macaroni or ditalini
- 1 pkg. (14 oz.) coleslaw mix
- 2 medium onions, finely chopped
- 2 celery ribs, finely chopped
- 1 medium cucumber, finely chopped
- 1 medium green pepper, finely chopped
- 1 can (8 oz.) whole water chestnuts, drained and chopped

DRESSING
- 1½ cups Miracle Whip Light
- ⅓ cup sugar
- ¼ cup cider vinegar
- ½ tsp. salt
- ¼ tsp. pepper

1. Cook macaroni according to package directions; drain and rinse in cold water. Transfer to a large bowl; add coleslaw mix, onions, celery, cucumber, green pepper and water chestnuts.
2. In a small bowl, whisk the dressing ingredients. Pour over salad; toss to coat. Cover and refrigerate for at least 1 hour.
¾ CUP: 150 cal., 5g fat (1g sat. fat), 6mg chol., 286mg sod., 24g carb. (12g sugars, 2g fiber), 3g pro.
DIABETIC EXCHANGES: 1 starch, 1 vegetable, 1 fat.:

THE SKINNY

The term "coleslaw" is derived from the Dutch word "koolsla," translated as cabbage salad. The term has evolved to refer to crunchy, shredded vegetable salads that hold up well after being dressed.

CUMIN-ROASTED CARROTS

Carrots make a super side—big on flavor and a breeze to cook. Plus, I can actually get my husband to eat these spiced veggies.
—Taylor Kiser, Brandon, FL

Prep: **20 min.** • Cook: **35 min.**
Makes: **12 servings**

- 2 Tbsp. coriander seeds
- 2 Tbsp. cumin seeds
- 3 lbs. carrots, peeled and cut into 4x½-in. sticks
- 3 Tbsp. coconut oil or butter, melted
- 8 garlic cloves, minced
- 1 tsp. salt
- ½ tsp. pepper
  Minced fresh cilantro, optional

1. Preheat oven to 400°. In a dry small skillet, toast coriander and cumin seeds over medium heat 45-60 seconds or until aromatic, stirring frequently. Cool slightly.

Grind seeds in a spice grinder, or with a mortar and pestle, until finely crushed.

2. Place carrots in a large bowl. Add the melted coconut oil, garlic, salt, pepper and crushed spices, and toss to coat. Divide carrots between two 15x10x1-in. baking pans coated with cooking spray, spreading evenly.

3. Roast 35-40 minutes or until crisp-tender and lightly browned, stirring and rotating pans halfway. Before serving, sprinkle with the cilantro if desired.

1 SERVING: 86 cal., 4g fat (3g sat. fat), 0 chol., 277mg sod., 13g carb. (5g sugars, 4g fiber), 1g pro.
DIABETIC EXCHANGES: 1 vegetable, 1 fat.

THE SKINNY
Two tablespoons each of ground coriander and ground cumin may be used in place of whole spices. Before using, toast ground spices in a dry skillet until aromatic, stirring frequently.

KIWI-STRAWBERRY SPINACH SALAD

This pretty salad is always a hit when I serve it! The recipe came from a cookbook, but I personalized it. Sometimes just a small change in ingredients can make a really big difference.
—*Laura Pounds, Andover, KS*

Takes: **20 min.** • Makes: **12 servings**

- ¼ cup canola oil
- ¼ cup raspberry vinegar
- ¼ tsp. Worcestershire sauce
- ⅓ cup sugar
- ¼ tsp. paprika
- 2 green onions, chopped
- 2 Tbsp. sesame seeds, toasted
- 1 Tbsp. poppy seeds
- 12 cups torn fresh spinach (about 9 oz.)
- 2 pints fresh strawberries, halved
- 4 kiwifruit, peeled and sliced

1. Place the first 5 ingredients in a blender; cover and process for 30 seconds or until blended. Transfer to a bowl; stir in the green onions, sesame seeds and poppy seeds.
2. In a large bowl, combine spinach, strawberries and kiwi. Drizzle with dressing; toss to coat.
1 CUP: 113 cal., 6g fat (1g sat. fat), 0 chol., 76mg sod., 15g carb. (10g sugars, 3g fiber), 2g pro. **DIABETIC EXCHANGES:** 1 vegetable, 1 fat, ½ starch, ½ fruit.

5-STAR SWEETS

EASTER MERINGUE CUPS

These sweet and crunchy meringue shells with a tart lemon curd filling will make guests stop to ooh and aah at your dessert table. Topped with fresh fruit, they're especially pretty when served with a spring meal.
—Taste of Home *Test Kitchen*

Prep: **25 min. + standing**
Bake: **45 min. + cooling**
Makes: **8 servings**

- 3 large egg whites
- ½ tsp. vanilla extract
- ¼ tsp. cream of tartar
- ¾ cup sugar
- ½ cup lemon curd
- 1 cup sliced fresh strawberries
- 2 medium kiwifruit, peeled and sliced
- ½ cup fresh raspberries
- ⅓ cup mandarin oranges
- ⅓ cup cubed fresh pineapple

1. Preheat oven to 275°. Place egg whites in a large bowl; let stand at room temperature for 30 minutes. Beat the egg whites, vanilla and cream of tartar on medium speed until soft peaks form. Gradually beat in the sugar, 1 Tbsp. at a time, on high until stiff peaks form.

2. Drop meringue into 8 mounds on a parchment-lined baking sheet. Shape into 3-in. cups with the back of a spoon.

3. Bake until set and dry, 45-50 minutes. Turn off oven and do not open door; leave meringues in oven for 1 hour. Spread cups with lemon curd and fill with fruit.

1 MERINGUE CUP: 180 cal., 1g fat (1g sat. fat), 15mg chol., 38mg sod., 40g carb. (37g sugars, 2g fiber), 2g pro.

TASTE OF HOME TALK

"I've always been afraid to try meringue recipes and now I know how easy it is. I will use this recipe again and again! Everyone loved it and I looked like a gourmet chef!"

SHARYNU, TASTEOFHOME.COM

CHOCOLATE SWIRLED CHEESECAKE

This cake tastes indulgent, but it's a light version you'll feel good serving.
—*Kathy Shan, Toledo, OH*

Prep: **30 min. + chilling**
Bake: **40 min. + cooling**
Makes: **12 servings**

- 2 cups 2% cottage cheese
- 1 cup crushed chocolate wafers (about 16 wafers)
- 1 pkg. (8 oz.) reduced-fat cream cheese, cubed
- ½ cup sugar
  Dash salt
- 1 Tbsp. vanilla extract
- 2 large eggs, room temperature, lightly beaten
- 1 large egg white, room temperature
- 2 oz. bittersweet chocolate, melted and cooled
  Fresh raspberries, optional

1. Line a strainer with 4 layers of cheesecloth or 1 coffee filter; place over a bowl. Place cottage cheese in the strainer; refrigerate, covered, 1 hour. Place a 9-in. springform pan on a double thickness of heavy-duty foil (about 18 in. square); wrap foil securely around pan. Coat inside of pan with cooking spray. Press crushed wafers onto bottom and 1 in. up sides; set aside.
2. Preheat oven to 350°. In a food processor, process drained cottage cheese until smooth. Add cream cheese, sugar and salt; process until blended. Transfer to a bowl; stir in vanilla, eggs and egg white. Remove 1 cup batter to a small bowl; stir in melted chocolate.

3. Pour plain batter into prepared crust. Drop chocolate batter by spoonfuls over plain batter. Cut through batter with a knife to swirl. Place springform pan in a larger baking pan; add 1 in. of boiling water to larger pan.
4. Bake until center is just set and top appears dull, about 40 minutes. Turn off oven; open door slightly. Let cheesecake cool in the oven for 30 minutes.

5. Remove springform pan from water bath; remove foil. Loosen sides with a knife; cool on a wire rack 30 minutes. Refrigerate overnight, covering when completely cooled.
6. Remove rim from pan. If desired, top with raspberries.
1 PIECE: 187 cal., 8g fat (5g sat. fat), 46mg chol., 378mg sod., 17g carb. (14g sugars, 1g fiber), 8g pro.
DIABETIC EXCHANGES: 1½ starch, 1 lean meat, ½ fat.

OATMEAL CAKE WITH CARAMEL ICING

This tastes anything but light. The icing sets up quick, so frost the cake immediately after it cools.
—*Summer Marks, Louisville, KY*

Prep: **30 min.**
Bake: **20 min. + cooling**
Makes: **20 servings**

- 1¼ **cups boiling water**
- 1 **cup quick-cooking oats**
- ¼ **cup butter, softened**
- 1 **cup packed brown sugar**
- ½ **cup sugar**
- 2 **large eggs, room temperature**
- ¼ **cup unsweetened applesauce**
- 1 **tsp. vanilla extract**
- 1½ **cups all-purpose flour**
- 2 **tsp. baking powder**
- ¾ **tsp. ground cinnamon**
- ½ **tsp. baking soda**
- ½ **tsp. salt**
- ¼ **tsp. ground nutmeg**

ICING
- ½ **cup packed brown sugar**
- ¼ **cup butter, cubed**
- ¼ **cup fat-free milk**
- ½ **tsp. vanilla extract**
- ⅛ **tsp. salt**
- 1½ **cups confectioners' sugar**

1. In a small bowl, pour boiling water over oats; let stand 10 minutes.
2. Meanwhile, preheat oven to 350°. In a large bowl, beat butter and sugars until crumbly, about 2 minutes. Add eggs, 1 at a time, beating well after each addition. Beat in applesauce and vanilla. Combine flour, baking powder, cinnamon, baking soda, salt and nutmeg. Gradually add to the creamed mixture. Stir in the oats.

Pour batter into a greased 13x9-in. baking pan.
3. Bake until a toothpick inserted in center comes out with moist crumbs, 18-22 minutes. Cool completely on a wire rack.
4. For icing, in a small saucepan, combine brown sugar and butter. Bring to a boil over medium heat, stirring constantly. Cook and stir 1 minute. Gradually whisk in milk. Return to a boil. Cook and stir for 1 minute. Transfer to a small bowl. Stir in vanilla and salt. Gradually beat in confectioners' sugar until smooth. Immediately spread icing over cake. Let stand until set.

1 PIECE: 218 cal., 5g fat (3g sat. fat), 31mg chol., 203mg sod., 41g carb. (30g sugars, 1g fiber), 2g pro.

PRESSURE-COOKER LAVA CAKE

Because I love chocolate, this decadent cake has long been a family favorite. It's even tasty cold the next day—assuming you have any leftovers!
—*Elizabeth Farrell, Hamilton, MT*

Prep: **15 min.**
Cook: **20 min. + standing**
Makes: **8 servings**

- 1 cup all-purpose flour
- 1 cup packed brown sugar, divided
- 5 Tbsp. baking cocoa, divided
- 2 tsp. baking powder
- ¼ tsp. salt
- ½ cup fat-free milk
- 2 Tbsp. canola oil
- ½ tsp. vanilla extract
- ⅛ tsp. ground cinnamon
- 1¼ cups hot water
  Optional: Fresh raspberries and ice cream

1. In a large bowl, whisk flour, ½ cup brown sugar, 3 Tbsp. cocoa, baking powder and salt. In another bowl, whisk milk, oil and vanilla until blended. Add to flour mixture; stir just until moistened.
2. Spread into a 1½-qt. baking dish coated with cooking spray. In a small bowl, mix cinnamon and remaining ½ cup brown sugar and 2 Tbsp. cocoa; stir in hot water. Pour over batter (do not stir).
3. Place trivet insert and 1 cup water in a 6-qt. electric pressure cooker. Cover baking dish with foil. Fold an 18x12-in. piece of foil lengthwise into thirds, making a sling. Use the sling to lower the dish onto the trivet. Lock lid; close pressure-release valve. Adjust to pressure-cook on high for 20 minutes. Quick-release pressure.
4. Using foil sling, carefully remove baking dish. Let stand 15 minutes. A toothpick inserted in cake portion should come out clean. If desired, serve with fresh raspberries and ice cream.
1 SERVING: 208 cal., 4g fat (0 sat. fat), 0 chol., 208mg sod., 42g carb. (28g sugars, 1g fiber), 3g pro.

BLUEBERRY & PEACH COBBLER

For a tasty finale to any meal, try this classic cobbler. Your family will be delighted by the sweet flavor.
—*Laura Jansen, Battle Creek, MI*

Prep: **15 min.** • Bake: **45 min.**
Makes: **6 servings**

- 2 Tbsp. sugar
- 2 Tbsp. brown sugar
- 1 Tbsp. cornstarch
- ½ cup water
- 1 Tbsp. lemon juice
- 2 cups sliced peeled fresh peaches
- 1 cup blueberries

TOPPING

- 1 cup all-purpose flour
- ¼ cup sugar
- 1½ tsp. baking powder
- ½ tsp. salt
- ½ cup 2% milk
- ¼ cup butter, softened

1. Preheat oven to 375°. In a saucepan, combine the first 5 ingredients. Bring to a boil. Cook, stirring constantly, until thickened, 1-2 minutes; stir in fruit. Pour into a 2-qt. baking dish.
2. For topping, in a small bowl, combine flour, sugar, baking powder and salt. Stir in milk and butter. Spread over the fruit mixture. Bake until topping is golden brown and filling is bubbly, 45-50 minutes. Serve warm.
1 SERVING: 260 cal., 9g fat (5g sat. fat), 22mg chol., 389mg sod., 44g carb. (25g sugars, 2g fiber), 4g pro.

TASTE OF HOME TALK

"I have made this several times—my family loves it. I used diet orange pop and it was just like an orange creamsicle. You can basically use whatever pop you like."

PENSGRL87, TASTEOFHOME.COM

ROOT BEER FLOAT PIE

This is the kind of recipe your kids will look back on and always remember. And you don't even need to use an oven.
—Cindy Reams, Philipsburg, PA

Prep: **15 min. + chilling**
Makes: **8 servings**

1 **carton (8 oz.) frozen reduced-fat whipped topping, thawed, divided**
¾ **cup cold diet root beer**
½ **cup fat-free milk**
1 **pkg. (1 oz.) sugar-free instant vanilla pudding mix**
1 **graham cracker crust (9 in.)**
  Maraschino cherries, optional

1. Set aside and refrigerate ½ cup whipped topping for garnish. In a large bowl, whisk the root beer, milk and pudding mix for 2 minutes. Fold in half the remaining whipped topping. Spread into the graham cracker crust.
2. Spread the remaining whipped topping over pie. Freeze for at least 8 hours or overnight.
3. Dollop reserved whipped topping over each serving; top with a maraschino cherry if desired.
1 PIECE: 185 cal., 8g fat (4g sat. fat), 0 chol., 275mg sod., 27g carb. (14g sugars, 0 fiber), 1g pro. **DIABETIC EXCHANGES:** 2 starch, 1 fat.

PINEAPPLE PUDDING CAKE

My mother used to love making this easy dessert in the summertime. It's so cool and refreshing that it never lasts very long!
—Kathleen Worden,
North Andover, MA

Prep: **25 min.**
Bake: **15 min. + chilling**
Makes: **20 servings**

1 **pkg. (9 oz.) yellow cake mix**
1½ **cups cold fat-free milk**
1 **pkg. (1 oz.) sugar-free instant vanilla pudding mix**
1 **pkg. (8 oz.) reduced-fat cream cheese**
1 **can (20 oz.) unsweetened crushed pineapple, well drained**
1 **carton (8 oz.) frozen reduced-fat whipped topping, thawed**
¼ **cup chopped walnuts, toasted**
20 **maraschino cherries, well drained**

1. Preheat oven to 350°. Prepare cake mix batter according to the package directions; pour into a greased 13x9-in. baking pan. Bake until a toothpick inserted near the center comes out clean, 15-20 minutes. Cool completely on a wire rack.
2. Whisk milk and pudding mix for 2 minutes. Let stand 2 minutes or until soft-set.
3. In a second bowl, beat cream cheese until smooth. Beat in the pudding mixture until blended. Spread evenly over cake. Sprinkle with pineapple; spread with whipped topping. Sprinkle with walnuts and garnish with cherries. Refrigerate until serving.
1 PIECE: 152 cal., 5g fat (3g sat. fat), 18mg chol., 173mg sod., 22g carb. (15g sugars, 1g fiber), 3g pro.
DIABETIC EXCHANGES: 1½ starch, ½ fat.

½ tsp. orange extract
¼ tsp. salt
1½ cups salted cashews, coarsely chopped

ICING
¾ cup confectioners' sugar
4 tsp. orange juice
1 tsp. grated orange zest

1. Preheat oven to 350°. In a large bowl, beat cream cheese and sugars until smooth. Beat in egg yolk and vanilla. Gradually beat in flour.

2. Press dough onto bottom and ¼ in. up sides of a 13x9-in. baking pan coated with cooking spray. Bake until the edges are light brown, 15-20 minutes. Cool 10 minutes on a wire rack.

3. For filling, in a large bowl, beat brown sugar, egg whites, egg, flour, extracts and salt until smooth. Stir in cashews. Pour into crust. Bake 15-20 minutes longer or until set.

4. Cool completely in pan on a wire rack. In a small bowl, mix icing ingredients; drizzle over top. Cut into bars.

1 BAR: 145 cal., 5g fat (1g sat. fat), 17mg chol., 98mg sod., 21g carb. (14g sugars, 0 fiber), 3g pro.

ORANGE CASHEW BARS

Two of my favorite ingredients, oranges and cashews, make a fantastic combination for a sweet-tart bar—especially when you use fresh-squeezed orange juice in the glaze.
—*Anna Wood, Cullowhee, NC*

Prep: **25 min.**
Bake: **15 min. + cooling**
Makes: **2½ dozen**

4 oz. reduced-fat cream cheese
½ cup confectioners' sugar
¼ cup packed brown sugar
1 large egg yolk
2 tsp. vanilla extract
1½ cups all-purpose flour
FILLING
1 cup packed brown sugar
3 large egg whites
1 large egg
3 Tbsp. all-purpose flour
2 tsp. vanilla extract

PUMPKIN CARAMEL CUPCAKES

Kids love to eat these cupcakes, and they can help bake them, too. To make things even easier, we dunk them in premade caramel apple dip instead of using frosting.
—*Donna Schaab, Belleville, IL*

Prep: **25 min.**
Bake: **20 min. + cooling**
Makes: **2 dozen**

1	pkg. yellow cake mix (regular size)
1	can (15 oz.) pumpkin
⅔	cup water
¼	cup maple syrup
3	large eggs, room temperature
4	tsp. sugar
4	tsp. ground cinnamon Dash salt
1	carton (16 oz.) caramel apple dip
	Optional: Chocolate frosting and decorating icing

1. Preheat oven to 350°. Line 24 muffin cups with paper liners. Combine the first 8 ingredients. Beat on low speed 30 seconds; beat on medium 2 minutes.
2. Fill prepared cups three-fourths full. Bake until a toothpick inserted in the center comes out clean, 18-22 minutes. Cool in pans for 10 minutes before removing to wire racks to cool completely.
3. Frost cupcakes with caramel apple dip. Decorate, if desired, with frosting and decorating icing. Refrigerate leftovers.
1 CUPCAKE: 178 cal., 5g fat (2g sat. fat), 26mg chol., 242mg sod., 31g carb. (22g sugars, 1g fiber), 2g pro.

TYPICAL	MAKEOVER
391 Calories	**178** Calories
22mg Fat	**5mg** Fat
10mg Saturated Fat	**2mg** Saturated Fat
70mg Cholesterol	**26mg** Cholesterol

THE SKINNY

Make portioning the batter easier by grabbing an ice cream scoop or measuring cup. Mashed cooked sweet potatoes can be used in place of the pumpkin.

GINGER PLUM TART

Sweet cravings, begone: This free-form plum tart is done in only 35 minutes. Plus, it's even more awesome served warm.
—Taste of Home *Test Kitchen*

Prep: **15 min.**
Bake: **20 min. + cooling**
Makes: **8 servings**

- 1 sheet refrigerated pie crust
- 3½ cups sliced fresh plums (about 10 medium)
- 3 Tbsp. plus 1 tsp. coarse sugar, divided
- 1 Tbsp. cornstarch
- 2 tsp. finely chopped crystallized ginger
- 1 large egg white
- 1 Tbsp. water

1. Preheat oven to 400°. On a work surface, unroll crust. Roll to a 12-in. circle. Transfer to a parchment-lined baking sheet.
2. In a large bowl, toss plums with 3 Tbsp. sugar and cornstarch. Arrange plums on crust to within 2 in. of edges; sprinkle with ginger. Fold crust edge over plums, pleating as you go.
3. In a small bowl, whisk egg white and water; brush over folded crust. Sprinkle with remaining 1 tsp. sugar.
4. Bake until crust is golden brown, 20-25 minutes. Cool in pan on a wire rack. Serve tart warm or at room temperature.
1 PIECE: 190 cal., 7g fat (3g sat. fat), 5mg chol., 108mg sod., 30g carb. (14g sugars, 1g fiber), 2g pro.
DIABETIC EXCHANGES: 1½ starch, 1 fat, ½ fruit.

DEVIL'S FOOD SNACK CAKE

My husband and his friends request this devil's food cake for camping trips because it's easy to transport. That makes it ideal for taking to potlucks and other events, too, as no frosting is involved. You can add frosting if you wish, of course, but it's fine without it!
—*Julie Danler, Bel Aire, KS*

Prep: **30 min.**
Bake: **35 min. + cooling**
Makes: **24 servings**

- 1 cup quick-cooking oats
- 1¾ cups boiling water
- ¼ cup butter, softened
- ½ cup sugar
- ½ cup packed brown sugar
- 2 large eggs, room temperature
- ⅓ cup buttermilk
- 3 Tbsp. canola oil
- 1 tsp. vanilla extract
- ¾ cup all-purpose flour
- ¾ cup whole wheat flour
- 2 Tbsp. dark baking cocoa
- 1 Tbsp. instant coffee granules
- 1 tsp. baking soda
- ⅛ tsp. salt
- 1 cup miniature semisweet chocolate chips, divided
- ¾ cup chopped pecans, divided

1. Preheat oven to 350°. Place oats in a large bowl. Cover with boiling water; let stand for 10 minutes.
2. Meanwhile, in a second large bowl, beat butter and sugars until crumbly, about 2 minutes. Add eggs, 1 at a time, beating well after each addition. Beat in buttermilk, oil and vanilla. Combine flours, cocoa, coffee granules, baking soda and salt. Gradually add dry mixture to the creamed mixture. Stir in the oat mixture, ½ cup chocolate chips and ⅓ cup pecans.
3. Pour batter into a greased 13x9-in. baking pan. Sprinkle with the remaining chips and pecans. Bake until a toothpick inserted in the center comes out clean, 35-40 minutes. Cool on a wire rack before cutting.
1 PIECE: 174 cal., 9g fat (3g sat. fat), 23mg chol., 91mg sod., 22g carb. (13g sugars, 2g fiber), 3g pro.
DIABETIC EXCHANGES: 2 fat, 1½ starch.

APPLE OATMEAL COOKIES

I took these cookies to work and they were gone in seconds. They're a welcome snack that's low in calories!
—*Nicki Woods, Springfield, MO*

Prep: **10 min.** • Bake: **15 min./batch**
Makes: **about 5 dozen**

- 1 pkg. yellow cake mix (regular size)
- 1½ cups quick-cooking oats
- ½ cup packed brown sugar
- 2 tsp. ground cinnamon
- 1 large egg, room temperature
- ¾ cup unsweetened applesauce
- 1 cup finely chopped peeled apple
- ½ cup raisins

1. Preheat oven to 350°. In a large bowl, combine cake mix, oats, brown sugar and cinnamon. In a small bowl, combine the egg, applesauce, apple and raisins. Stir into the oat mixture; mix well.

2. Drop by heaping teaspoonfuls 2 in. apart onto baking sheets coated with cooking spray. Bake until golden brown, 12-14 minutes. Let stand for 2 minutes before removing to wire racks to cool.

1 COOKIE: 57 cal., 1g fat (0 sat. fat), 0 chol., 55mg sod., 12g carb. (7g sugars, 1g fiber), 1g pro. **DIABETIC EXCHANGES:** 1 starch.

CHOCOLATE-DIPPED PHYLLO STICKS

Looking for something light and special to bake up for a holiday or special occasion? Try these crunchy treats. They're delicious with coffee or alongside sorbet and sherbet.
—*Peggy Woodward, Shullsburg, WI*

Prep: **30 min.** • Bake: **5 min./batch**
Makes: **20 sticks**

- 4 sheets phyllo dough (14x9-in. size)
- 2 Tbsp. butter, melted
- 1 Tbsp. sugar
- ¼ tsp. ground cinnamon Cooking spray
- 2 oz. semisweet chocolate, finely chopped
- ½ tsp. shortening
- ½ oz. white baking chocolate, melted

1. Preheat oven to 425°. Place 1 sheet of phyllo dough on a work surface; brush with butter. Cover with a second sheet of phyllo; brush with butter. (Keep remaining phyllo dough covered with a damp towel to prevent it from drying out.) Cut phyllo lengthwise in half; cut each half crosswise into 5 rectangles (4½x2¾ in.). Tightly roll up the rectangles jelly-roll style, starting with a long side.

2. Mix sugar and cinnamon. Lightly coat phyllo sticks with cooking spray; sprinkle with 1½ tsp. sugar mixture. Place on an ungreased baking sheet. Bake until lightly browned, 3-5 minutes. Remove to a wire rack to cool. Repeat with the remaining ingredients.

3. In a microwave, melt semisweet chocolate and shortening; stir until smooth. Dip 1 end of each phyllo stick into the chocolate; allow extra to drip off. Place on waxed paper; let stand until set. Drizzle with white chocolate.

1 PHYLLO STICK: 42 cal., 3g fat (2g sat. fat), 3mg chol., 19mg sod., 3g carb. (2g sugars, 0 fiber), 0 pro.

BANANA NUT BROWNIES

This recipe comes from my Grandma Schlientz. Any time there are ripe bananas around our house, it's Banana Nut Brownie time! People are always surprised to learn there are bananas in the brownies.

Christine Mol, Grand Rapids, MI

Prep: **10 min.**
Bake: **40 min. + cooling**
Makes: **16 brownies**

- ½ cup butter, melted, cooled
- 1 cup sugar
- 3 Tbsp. baking cocoa
- 2 large eggs, room temperature, lightly beaten
- 1 Tbsp. 2% milk
- 1 tsp. vanilla extract
- ½ cup all-purpose flour
- 1 tsp. baking powder
- ¼ tsp. salt
- 1 cup mashed ripe bananas (2½ to 3 medium)
- ½ cup chopped walnuts
  Confectioners' sugar, optional

1. Preheat oven to 350°. In a bowl, combine butter, sugar and cocoa. Stir in eggs, milk and vanilla. Blend in flour, baking powder and salt. Stir in bananas and nuts.

2. Pour into a greased 9-in. square baking pan. Bake until a toothpick comes out with moist crumbs, 40-45 minutes. Cool on a wire rack. Just before serving, dust with confectioners' sugar if desired.

1 BROWNIE: 163 cal., 9g fat (4g sat. fat), 42mg chol., 128mg sod., 20g carb. (15g sugars, 1g fiber), 3g pro.

THE SKINNY

Bake brownies for the amount of time specified in the recipe—no longer. (Overcooking is a common brownie-baking mistake.) For a fudgy texture, take the brownies out of the oven when a toothpick inserted in the center turns up streaks of batter and a few moist crumbs. For more cake-like brownies, bake until you see just a few moist crumbs on the toothpick.

ICE CREAM CONE TREATS

I came up with these as a way for my grandkids to enjoy Rice Krispies treats without getting sticky hands. You can also pack the cereal mixture into paper cups and insert a wooden pop stick to create cute pops.
—*Mabel Nolan, Vancouver, WA*

Takes: **20 min.** • Makes: **12 dozen**

- 12 ice cream sugar cones
     Melted semisweet chocolate, optional
     Colored sprinkles
- 4 cups miniature marshmallows
- 3 Tbsp. butter
- 6 cups Rice Krispies

1. If desired, dip ice cream cones in melted chocolate to coat the edges; stand in juice glasses or coffee mugs to set.
2. Place sprinkles in a shallow bowl. In a microwave or in a large saucepan over low heat, melt marshmallows and butter; stir until smooth. Remove from heat; stir in cereal.
3. Working quickly, with buttered hands, shape mixture into 12 balls; pack balls firmly into cones. Dip tops in sprinkles.
1 FILLED CONE: 174 cal., 4g fat (2g sat. fat), 8mg chol., 142mg sod., 34g carb. (14g sugars, 0 fiber), 2g pro.

BANANA PUDDING

I didn't see my son for more than two years after he enlisted in the Marines after high school. When he got home, the first thing he ate was two bowls of my easy banana pudding. He's a true southern boy! It's a dessert, but you can have it for breakfast, lunch or dinner.
—*Stephanie Harris, Montpelier, VA*

Prep: **35 min. + chilling**
Makes: **9 servings**

- ¾ cup sugar
- ¼ cup all-purpose flour
- ¼ tsp. salt
- 3 cups 2% milk
- 3 large eggs
- 1½ tsp. vanilla extract
- 8 oz. vanilla wafers (about 60 cookies), divided
- 4 large ripe bananas, cut into ¼-in. slices

1. In a large saucepan, mix sugar, flour and salt. Whisk in milk. Cook and stir over medium heat until thickened and bubbly. Reduce heat to low; cook and stir 2 minutes longer. Remove from heat.
2. In a small bowl, whisk eggs. Whisk a small amount of hot mixture into the eggs; return all to pan, whisking constantly. Bring to a gentle boil; cook and stir 2 minutes. Remove from heat. Stir in vanilla. Cool 15 minutes, stirring occasionally.
3. In an ungreased 8-in. square baking dish, layer 25 vanilla wafers, half the banana slices and half the pudding. Repeat layers.
4. Press plastic wrap onto surface of pudding. Refrigerate 4 hours or overnight. Just before serving, remove wrap; crush remaining wafers and sprinkle over top.
1 SERVING: 302 cal., 7g fat (2g sat. fat), 80mg chol., 206mg sod., 55g carb. (37g sugars, 2g fiber), 7g pro.

THE SKINNY
Leave the bottom of the apple intact when you core it so the sugar doesn't leak as it melts. If you don't have an apple corer, you can use a melon baller for this task.

LEMON-BERRY SHORTCAKE

Bake a simple cake using fresh strawberries, and enjoy this summertime classic with a layer of whipped topping and more berries.
—*Meryl Herr, Grand Rapids, MI*

- -

Prep: 30 min.
Bake: 20 min. + cooling
Makes: 8 servings

- 1⅓ cups all-purpose flour
- ½ cup sugar
- 2 tsp. baking powder
- ¼ tsp. salt
- 1 large egg, room temperature
- ⅔ cup buttermilk
- ¼ cup butter, melted
- 1 tsp. grated lemon zest
- 1 Tbsp. lemon juice
- 1 tsp. vanilla extract
- 1 cup sliced fresh strawberries

TOPPING
- 1 cup fresh blackberries
- 1 cup sliced fresh strawberries
- 1 Tbsp. lemon juice
- 1 tsp. sugar
- 2 cups reduced-fat whipped topping

1. Preheat oven to 350°. Grease and flour a 9-in. round baking pan.

2. In a large bowl, whisk flour, sugar, baking powder and salt. In another bowl, whisk egg, buttermilk, melted butter, lemon zest, lemon juice and vanilla. Add to the dry ingredients; stir just until moistened. Fold in 1 cup strawberries. Transfer to prepared pan.

3. Bake 20-25 minutes or until a toothpick inserted in center comes out clean. Cool 10 minutes before removing from pan to a wire rack to cool completely.

4. For topping, toss berries with lemon juice and sugar. To serve, spread whipped topping over cake. Top with berries.

1 PIECE: 252 cal., 9g fat (6g sat. fat), 42mg chol., 245mg sod., 40g carb. (19g sugars, 2g fiber), 4g pro.

SLOW-COOKER BAKED APPLES

On a cool fall day, coming home to the scent of apple dessert cooking and then eating it is a double dose of just plain wonderful.
—*Evangeline Bradford, Covington, KY*

Prep: **25 min.** • Cook: **4 hours**
Makes: **6 servings**

- 6 medium tart apples
- ½ cup raisins
- ⅓ cup packed brown sugar
- 1 Tbsp. grated orange zest
- 1 cup water
- 3 Tbsp. thawed orange juice concentrate
- 2 Tbsp. butter

1. Core apples and, if desired, peel the top third of each. Combine the raisins, brown sugar and orange zest; spoon into apples. Place in a 5-qt. slow cooker.
2. Pour water around apples. Drizzle apples with orange juice concentrate. Dot with butter. Cover and cook on low until apples are tender, 4-5 hours.
1 FILLED APPLE: 203 cal., 4g fat (2g sat. fat), 10mg chol., 35mg sod., 44g carb. (37g sugars, 4g fiber), 1g pro.

TROPICAL PARADISE MILKSHAKES

Slip away to paradise without leaving home with these fruity, coconutty milkshakes.
—Taste of Home *Test Kitchen*

Takes: **15 min.** • Makes: **6 servings**

- 2 medium limes, divided
- ¼ cup unsweetened shredded coconut, toasted
- 1½ cups frozen pineapple chunks
- 1½ cups frozen mango chunks
- 1 medium banana, sliced and frozen
- 1½ cups vanilla ice cream
- 1 cup light coconut milk
- ½ cup fat-free milk

- 1 cup frozen unsweetened strawberries
  Optional: Fresh pineapple, kiwifruit, strawberries, mango, starfruit and edible blossoms

1. Cut 1 lime into wedges. Moisten rims of 6 margarita or cocktail glasses with a lime wedge. Sprinkle shredded coconut on a plate; dip rims in coconut.
2. Zest and juice remaining lime. Place zest and juice in a blender. Add pineapple, mango, banana, ice cream and milks; cover and process until smooth. Pour ⅔ cup mixture into each prepared glass. Add strawberries to remaining mixture in blender; cover and process until smooth. Pour into glasses; garnish as desired optional ingredients.
1 CUP: 198 cal., 6g fat (4g sat. fat), 15mg chol., 44mg sod., 33g carb. (23g sugars, 3g fiber), 3g pro.

MAKE IT YOUR OWN
Make a grown-up version of these shakes by adding pineapple or coconut rum to the mix!

HOT FUDGE CAKE

What better way to top off a meal than with a rich chocolaty cake? Mom served this dessert with a scoop of ice cream or with cream poured over—and no matter what, I'd always have room for it.
—*Vera Reid, Laramie, WY*

Prep: **20 min.** • Bake: **35 min.**
Makes: **9 servings**

- 1 cup all-purpose flour
- ¾ cup sugar
- 6 Tbsp. baking cocoa, divided
- 2 tsp. baking powder
- ¼ tsp. salt
- ½ cup 2% milk
- 2 Tbsp. canola oil
- 1 tsp. vanilla extract
- 1 cup packed brown sugar
- 1¾ cups hot water
  Optional: Ice cream or whipped cream

1. Preheat oven to 350°. In a large bowl, whisk flour, sugar, 2 Tbsp. cocoa, baking powder and salt. In another bowl, whisk milk, oil and vanilla until blended. Add to flour mixture; stir just until moistened.
2. Transfer to an ungreased 9-in. square baking pan. In a small bowl, mix brown sugar and remaining 4 Tbsp. cocoa; sprinkle over batter. Pour hot water over all; do not stir.
3. Bake 35-40 minutes. Serve warm. If desired, top with ice cream.
1 PIECE: 253 cal., 4g fat (1g sat. fat), 2mg chol., 171mg sod., 54g carb. (41g sugars, 1g fiber), 3g pro.

MULLED WINE-POACHED APPLES

For a satisfying touch of sweetness at the end of a meal without a heavy dessert, try these ruby red apples. The spice and wine sauce makes them very special.
—Taste of Home *Test Kitchen*

Prep: **20 min.**
Cook: **20 min. + chilling**
Makes: **6 servings**

- 6 **medium apples, peeled**
- 1 **bottle (750 milliliters) merlot**
- ½ **cup mulling spices**

1. Core apples from bottom, leaving stems intact if desired. In a Dutch oven, bring wine and mulling spices to a boil. Reduce heat; carefully add apples. Cover and simmer just until apples are tender, 15-20 minutes, turning once.
2. With a slotted spoon, remove apples to a large bowl. Strain using a fine mesh strainer to remove spices; return wine to pan. Bring wine to a boil; cook, uncovered, until liquid is reduced to about ½ cup. Cool. Pour over apples; cover and refrigerate at least 1 hour before serving.
1 POACHED APPLE WITH 4 TSP. SAUCE: 240 cal., 0 fat (0 sat. fat), 0 chol., 12mg sod., 38g carb. (32g sugars, 2g fiber), 0 pro.

THE SKINNY
If using frozen blueberries, do not thaw before using.

BLUEBERRY PUDDING CAKE

We have many acres of blueberry bushes in the area where I live. My father-in-law has a number near his house, so I have an abundant supply every year and I'm always looking for new ways to use them. This is new recipe I found and it's been very popular.
—Jan Bamford, Sedgwick, ME

Prep: **15 min.** • Bake: **45 min.**
Makes: **9 servings**

- 2 **cups fresh or frozen blueberries**
- 1 **tsp. ground cinnamon**
- 1 **tsp. lemon juice**
- 1 **cup all-purpose flour**
- ¾ **cup sugar**
- 1 **tsp. baking powder**
- ½ **cup 2% milk**
- 3 **Tbsp. butter, melted**

TOPPING
- ¾ **cup sugar**
- 1 **Tbsp. cornstarch**
- 1 **cup boiling water**
  Whipped cream, optional

1. Preheat oven to 350°. Toss blueberries with cinnamon and lemon juice; pour into a greased 8-in. square baking dish. In a small bowl, combine flour, sugar and baking powder; stir in milk and melted butter. Spoon over berries.
2. Combine sugar and cornstarch; sprinkle over batter. Slowly pour boiling water over all. Bake until a toothpick inserted into the cake portion comes out clean, 45-50 minutes. Serve warm. If desired, top with whipped cream and additional blueberries.
1 PIECE: 244 cal., 4g fat (3g sat. fat), 11mg chol., 91mg sod., 51g carb. (37g sugars, 1g fiber), 2g pro.

4-INGREDIENT WATERMELON SORBET

You don't need an ice cream maker to make this easy, 4-ingredient sorbet. My family loves it so much that I can never keep enough watermelon in the house to meet their demand for it!
—*Kory Figura, Waverly, IA*

Prep: **35 min. + freezing**
Makes: **1½ qt.**

- 1 **cup sugar**
- 1 **cup water**
- 8 **cups cubed seedless watermelon**
- 2 **Tbsp. lemon juice**
  Fresh mint leaves, optional

1. In a small saucepan, bring sugar and water to a boil. Cook and stir until sugar is dissolved; set aside.
2. In a blender or food processor, process the watermelon in batches until pureed. Transfer to a large bowl; stir in the sugar syrup and lemon juice.
3. Pour into a 13x9-in. dish; cover and freeze for 8 hours or until firm. Just before serving, puree the watermelon mixture in batches until smooth. If desired, garnish with fresh mint.
1 CUP: 184 cal., 0 fat (0 sat. fat), 0 chol., 7mg sod., 52g carb. (49g sugars, 1g fiber), 1g pro.

TASTE OF HOME TALK
"This was my first sorbet at home. It was actually really easy. I will definitely be trying different flavors. I'm thinking lemon and strawberry would be a nice combo."
CYNANDTOM, TASTEOFHOME.COM

CARAMEL APPLE DESSERT PIZZA

I made a favorite dessert recipe a little bit lighter by using healthier ingredients. Slice up this fun take on pizza and see what you think!
—*Tari Ambler, Shorewood, IL*

Prep: **40 min. + cooling**
Makes: **12 slices**

- ¼ cup butter, softened
- ¼ cup sugar
- ¼ cup packed brown sugar
- 1 large egg, room temperature
- 2 Tbsp. canola oil
- 1 Tbsp. light corn syrup
- 1 tsp. vanilla extract
- 1 cup whole wheat pastry flour
- ¾ cup all-purpose flour
- ½ tsp. baking powder
- ¼ tsp. salt
- ¼ tsp. ground cinnamon

TOPPING

- 1 pkg. (8 oz.) fat-free cream cheese
- ¼ cup packed brown sugar
- ½ tsp. ground cinnamon
- ½ tsp. vanilla extract
- 3 medium tart apples, thinly sliced
- ¼ cup fat-free caramel ice cream topping
- ¼ cup chopped unsalted dry roasted peanuts

1. Cream butter and sugars until light and fluffy, 5-7 minutes. Beat in the egg, oil, corn syrup and vanilla. Combine the flours, baking powder, salt and cinnamon; gradually add to creamed mixture and mix well.

2. Press dough onto a 14-in. pizza pan coated with cooking spray. Bake at 350° until lightly browned, 12-15 minutes. Cool on a wire rack.

3. In a small bowl, beat the cream cheese, brown sugar, cinnamon and vanilla until smooth. Spread over crust. Arrange apples over the top. Drizzle with caramel topping; sprinkle with peanuts. Serve immediately.

1 PIECE: 238 cal., 9g fat (3g sat. fat), 29mg chol., 228mg sod., 36g carb. (20g sugars, 2g fiber), 6g pro.

JELLIED CHAMPAGNE DESSERT

This refreshing dessert looks just like a glass of bubbling champagne.
—*Vickie McLaughlin, Kingsport, TN*

Prep: **20 min. + chilling**
Makes: **8 servings**

- 1 envelope unflavored gelatin
- 2 cups cold white grape juice, divided
- 2 Tbsp. sugar
- 2 cups champagne or club soda
- 8 fresh strawberries, hulled

1. In a small saucepan, sprinkle gelatin over 1 cup cold grape juice; let stand for 1 minute. Heat over low heat, stirring until gelatin is dissolved. Stir in sugar. Remove from the heat; stir in remaining 1 cup grape juice. Let cool to room temperature.

2. Transfer gelatin mixture to a large bowl. Slowly stir in champagne. Pour half of the champagne mixture into 8 champagne or parfait glasses. Add 1 strawberry to each glass. Refrigerate glasses and remaining champagne mixture until almost set, about 1 hour.

3. Place reserved champagne mixture in a blender; cover and process until foamy. Pour into glasses. Chill until set, about 3 hours.

1 SERVING: 96 cal., 0 fat (0 sat. fat), 0 chol., 9mg sod., 13g carb. (12g sugars, 0 fiber), 1g pro. **DIABETIC EXCHANGES:** 1 starch.

STRAWBERRY-BANANA GRAHAM PUDDING

I add more fruit to get a little closer to all those servings you need every day. You can also try using different flavored puddings and fruit to switch up the recipe.
—*Jackie Termont, Ruther Glen, VA*

Prep: **20 min. + chilling**
Makes: **12 servings**

- 9 whole reduced-fat cinnamon graham crackers
- 1¾ cups cold fat-free milk
- 1 pkg. (1 oz.) sugar-free instant cheesecake or vanilla pudding mix
- 1 large firm banana, sliced
- ½ tsp. lemon juice
- 2 cups sliced fresh strawberries, divided
- 2½ cups reduced-fat whipped topping, divided
  Mint sprigs, optional

1. Line the bottom of a 9-in. square pan with 4½ graham crackers; set aside.

2. In a small bowl, whisk milk and pudding mix for 2 minutes. Let stand until soft-set, 2 minutes. Place banana slices in another small bowl; toss with lemon juice. Stir bananas and 1 cup strawberries into the pudding. Fold in 1¾ cups whipped topping.

3. Spread half the pudding mixture over the graham crackers; repeat layers. Cover and refrigerate overnight. Refrigerate remaining berries and whipped topping. Just before serving, top with remaining berries and topping. If desired, garnish with mint.

1 PIECE: 117 cal., 2g fat (2g sat. fat), 1mg chol., 171mg sod., 20g carb. (11g sugars, 1g fiber), 2g pro.
DIABETIC EXCHANGES: 1 starch, ½ fat.

NO-CRUST PUMPKIN PIE

Baked in a water bath, this pie has a texture that's more like a custard than a traditional pie. In place of pumpkin, I sometimes use cushaw, a type of crookneck squash.
—Linda McClung, Robbinsville, NC

Prep: **5 min.** • Bake: **50 min.**
Makes: **8 servings**

- 1¼ cups sugar
- 3 Tbsp. all-purpose flour
- 3 large eggs, room temperature
- 2 cups canned pumpkin
- ¾ cup evaporated milk
- 1½ tsp. vanilla extract
- ¼ tsp. ground cinnamon, optional

1. Combine the sugar and flour. Add eggs; mix well. Stir in pumpkin, milk, vanilla and, if desired, cinnamon; mix until well blended.

2. Pour into a greased 9-in. pie plate. Place pie plate in a 15x10x1-in. baking pan; add ½ in. of hot water to pan.

3. Bake at 350° until a knife inserted in center of the pie comes out clean, 50-55 minutes. Cool on a wire rack.

1 PIECE: 211 cal., 4g fat (2g sat. fat), 87mg chol., 49mg sod., 40g carb. (35g sugars, 3g fiber), 5g pro.

TYPICAL	MAKEOVER
345 Calories	**211** Calories
16mg Fat	**4**mg Fat
5mg Saturated Fat	**2**mg Saturated Fat
244mg Sodium	**49**mg Sodium

THE SKINNY
Using rum in place
of the extract might
seem like a fun idea,
but the alcohol will
keep your dessert
from freezing solid.

BLACKBERRY DAIQUIRI SHERBET

The summer I decided to try to make sherbet—one of my favorite desserts—blackberries were in season in my mom's garden. I love the flavor of daiquiris, and the two blend together beautifully!
—*Shelly Bevington, Hermiston, OR*

Prep: **15 min.**
Process: **30 min. + freezing**
Makes: **1¼ qt.**

- 3 **cups fresh or frozen blackberries, thawed**
- 1 **cup sugar**
- ¼ **tsp. salt**
- 1 **can (12 oz.) evaporated milk**
- 2 **Tbsp. lime juice**
- 1 **tsp. rum extract**
- ⅓ **tsp. citric acid**

1. Place blackberries, sugar and salt in a food processor; process until smooth. Press through a fine-mesh strainer into a bowl; discard seeds and pulp. Stir remaining ingredients into the puree.

2. Fill cylinder of ice cream maker no more than two-thirds full; freeze according to the manufacturer's directions. Transfer sherbet to freezer containers, allowing headspace for expansion. Freeze until firm, 8 hours or overnight.

½ CUP: 147 cal., 3g fat (2g sat. fat), 12mg chol., 96mg sod., 28g carb. (26g sugars, 2g fiber), 3g pro.

APPLE PANDOWDY

This apple pandowdy, which comes from a very old cookbook, is tangy and delicious.
—*Doreen Lindquist, Thompson, MB*

- -

Prep: **25 min.** • Bake: **55 min.**
Makes: **9 servings**

- 1 **cup packed brown sugar**
- 1¼ **cups all-purpose flour, divided**
- ½ **tsp. salt, divided**
- 1 **cup water**
- 1 **tsp. lemon juice**
- 2 **tsp. baking powder**
- 5 **Tbsp. butter, divided**
- ¾ **cup 2% milk**
- 5 **cups sliced peeled apples**
- ½ **tsp. plus ⅛ tsp. ground cinnamon, divided**
- ½ **tsp. ground nutmeg**
- 1 **tsp. vanilla extract**
- 1 **Tbsp. coarse sugar**
  Whipped cream, optional

1. In a saucepan, combine brown sugar, ¼ cup flour and ¼ tsp. salt. Add water and lemon juice; cook and stir over medium heat until thick. Cover and set aside.
2. Combine baking powder and remaining 1 cup flour and ¼ tsp. salt. Cut in 3 Tbsp. butter. Add milk and mix just until moistened (a few lumps will remain); set aside.
3. Arrange apples in a 1½-qt. baking dish; sprinkle with ½ tsp. cinnamon. Add nutmeg, vanilla and remaining 2 Tbsp. butter to sauce; pour over apples. Drop dough by spoonfuls over sauce. Combine remaining ⅛ tsp. cinnamon and the coarse sugar; sprinkle over dough.
4. Bake at 350° until top is brown and apples are tender, about 55 minutes. Serve warm, with whipped cream if desired.
1 SERVING: 260 cal., 7g fat (4g sat. fat), 20mg chol., 304mg sod., 47g carb. (33g sugars, 2g fiber), 3g pro.

AIR-FRYER MOCHA PUDDING CAKES

My mom used to make these mouthwatering mini cakes when I was little. Now I whip them up in my air fryer for a speedy dessert.
—*Debora Simmons, Eglon, WV*

- -

Takes: **30 min.** • Makes: **2 servings**

- ¼ **cup all-purpose flour**
- 3 **Tbsp. sugar**
- 1½ **tsp. baking cocoa**
- ½ **tsp. baking powder**
- ⅛ **tsp. salt**
- 3 **Tbsp. 2% milk**
- 1½ **tsp. butter, melted**
- ¼ **tsp. vanilla extract**

TOPPING

- 2 **Tbsp. brown sugar**
- 1½ **tsp. baking cocoa**
- 3 **Tbsp. hot brewed coffee**
- 1 **Tbsp. hot water**
  Whipped topping, optional

1. Preheat air fryer to 350°. In a small bowl, combine flour, sugar, cocoa, baking powder and salt. Stir in the milk, butter and vanilla until smooth. Spoon into 2 lightly greased 4-oz. ramekins. Combine brown sugar and cocoa; sprinkle over batter. Combine coffee and water; pour over topping.
2. Place ramekins on tray in air-fryer basket. Cook until a knife inserted in the center comes out clean, 15-20 minutes. Serve warm or at room temperature, with whipped topping if desired.
1 PUDDING CAKE: 229 cal., 4g fat (2g sat. fat), 9mg chol., 306mg sod., 47g carb. (33g sugars, 1g fiber), 3g pro.

CHERRY CHOCOLATE CAKE

I've had the recipe for this lovely cake for years. It's a chocolate lover's delight! It's so easy to make, and it's easy to take along to potlucks, too. Just spread the second can of pie filling right over the top.

—Ann Purchase, Panama City, FL

Prep: **15 min.**
Bake: **30 min. + cooling**
Makes: **18 servings**

- 1 **pkg. chocolate cake mix (regular size)**
- 3 **large eggs, room temperature, lightly beaten**
- 1 **tsp. almond extract**
- 2 **cans (20 oz. each) reduced-sugar cherry pie filling, divided**
- ¾ **tsp. confectioners' sugar**

1. Preheat oven to 350°. In a large bowl, combine the cake mix, eggs and extract until well blended. Stir in 1 can of pie filling until blended. Transfer to a 13x9-in. baking pan coated with cooking spray.
2. Bake for 30-35 minutes or until a toothpick inserted in the center comes out clean. Set cake on a wire rack to cool completely. Dust with confectioners' sugar. Top individual servings with remaining pie filling.
1 PIECE: 187 cal., 6g fat (1g sat. fat), 35mg chol., 253mg sod., 33g carb., 1g fiber), 3g pro.

CHOCOLATE-GLAZED BROWNIES

These moist and fudgy squares are bursting with such rich chocolate flavor that you'd never know they're low in fat. They're ideal for taking to bake sales and family gatherings. For holidays, I dress them up with colorful candy sprinkles.

—Deb Anderson, Joplin, MO

Prep: **15 min.**
Bake: **20 min. + cooling**
Makes: **1 dozen**

- ⅓ **cup butter, softened**
- 1 **cup sugar**
- 1 **tsp. vanilla extract**
- 3 **large egg whites, room temperature**
- ⅔ **cup all-purpose flour**
- ½ **cup baking cocoa**
- ½ **tsp. baking powder**
- ¼ **tsp. salt**

GLAZE
- ⅔ **cup confectioners' sugar**
- 2 **Tbsp. baking cocoa**
- ¼ **tsp. vanilla extract**
- 3 **to 4 tsp. hot water**

1. Preheat oven to 350°. Cream butter and sugar until light and fluffy, 5-7 minutes. Beat in vanilla and egg whites, 1 at a time. In a small bowl, whisk together flour, cocoa, baking powder and salt; gradually add to creamed mixture. Spread into an 8-in. square baking pan coated with cooking spray.
2. Bake until a toothpick inserted in the center comes out clean, 20-25 minutes. Cool completely on a wire rack.
3. Mix glaze ingredients; spread over cool brownies. Cut into bars.
1 BROWNIE: 180 cal., 6g fat (3g sat. fat), 14mg chol., 124mg sod., 31g carb. (23g sugars, 1g fiber), 3g pro.

HOT COCOA SOUFFLE

A friend invited me to go to a church cooking demo years ago, and one of the recipes we prepared was this luscious souffle. It's decadent and delicious.
—*Joan Hallford,*
North Richland Hills, TX

- -

Prep: **20 min.** • Bake: **40 min.**
Makes: **6 servings**

- 5 **large eggs**
- 4 **tsp. plus ¾ cup sugar, divided**
- ½ **cup baking cocoa**
- 6 **Tbsp. all-purpose flour**
- ¼ **tsp. salt**
- 1½ **cups fat-free milk**
- 2 **Tbsp. butter**
- 1½ **tsp. vanilla extract**
  Confectioners' sugar, optional

1. Separate eggs; let stand at room temperature for 30 minutes. Coat a 2-qt. souffle dish with cooking spray and lightly sprinkle with 4 tsp. sugar; set aside. Preheat oven to 350°.

2. In a small saucepan, combine the cocoa, flour, salt and remaining ¾ cup sugar. Gradually whisk in milk. Bring to a boil, stirring constantly. Cook and stir until thickened, 1-2 minutes longer. Stir in butter. Transfer to a large bowl.

3. Stir a small amount of hot mixture into the egg yolks; return all to the bowl, stirring constantly. Add vanilla; cool slightly.

4. In a second large bowl, with clean beaters, beat egg whites until stiff peaks form. With a spatula, stir a fourth of the egg whites into the chocolate mixture until no white streaks remain. Fold in remaining egg whites until combined.

5. Transfer to prepared dish. Bake until the top is puffed and the center appears set, 40-45 minutes. If desired, dust with confectioners' sugar. Serve immediately.

1 SERVING: 272 cal., 9g fat (4g sat. fat), 188mg chol., 209mg sod., 41g carb. (31g sugars, 2g fiber), 9g pro.

OLD-FASHIONED RICE PUDDING

This dessert is a wonderful way to end any meal. As a young girl, I always waited eagerly for the first heavenly bite. Today, my husband likes to top his with a scoop of ice cream.
—*Sandra Melnychenko, Grandview, MB*

Prep: **10 min.** • Bake: **1 hour**
Makes: **6 servings**

- 3½ cups 2% milk
- ½ cup uncooked long grain rice
- ⅓ cup sugar
- ½ tsp. salt
- ½ cup raisins
- 1 tsp. vanilla extract
  Ground cinnamon, optional

1. Preheat oven to 325°. Place the first 4 ingredients in a large saucepan; bring to a boil over medium heat, stirring constantly. Transfer to a greased 1½-qt. baking dish.
2. Bake, covered, 45 minutes, stirring every 15 minutes. Stir in raisins and vanilla; bake, covered, until rice is tender, about 15 minutes longer. If desired, sprinkle with cinnamon. Serve warm or refrigerate and serve cold.
¾ CUP: 214 cal., 3g fat (2g sat. fat), 11mg chol., 266mg sod., 41g carb. (25g sugars, 1g fiber), 6g pro.

THE SKINNY

For a super creamy rice pudding, add 1-2 egg yolks. Whisk a small amount of the hot mixture into the yolks, then add it all back to the saucepan and stir it in before transferring to the baking dish. After baking, make sure a thermometer inserted in the pudding reads 160°; that's how you know the yolk has cooked long enough to be safely eaten.

BONUS: SPECIAL VEGAN DISHES

SMOKY VEGAN BACON

This recipe is a must for any vegetarian! You won't believe how similar it is to the real thing.
—Taste of Home *Test Kitchen*

Prep: 15 min. • **Cook:** 5 min./batch
Makes: 12 servings

1	large carrot
2	Tbsp. maple syrup
1	tsp. smoked paprika
½	tsp. garlic powder
¼	tsp. onion powder
⅛	tsp. salt
⅛	tsp. liquid smoke
2	Tbsp. olive oil

1. With a mandoline or vegetable peeler, cut carrot into long, thin strips. In a shallow bowl, whisk maple syrup, paprika, garlic powder, onion powder, salt and liquid smoke. Dip carrot slices into the syrup mixture, allowing excess to drip off.
2. In a large skillet, heat oil over medium heat. Cook carrot slices in batches until browned, 4-6 minutes, turning once.
1 PIECE: 32 cal., 2g fat (0 sat. fat), 0 chol., 29mg sod., 3g carb. (2g sugars, 0 fiber), 0 pro.

THE SKINNY

It may seem hard to believe, but these thin carrot slices really do fill the bill when you're craving bacon. The caramelized maple syrup and liquid smoke do the trick.

VEGAN TACO SALAD

The best salads are made with ingredients that have different textures and complementary flavors. In this salad, you'll love the crunch of the tortilla chips mixed with the sweet, crisp lettuce and "meaty" crumble mixture.
—Taste of Home *Test Kitchen*

- -

Takes: **30 min.** • Makes: **6 servings**

1	Tbsp. canola oil
1	medium sweet red pepper, chopped
1	small onion, chopped
3	garlic cloves, minced
1	pkg. (12 oz.) frozen vegetarian meat crumbles
1½	cups salsa, divided
1	Tbsp. chili powder
1	tsp. ground cumin
8	cups torn romaine
1	can (15 oz.) black beans, rinsed and drained
1	cup coarsely crushed tortilla chips
1	cup frozen corn, thawed
2	plum tomatoes, chopped
1	medium ripe avocado, peeled and cubed
¼	cup chopped fresh cilantro
¼	cup vegan ranch salad dressing
	Lime wedges, optional

1. In a large skillet, heat oil over medium heat. Add pepper and onion; cook and stir until tender, 5-7 minutes. Add garlic; cook 1 minute longer. Stir in crumbles, ¾ cup salsa, chili powder and cumin; cook and stir until heated through, 3-5 minutes.

2. In a large bowl, combine lettuce, beans, tortilla chips, corn, tomatoes, avocado, cilantro and crumble mixture. Combine remaining salsa and vegan ranch, pour over salad and toss to coat. If desired, serve with lime wedges.

2 CUPS: 354 cal., 15g fat (2g sat. fat), 1mg chol., 807mg sod., 40g carb. (7g sugars, 11g fiber), 17g pro. **DIABETIC EXCHANGES:** 2½ starch, 2 lean meat, 2 fat.

VEGETARIAN CHILI OLE!

I combine ingredients for this hearty chili the night before, start my trusty slow cooker in the morning and come home to a rich, spicy meal in the evening!
—*Marjorie Au, Honolulu, HI*

Prep: **35 min.** • Cook: **6 hours**
Makes: **7 servings**

- 1   can (16 oz.) kidney beans, rinsed and drained
- 1   can (15 oz.) black beans, rinsed and drained
- 1   can (14½ oz.) diced tomatoes, undrained
- 1½ cups frozen corn
- 1   large onion, chopped
- 1   medium zucchini, chopped
- 1   medium sweet red pepper, chopped
- 1   can (4 oz.) chopped green chiles
- 1   oz. Mexican chocolate, chopped
- 1   cup water
- 1   can (6 oz.) tomato paste
- 1   Tbsp. cornmeal
- 1   Tbsp. chili powder
- ½   tsp. salt
- ½   tsp. dried oregano
- ½   tsp. ground cumin
- ¼   tsp. hot pepper sauce, optional
     Optional toppings: Diced tomatoes and chopped green onions

1. In a 4-qt. slow cooker, combine the first 9 ingredients. Combine the water, tomato paste, cornmeal, chili powder, salt, oregano, cumin and, if desired, pepper sauce until smooth; stir into slow cooker. Cover and cook on low until vegetables are tender, 6-8 hours.

2. Serve with toppings of your choice.

FREEZE OPTION: Freeze chili in freezer containers. To use, partially thaw in the refrigerator overnight. Heat through in a saucepan, stirring occasionally; add water or broth if necessary.

1 CUP: 216 cal., 1g fat (0 sat. fat), 0 chol., 559mg sod., 43g carb. (11g sugars, 10g fiber), 11g pro. **DIABETIC EXCHANGES:** 2½ starch, 1 lean meat.

THE SKINNY

Make your vegan chili even more rich and satisfying by adding a can of chickpeas, rinsed and drained. Instead of frozen veggies, reach for in-season fresh corn, cut off the cobs. Roasted red or green Hatch chiles would be a wonderful spicy addition to this chili. For a crispy crunch, top with homemade tortilla chips.

STUFFED MUSHROOMS

Mixed with a blend of parsley, basil, oregano and bread crumbs, soy crumbles make a delightful addition to these savory stuffed mushrooms.
—*Arline Aaron, Brooklyn, NY*

Prep: **15 min.** • Bake: **25 min.**
Makes: **14 appetizers**

- 14 large fresh mushrooms
- 1 small onion, finely chopped
- 4 tsp. canola oil
- ¾ cup soft bread crumbs
- ½ cup frozen vegetarian meat crumbles, thawed
- 1 tsp. minced fresh parsley
- 1 tsp. dried basil
- ½ tsp. dried oregano
- ½ tsp. salt
- ½ tsp. pepper
  Chopped fresh basil, optional

1. Remove stems from mushrooms and chop; set mushroom caps aside. In a large nonstick skillet coated with cooking spray, saute the stems and onion in oil until tender. Stir in the bread crumbs, crumbles and next 5 seasonings; cook until bread crumbs are lightly browned. Cool slightly.
2. Stuff into mushroom caps. Place in a 15x10x1-in. baking pan coated with cooking spray. Bake at 350° for 25-30 minutes or until heated through and mushrooms are tender. If desired, top with chopped fresh basil. Serve warm.
1 STUFFED MUSHROOM: 34 cal., 2g fat (0 sat. fat), 0 chol., 111mg sod., 3g carb. (1g sugars, 1g fiber), 2g pro.
DIABETIC EXCHANGES: ½ starch, ½ fat.

VEGAN GRAVY

This vegan gravy is really easy to make. I like to serve it over poutine, but it is perfect with mashed potatoes, stuffing and other foods, too. The entire family will love it!
—*Lisa Grant, Kingston, ON*

Takes: **30 min.** • Makes: **1¾ cups**

- 2 Tbsp. vegan butter-style sticks
- 1 medium onion, finely chopped
- 2 Tbsp. all-purpose flour
- 2 Tbsp. cornstarch
- 1½ cups vegetable broth
- 1 to 2 Tbsp. soy sauce
- 1 tsp. yeast extract (such as Vegemite)
- ½ tsp. garlic salt
- ¼ tsp. pepper

1. In a small saucepan, melt butter over medium heat. Add onion; cook and stir until tender, 3-5 minutes. Stir in flour until blended; cook and stir until lightly golden brown, 8-9 minutes (do not burn).
2. Whisk cornstarch and broth. Gradually whisk into flour mixture. Bring to a boil, stirring constantly; cook and stir until thickened, 2-3 minutes. Stir in the soy sauce, yeast extract, garlic salt and pepper.
2 TBSP.: 28 cal., 2g fat (1g sat. fat), 0 chol., 295mg sod., 3g carb. (0 sugars, 0 fiber), 0 pro.

THE SKINNY
You can customize this recipe by adding in your favorite herbs. Rosemary, fresh thyme or oregano would be perfect for this gravy recipe.

THE SKINNY

These stuffed mushrooms are vegan as is, but other vegan swaps you could make include skipping the vegetarian meat crumbles and instead using a different protein like white navy beans, crumbled tofu, sauteed seitan or vegan sausage.

VEGAN CHOCOLATE CHIP COOKIES

As a competitive figure skater, I came up with this high-energy recipe. Whenever I bring these cookies to the rink, coaches are always sneaking two or three.
—*Cassandra Brzycki, Wauwatosa, WI*

Prep: **15 min. + chilling**
Bake: **10 min./batch**
Makes: **3½ dozen**

- 1¼ **cups packed dark brown sugar**
- ½ **cup canola oil**
- 6 **Tbsp. vanilla soy milk**
- ¼ **cup sugar**
- ¼ **cup unsweetened applesauce**
- 2 **tsp. vanilla extract**
- 2¼ **cups all-purpose flour**
- 1 **tsp. baking soda**
- ¾ **tsp. salt**
- 1 **cup dairy-free semisweet chocolate chips**
- ½ **cup finely chopped walnuts**

1. In a large bowl, beat the first 6 ingredients until well blended. Combine the flour, baking soda and salt; gradually add to sugar mixture and mix well. Stir in chocolate chips and nuts. Cover and refrigerate for 1 hour.

2. Drop by rounded tablespoonfuls 2 in. apart onto parchment-lined baking sheets. Bake at 375° for 10-12 minutes or until edges are lightly browned. Cool for 1 minute before removing from pans to wire racks.

1 COOKIE: 111 cal., 5g fat (1g sat. fat), 0 chol., 76mg sod., 16g carb. (10g sugars, 1g fiber), 1g pro.

VEGAN GREEN GODDESS POTATO SALAD

Don't be fooled by the green color—this salad is absolutely delicious! It is perfect for potlucks and for those with dietary restrictions.
—*Laura Wilhelm, West Hollywood, CA*

Prep: **30 min. + chilling**
Makes: **8 servings**

- 2 **lbs. baby red potatoes, halved**
- 4 **green onions**
- 2 **medium ripe avocados, peeled and pitted**
- ½ **cup sprigs fresh parsley, stems removed**
- ½ **cup vegan mayonnaise**
- 3 **tarragon sprigs, stems removed**
- 2 **tsp. capers, drained**
- 1 **tsp. seasoned salt**
- 1 **celery rib, finely chopped Sliced radishes**

1. Place potatoes in large saucepan; add water to cover. Bring to a boil. Reduce heat; cook, uncovered, until tender, 8-10 minutes.

2. Meanwhile, chop green onions, reserving white portions for the salad. Add green portions to a blender. Add the avocados, parsley, mayonnaise, tarragon, capers and seasoned salt. Cover and process until blended, scraping down sides as needed.

3. Drain potatoes; transfer to a large bowl. Add celery, white portions of green onions, and dressing; toss to coat. Refrigerate, covered, at least 1 hour. Top with radishes and additional parsley.

¾ CUP: 235 cal., 15g fat (2g sat. fat), 0 chol., 295mg sod., 24g carb. (1g sugars, 4g fiber), 3g pro. **DIABETIC EXCHANGES:** 3 fat, 1½ starch.

1. In a blender, puree the drained cashews and next 7 ingredients until smooth; mix in crushed red pepper flakes if desired. Set aside.

2. In a Dutch oven or large skillet, heat oil over medium heat. Add onion; cook and stir until browned, 4-5 minutes. Stir in garlic; cook 1 minute longer. Add asparagus, Broccolini and carrots; cook until tender, 10-12 minutes. Remove from pan; set aside.

3. In same pan, add tomato mixture and cook for 2 minutes. Add water, sun-dried tomatoes and pasta. Bring to a boil; reduce heat and simmer until pasta is al dente, 10-12 minutes, adding additional water as necessary and stirring occasionally. Stir in the cooked vegetables and toss to coat. Serve immediately.

1¾ CUPS: 500 cal., 21g fat (3g sat. fat), 0 chol., 712mg sod., 72g carb. (13g sugars, 10g fiber), 10g pro.

ONE-POT CREAMY TOMATO PASTA

Here's a creamy vegan recipe with tons of fresh sauteed vegetables. The spicy tomato sauce with sweet sun-dried tomatoes is the highlight of this dish. It's the perfect meal for when you just don't feel like cooking.
—*Michelle Miller, Sunkissedkitchen.com*

Prep: **20 min.** • Cook: **30 min.**
Makes: **4 servings**

- ⅓ cup unsalted cashews, soaked overnight
- 1 can (14½ oz.) diced tomatoes, undrained
- 2 Tbsp. tomato paste
- 1½ tsp. dried oregano
- 1 tsp. garlic powder
- 1 tsp. onion powder
- 1 tsp. sea salt
- ½ tsp. ground cumin
- ¼ tsp. crushed red pepper flakes, optional
- ¼ cup olive oil
- 1 medium red onion, thinly sliced
- 2 garlic cloves, minced
- ½ lb. fresh asparagus, trimmed and cut into 2-in. pieces
- ½ lb. Broccolini or broccoli spears, cut into 3-in. pieces
- 1 cup sliced fresh carrots
- 2½ to 3 cups water
- ½ cup julienned soft sun-dried tomatoes (not packed in oil)
- 8 oz. uncooked gluten-free spiral pasta

THE SKINNY

To soak the cashews, simply place them in a bowl and fill it with warm water to cover the nuts completely. Let the cashews soak overnight, and drain them before using.

THE SKINNY

Similar cake recipes sometimes suggest mixing the ingredients directly in the baking pan. We find that first mixing it in a bowl ensures equal distribution of the ingredients and no burnt edges where the batter could have splashed up the sides of the pan. Using a mixer in your baking pan can also ruin any nonstick finishes.

MOIST CHOCOLATE SNACK CAKE

I have made this dessert—otherwise known as crazy cake—for more than 50 years. It is classic, tender and moist, and requires only three easy steps.
—*Devota Angell, Allenstown, NH*

- -

Prep: **10 min.**
Bake: **25 min. + cooling**
Makes: **4 servings**

- ½ cup sugar
- ½ cup water
- 2 Tbsp. plus 1 tsp. canola oil
- 1½ tsp. white vinegar
- ½ tsp. vanilla extract
- ¾ cup all-purpose flour
- 4½ tsp. baking cocoa
- ½ tsp. baking soda
- ¼ tsp. salt
  Confectioners' sugar, optional

1. Preheat oven to 350°. Grease a 8½x4½-in. loaf pan. In a small bowl, beat the sugar, water, oil, vinegar and vanilla until well blended. Combine flour, cocoa, baking soda and salt; gradually beat into sugar mixture until blended.
2. Pour into prepared pan. Bake until a toothpick inserted in center comes out clean, 25-30 minutes.
3. Cool 10 minutes before removing from the pan to a wire rack to cool completely. Dust with confectioners' sugar if desired.
1 PIECE: 262 cal., 9g fat (1g sat. fat), 0 chol., 306mg sod., 44g carb. (25g sugars, 1g fiber), 3g pro.

VEGETARIAN WHITE BEAN SOUP

Our Test Kitchen simmered up this fresh-tasting meatless soup. Hearty with two kinds of beans, it makes a satisfying entree. Round out the meal with warm dinner rolls.
—Taste of Home *Test Kitchen*

- -

Takes: **30 min.** • Makes: **10 servings**

- 2 small zucchini, quartered lengthwise and sliced
- 1 cup each chopped onion, celery and carrot
- 2 Tbsp. canola oil
- 3 cans (14½ oz. each) vegetable broth
- 1 can (15½ oz.) great northern beans, rinsed and drained
- 1 can (15 oz.) cannellini beans, rinsed and drained
- 1 can (14½ oz.) diced tomatoes, undrained
- ½ tsp. dried thyme
- ½ tsp. dried oregano
- ¼ tsp. pepper
  Minced fresh oregano, optional

In a large saucepan, saute zucchini, onion, celery and carrot in oil over medium heat until crisp-tender, 5-7 minutes. Add the remaining ingredients except fresh oregano. Bring to a boil. Reduce heat; cover and simmer until the vegetables are tender, 5 minutes. If desired, garnish with fresh oregano.
1 CUP: 117 cal., 3g fat (0 sat. fat), 0 chol., 555mg sod., 17g carb. (3g sugars, 5g fiber), 5g pro. **DIABETIC EXCHANGES:** 1 starch, ½ fat.

¼ tsp. pepper
2 green onions, thinly sliced
1 plum tomato,
seeded and chopped

1. Place sweet potato in a small saucepan and cover with water. Bring to a boil. Reduce the heat; cover and cook until tender, 13-18 minutes. Drain, reserving ¼ cup liquid. Cool slightly. Place sweet potato and reserved liquid in a blender or food processor; cover and process until smooth. Set aside.
2. In a small saucepan coated with cooking spray, cook green pepper, onion and garlic until almost tender, 2-3 minutes. Stir in cilantro and cumin; cook and stir until vegetables are tender, 1-2 minutes. Add the beans, water, corn, tomato sauce, pepper and reserved sweet potato puree; heat through. Top with green onions and tomato.
1½ CUPS: 211 cal., 1g fat (0 sat. fat), 0 chol., 472mg sod., 44g carb. (10g sugars, 9g fiber), 9g pro. **DIABETIC EXCHANGES:** 2½ starch, 1 lean meat, 1 vegetable.

MAKE IT YOUR OWN
If you don't have any black beans on hand, white cannellini beans will also work.

SWEET POTATO BEAN SOUP
I felt like making some black bean soup, but I had a sweet potato that needed to be used, so I combined the two and created this delicious option. It joins the creaminess of the sweet potato with the crunch of corn and bell pepper.
—*Michelle Sweeny, Bloomington, IN*

Takes: **30 min.** • Makes: **4 servings**

1 medium sweet potato, peeled and cubed
1 small green pepper, chopped
1 small onion, chopped
2 garlic cloves, minced
1 tsp. minced fresh cilantro
1 tsp. ground cumin
1 can (15 oz.) black beans, rinsed and drained
2 cups water
1½ cups frozen corn
1 can (8 oz.) tomato sauce

VEGAN PUMPKIN PIE

Rich, creamy and wonderfully spiced for the holidays, this vegan pie is perfect for all your guests.
—*Justin Weber, Kenosha, WI*

Prep: **20 min. + chilling**
Bake: **1 hour + cooling**
Makes: **8 servings**

- 1¼ cups all-purpose flour
- 2 tsp. sugar
- ¼ tsp. salt
- ½ cup coconut oil or shortening, cold
- 3 to 4 Tbsp. ice water

FILLING

- 2½ cups canned pumpkin
- ¼ cup packed brown sugar
- ¼ cup maple or agave syrup
- ¾ cup oat milk
- 1 tsp. vanilla extract
- 2 tsp. pumpkin pie spice
- ½ tsp. ground cinnamon
- ½ tsp. salt
- 3 Tbsp. tapioca flour or arrowroot flour

1. In a food processor, mix flour, sugar and salt; pulse in coconut oil until crumbly. Gradually add ice water, pulsing until dough holds together when pressed. Shape into a disk. Cover and refrigerate for 30 minutes or up to 2 hours.
2. On a lightly floured surface, roll the dough into a ⅛-in.-thick circle; transfer to 9-in. pie plate. Trim crust to ½ in. beyond rim of plate; flute the edge. Refrigerate 30 minutes. Preheat oven to 425°.
3. Line crust with a double thickness of foil. Fill with pie weights, dried beans or uncooked rice. Bake on a lower oven rack until crust is set, about 5 minutes. Remove foil and weights; bake until crust just starts to brown, about 10 minutes. Reduce oven temperature to 350°.
4. In a blender, combine the filling ingredients. Puree until smooth. Pour the filling into crust. Bake for 45-50 minutes or until the center is set and filling is beginning to crack (cover edges with foil during the last 15 minutes to prevent overbrowning if necessary). Cool on a wire rack for 1 hour. Refrigerate pie overnight or until set.
1 PIECE: 298 cal., 15g fat (12g sat. fat), 0 chol., 239mg sod., 41g carb. (18g sugars, 3g fiber), 3g pro.

THE SKINNY
Otherwise known as the coriander leaf, cilantro is bright and refreshing with a zesty lemon flavor.

FRESH FROM THE GARDEN WRAPS

We moved into a new house with a garden. Using the herbs we found, we made these fresh-tasting wraps.
—*Chris Bugher, Fairview, NC*

Prep: **20 min. + standing**
Makes: **8 servings**

- 1 **medium ear sweet corn**
- 1 **medium cucumber, chopped**
- 1 **cup shredded cabbage**
- 1 **medium tomato, chopped**
- 1 **small red onion, chopped**
- 1 **jalapeno pepper, seeded and minced**
- 1 **Tbsp. minced fresh basil**
- 1 **Tbsp. minced fresh cilantro**
- 1 **Tbsp. minced fresh mint**
- ⅓ **cup Thai chili sauce**
- 3 **Tbsp. rice vinegar**
- 2 **tsp. reduced-sodium soy sauce**
- 2 **tsp. creamy peanut butter**
- 8 **Bibb or Boston lettuce leaves**

1. Cut corn from cob and place in a large bowl. Add cucumber, cabbage, tomato, onion, jalapeno and herbs.
2. Whisk together the chili sauce, vinegar, soy sauce and peanut butter. Pour over vegetable mixture; toss to coat. Let stand 20 minutes.
3. Using a slotted spoon, place ½ cup mixture in each lettuce leaf. Fold lettuce over filling.
NOTE: Wear disposable gloves when cutting hot peppers; the oils can burn skin. Avoid touching your face.
1 FILLED LETTUCE WRAP: 64 cal., 1g fat (0 sat. fat), 0 chol., 319mg sod., 13g carb. (10g sugars, 2g fiber), 2g pro.

BEST EVER CASHEW CHEESE SAUCE

Here's a versatile cashew cream sauce that's plant-based. I use it as a pasta sauce, as a pizza topping, over roasted veggies, on tacos and for grilled cheese. It doesn't reheat well, so I don't suggest making a double batch to use throughout the week.
—*Max Gregor, Santa Fe, NM*

Prep: **15 min. + soaking**
Cook: **10 min. •** Makes: **4 cups**

- 2 **cups organic raw cashews**
- 1 **Tbsp. olive oil**
- ½ **medium onion, chopped**
- 2 **garlic cloves, minced**
- ¼ **tsp. salt**
- ¼ **tsp. pepper**
- 2 **cups vegetable broth, divided**
- 1 **Tbsp. nutritional yeast**
  Paprika, optional

1. Rinse cashews in cold water; drain. Place in a large bowl, add enough water to cover by 3 in. Cover and let stand overnight.
2. In a large skillet, heat oil over medium heat. Add the onion; cook and stir until tender, 4-6 minutes. Add garlic, salt and pepper; cook 1 minute longer. Add 1½ cups vegetable broth; bring to a boil. Reduce the heat to a simmer.
3. Drain and rinse the cashews, discarding liquid. Add cashews to skillet; heat through. Transfer the mixture to a blender. Add the nutritional yeast; cover and process until cashews are pureed, adding enough remaining broth to achieve the desired consistency. If desired, sprinkle with paprika.
⅔ CUP: 245 cal., 18g fat (3g sat. fat), 0 chol., 329mg sod., 13g carb. (3g sugars, 2g fiber), 7g pro.

HUMMUS PASTA SALAD

Here's a hearty side that could also be enjoyed as a tasty meatless main dish. Add the homemade dressing to the pasta while it's still warm so the noodles absorb some of the liquid.
—*Michelle Morrow, Newmarket, NH*

- -

Prep: **25 min.**
Bake: **20 min. + chilling**
Makes: **18 servings**

2   cans (16 oz. each) garbanzo beans or chickpeas, rinsed and drained
2   Tbsp. olive oil
¾   tsp. salt, divided
½   tsp. pepper, divided
1   pkg. (16 oz.) uncooked whole wheat spiral pasta
4   cups chopped fresh kale
2   medium lemons
½   cup water
6   Tbsp. tahini
4   garlic cloves, minced
2   Tbsp. Greek olive juice
1   pint cherry tomatoes, quartered
1   cup Greek olives, chopped

1. Preheat oven to 350°. Place garbanzo beans on a parchment-lined rimmed baking sheet. Drizzle with oil and sprinkle with ½ tsp. salt and ¼ tsp. pepper; toss to coat. Bake until beans are golden brown, about 20 minutes.

2. Meanwhile, cook pasta according to package directions for al dente. Drain pasta; rinse with cold water and drain well. Place kale in a large mixing bowl; massage until tender, 3-5 minutes. Add pasta.

3. Finely grate zest from 1 lemon. Cut the lemons crosswise in half; squeeze juice from lemons. In a small bowl, whisk water, tahini, garlic, olive juice, lemon juice and zest, and remaining ¼ tsp. salt and ¼ tsp. pepper. Pour over pasta mixture; toss to coat. Stir in the garbanzo beans, tomatoes and olives. Refrigerate, covered, at least 3 hours.

¾ CUP: 219 cal., 8g fat (1g sat. fat), 0 chol., 316mg sod., 30g carb. (2g sugars, 6g fiber), 7g pro. **DIABETIC EXCHANGES:** 2 starch, 1½ fat.

MAKE IT YOUR OWN
Feel free to toss other veggies, such as chopped cucumbers, bell peppers, onions or broccoli, into this salad.

CHOCOLATE DATE ENERGY BALLS

Eating just one of these healthy treats satisfies my sweet tooth without adding any refined sugar. My recipe is a spinoff of an energy ball my daughter made for me when I was testing for my tae kwon do black belt.

—*Barbara Estabrook, Appleton, WI*

Prep: **20 min. + chilling**
Makes: **1 dozen**

- 1¼ **cups pitted medjool dates, roughly chopped**
- 3 **oz. 60% bittersweet chocolate, coarsely chopped**
- ¼ **cup dried unsweetened tart cherries, chopped**
- ¼ **cup deluxe mixed nuts, coarsely chopped**
- 3 **Tbsp. unsweetened coconut flakes**
- 3 **Tbsp. sunflower kernels**
- 1½ **tsp. olive oil**
- 1 **tsp. vanilla extract**

Place dates, chocolate and cherries in a food processor; process until finely chopped, about 1 minute. Add nuts, coconut and sunflower kernels; process until blended. Add oil and vanilla; process until mixture comes together. Roll into 12 balls. Refrigerate, covered, for at least 30 minutes before serving. Store any leftovers in an airtight container in the refrigerator.

1 BALL: 125 cal., 6g fat (2g sat. fat), 0 chol., 25mg sod., 14g carb. (11g sugars, 2g fiber), 2g pro.

BONUS: GLUTEN-FREE BAKING

GLUTEN-FREE CHOCOLATE CAKE COOKIES

I can't consume gluten, so I've transformed my favorite recipes to fit my diet. I came up with these cakelike cookies, and no one ever guesses they're gluten free.
—*Becki DiMercurio, Martinez, CA*

- -

Prep: **30 min.**
Bake: **10 min./batch + cooling**
Makes: **2 dozen**

2	cups confectioners' sugar
½	cup plus 3 Tbsp. Dutch-processed cocoa powder
2¼	tsp. cornstarch
¼	tsp. salt
2	large egg whites
2½	tsp. Kahlua coffee liqueur
1	cup chopped walnuts, toasted Additional confectioners' sugar

1. In a large bowl, combine confectioners' sugar, cocoa powder, cornstarch and salt. Stir in the egg whites and coffee liqueur until the batter resembles frosting. Add the walnuts.

2. Drop batter by tablespoonfuls 3 in. apart onto parchment-lined baking sheets. Bake at 300° until set, 10-14 minutes. Cool for 2 minutes before removing from pans to wire racks to cool completely. Dust with additional confectioners' sugar.

1 COOKIE: 82 cal., 3g fat (0 sat. fat), 0 chol., 29mg sod., 12g carb. (10g sugars, 1g fiber), 2g pro. **DIABETIC EXCHANGES:** 1 starch, ½ fat.

GLUTEN-FREE CHICKEN POTPIE

This gluten-free potpie is just as comforting as the original. The filling is creamy and flavorful from the seasonings.
—Taste of Home *Test Kitchen*

- -

Prep: 30 min.
Bake: 35 min. + standing
Makes: 8 servings

- 1¼ cups gluten-free all-purpose baking flour
- ⅓ cup ground almonds
- 2 tsp. sugar
- ¼ tsp. salt
- ¼ tsp. xanthan gum
- 6 Tbsp. cold butter, cubed
- 1 large egg, lightly beaten
- 1 to 2 Tbsp. ice water

FILLING
- 1 cup cubed peeled potato
- ¼ cup butter, cubed
- 1 small onion, chopped
- ¼ cup cornstarch
- ¾ tsp. salt
- ½ tsp. dried thyme
- ¼ tsp. pepper
- 1 cup chicken broth
- 1 cup whole milk
- 2 cups cubed cooked chicken
- 1 cup frozen peas and carrots

1. In a large bowl, combine flour, almonds, sugar, salt and xanthan gum. Cut in butter until crumbly. Stir in the egg. Gradually add water, tossing with a fork until dough holds together when pressed. Shape into a disk; wrap and refrigerate for 30 minutes or until easy to handle.
2. Preheat oven to 425°. Place potato cubes in a small saucepan; add water to cover. Bring to a boil. Reduce the heat; cook, covered, 8-10 minutes or until cubes are crisp-tender; drain.
3. In a large skillet, heat butter over medium-high heat. Add onion; cook and stir until tender, 3-5 minutes. Stir in cornstarch and seasonings until blended. Gradually stir in broth and milk. Bring to a boil, stirring constantly; cook and stir 2 minutes or until thickened. Stir in chicken, peas and carrots, and potato; remove from heat. Spoon into 9-in. pie plate.
4. On a lightly floured surface, roll out dough to fit plate; place over filling. Cut several 1-in. slits in the top. Bake 35-40 minutes or until crust is lightly browned. Let stand 15 minutes before serving.
1 SERVING: 358 cal., 21g fat (11g sat. fat), 96mg chol., 600mg sod., 28g carb. (4g sugars, 4g fiber), 16g pro.

GLUTEN-FREE FIG COOKIES

These goodies definitely don't taste like typical gluten-free cookies. For added flavor, I soak the figs in wine and pomegranate juice.
—*Alissa Stehr,*
Gau-Odernheim, Germany

- -

Prep: 30 min. + chilling
Bake: 15 min. + cooling
Makes: **3 dozen**

- ½ lb. dried figs, quartered
- ½ cup pomegranate juice
- ½ cup port wine or additional pomegranate juice
- ¼ cup lemon juice

DOUGH

- ½ cup unsalted butter, softened
- ½ cup sugar
- ½ cup packed brown sugar
- 1 large egg, room temperature
- 2 Tbsp. molasses
- 1 tsp. vanilla extract
- 1 cup sorghum flour
- 1 cup brown rice flour
- ½ cup tapioca flour
- 1 tsp. baking powder
- 1 tsp. ground nutmeg
- ¾ tsp. salt
- ½ tsp. baking soda
- ½ tsp. xanthan gum

1. Place figs in a small bowl. Add the pomegranate juice, port wine and lemon juice. Cover and refrigerate for 8 hours or overnight. Drain, reserving ¼ cup juice. Transfer figs and reserved juice to a small food processor; cover and process until a thick paste is formed. Set aside.
2. In a large bowl, cream butter and sugars until light and fluffy, 5-7 minutes. Beat in egg, molasses and vanilla. Combine the flours, baking powder, nutmeg, salt, baking soda and xanthan gum. Gradually add to creamed mixture and mix well. Divide dough into 4 portions; cover and refrigerate for 1 hour.
3. Roll out each portion of dough between 2 sheets of waxed paper into a 9x4-in. rectangle. Transfer 2 rectangles to a parchment-lined baking sheet; remove waxed paper. Spread reserved fig mixture evenly over both rectangles to within ½ in. of edges. Top with remaining crust; remove waxed paper. Using a fork, crimp edges to seal.
4. Bake at 350° until the edges are golden brown, 15-18 minutes. Cool for 10 minutes before removing from pan to a wire rack to cool completely. Transfer to a cutting board. Cut each in half lengthwise; cut widthwise into slices. Store in an airtight container.

1 COOKIE: 105 cal., 3g fat (2g sat. fat), 13mg chol., 83mg sod., 19g carb. (10g sugars, 1g fiber), 1g pro.
DIABETIC EXCHANGES: 1 starch, ½ fat.

GLUTEN-FREE PANCAKES

Since being diagnosed with celiac disease, I've made my gluten-free flapjacks dozens of times. My kids like them best with chocolate chips and maple syrup.
—*Kathy Rairigh, Milford, IN*

Prep: **15 min.** • Cook: **10 min./batch**
Makes: **12 pancakes**

- 1 **cup brown rice flour**
- ½ **cup potato starch**
- ½ **cup ground almonds**
- 3 **tsp. sugar**
- 3 **tsp. baking powder**
- ½ **tsp. salt**
- 2 **large eggs, room temperature**
- 1 **cup fat-free milk**
- 2 **Tbsp. butter, melted**
- 1 **tsp. vanilla extract**
- ⅓ **cup miniature semisweet chocolate chips, optional**

1. In a large bowl, combine rice flour, potato starch, almonds, sugar, baking powder and salt.

2. In another bowl, whisk eggs, milk, butter and vanilla; stir into dry ingredients just until moistened. If desired, stir in chocolate chips.

3. Preheat griddle over medium heat. Lightly grease griddle. Pour batter by ¼ cupfuls onto a hot griddle; cook until bubbles on top start to pop and bottoms are golden brown. Turn; cook until second side is golden brown. If desired, serve with additional mini chocolate chips.

FREEZE OPTION: Arrange cooled pancakes in a single layer on sheet pans. Freeze overnight or until frozen. Transfer frozen pancakes to an airtight freezer container; freeze for up to 2 months. To use, place a pancake on a microwave-safe plate; microwave on high for 40-50 seconds or until heated through.

2 PANCAKES: 233 cal., 10g fat (3g sat. fat), 73mg chol., 508mg sod., 30g carb. (5g sugars, 2g fiber), 7g pro. **DIABETIC EXCHANGES:** 2 starch, 2 fat.

GLUTEN-FREE SNACK MIX

The buttery, sweet cinnamon coating on this crunchy mix makes the snack addicting. It travels well, making it an easy on-the-go treat.
—Taste of Home *Test Kitchen*

Prep: **15 min.**
Bake: **15 min. + cooling**
Makes: **10 cups**

- 8 **cups popped popcorn**
- 2 **cups Koala Crisp cereal**
- 1 **pkg. (5 oz.) dried cherries**
- ⅓ **cup butter, cubed**
- ⅓ **cup honey**
- ½ **tsp. ground cinnamon**

1. In a large ungreased roasting pan, combine the popcorn, cereal and cherries. In a small saucepan, melt butter. Add honey and cinnamon; cook and stir until heated through. Pour over popcorn mixture and toss to coat.

2. Bake at 325° for 15 minutes, stirring every 5 minutes. Cool completely. Store mix in airtight containers.

½ CUP: 110 cal., 5g fat (2g sat. fat), 8mg chol., 89mg sod., 16g carb. (11g sugars, 1g fiber), 1g pro. **DIABETIC EXCHANGES:** 1 starch, 1 fat.

GLUTEN-FREE FLOUR MIX

My son and I have celiac disease, and I use this flour mix to make our favorite dishes. I prepare it in 2-quart batches and store it in airtight jars.
—Bernice Fenskie, Wexford, PA

Takes: **5 min.** • Makes: **3 cups**

- 2 **cups white rice flour**
- ⅔ **cup potato starch flour**
- ⅓ **cup tapioca flour**

In a bowl, combine all ingredients. Store in an airtight container in a cool, dry place for up to 1 year.

1 TBSP.: 29 cal., 0 fat (0 sat. fat), 0 chol., 0 sod., 7g carb. (0 sugars, 0 fiber), 0 pro.

GLUTEN-FREE ANADAMA BREAD

Anadama bread has been a New England mainstay for generations. This version substitutes gluten-free flour for regular all-purpose but keeps the loaf's slightly sweet flavor and hearty texture.
—Doris Kinney, Merrimack, NH

Prep: **25 min. + rising**
Bake: **30 min. + cooling**
Makes: **1 loaf (12 pieces)**

- 1 **pkg. (¼ oz.) active dry yeast**
- 1 **Tbsp. sugar**
- 1 **cup warm water (110° to 115°)**
- 2 **large eggs, room temperature**
- 3 **Tbsp. canola oil**
- 1 **Tbsp. molasses**
- 1 **tsp. white vinegar**
- 1½ **cups gluten-free all-purpose baking flour**

- ¾ **cup cornmeal**
- 1½ **tsp. xanthan gum**
- ½ **tsp. salt**

1. Grease an 8x4-in. loaf pan and sprinkle with gluten-free flour; set aside.

2. In a bowl, dissolve yeast and sugar in warm water. In the bowl of a stand mixer with a paddle attachment, combine eggs, oil, molasses, vinegar and yeast mixture. Gradually beat in flour, cornmeal, xanthan gum and salt. Beat on low speed for 1 minute. Next, beat on medium for 2 minutes. (Dough will be softer than yeast bread dough with gluten.)

3. Transfer to prepared pan. Smooth the top with a wet spatula. Cover and let rise in a warm place until the dough reaches the top of pan, about 40 minutes.

4. Bake at 375° for 20 minutes; cover loosely with foil. Bake for 10-15 minutes longer or until golden brown. Turn oven off. Leave bread in oven with door ajar for 15 minutes. Remove bread from pan to a wire rack to cool.

1 PIECE: 136 cal., 5g fat (1g sat. fat), 35mg chol., 115mg sod., 21g carb. (3g sugars, 3g fiber), 4g pro. **DIABETIC EXCHANGES:** 1½ starch, ½ fat.

GLUTEN-FREE CORNMEAL MUFFINS

Serve these golden bites warm with butter, honey or even salsa! Any leftovers are terrific—just wrap in foil and reheat in the oven.
—*Laura Fall-Sutton, Buhl, ID*

Prep: **20 min.** • Bake: **15 min.**
Makes: **1 dozen**

- ¾ cup fat-free milk
- ¼ cup honey
- 2 Tbsp. canola oil
- 1 large egg, room temperature
- 1 large egg white
- 1½ cups cornmeal
- ½ cup amaranth flour
- 2½ tsp. baking powder
- ½ tsp. xanthan gum
- ½ tsp. salt
- 1 cup frozen corn, thawed
- ¾ cup shredded reduced-fat Monterey Jack cheese or Mexican cheese blend

1. In a large bowl, beat the first 5 ingredients until well blended. Combine the cornmeal, amaranth flour, baking powder, xanthan gum and salt; gradually beat into milk mixture until blended. Stir in corn and cheese.

2. Coat muffin cups with cooking spray or use foil muffin liners; fill three-fourths full with batter. Bake at 375° until a toothpick inserted in the center comes out clean, 15-18 minutes.

3. Cool for 5 minutes before removing from pan to a wire rack.

1 MUFFIN: 169 cal., 5g fat (1g sat. fat), 23mg chol., 263mg sod., 27g carb. (7g sugars, 2g fiber), 6g pro.

GLUTEN-FREE PEANUT BUTTER BLONDIES

I converted these blondies to be gluten free so that my family could enjoy a comforting dessert. We were craving brownies one night, and these cakelike treats hit the spot. They are a fantastic spin on gluten-free peanut butter chocolate chip cookies.
—*Becky Klope, Loudonville, NY*

Prep: **15 min.**
Bake: **20 min. + cooling**
Makes: **16 servings**

- ⅔ cup creamy peanut butter
- ½ cup packed brown sugar
- ¼ cup sugar
- ¼ cup unsweetened applesauce
- 2 large eggs, room temperature
- 1 tsp. vanilla extract
- 1 cup gluten-free all-purpose baking flour
- 1¼ tsp. baking powder
- 1 tsp. xanthan gum
- ¼ tsp. salt
- ½ cup semisweet chocolate chips
- ¼ cup salted peanuts, chopped

1. In a large bowl, combine peanut butter, sugars and applesauce. Beat in eggs and vanilla until blended. Combine the flour, baking powder, xanthan gum and salt; gradually add to peanut butter mixture and mix well. Stir in the chocolate chips and chopped peanuts.

2. Transfer to a 9-in. square baking pan coated with cooking spray. Bake at 350° until a toothpick inserted in the center comes out clean, 20-25 minutes. Cool on a wire rack. Cut into squares.

1 BAR: 176 cal., 9g fat (2g sat. fat), 26mg chol., 142mg sod., 22g carb. (14g sugars, 2g fiber), 5g pro. **DIABETIC EXCHANGES:** 1½ starch, 1½ fat.

GLUTEN-FREE ALMOND CRISPIES

Every bite of these cookies contains cinnamon and maple. Your whole family will love them.
—*Jean Ecos, Hartland, WI*

Prep: **20 min.**
Bake: **10 min./ batch**
Makes: **3 dozen**

- ⅓ cup maple syrup
- ¼ cup canola oil
- 1 Tbsp. water
- 1 tsp. almond extract
- 1 cup brown rice flour
- ½ cup almond flour
- ¼ cup sugar
- 1 tsp. baking powder
- 1 tsp. ground cinnamon
- ⅛ tsp. salt
- ½ cup finely chopped almonds

1. In a small bowl, beat the syrup, oil, water and extract until well blended. Combine the flours, sugar, baking powder, ground cinnamon and salt; gradually beat into syrup mixture until blended. Stir in the almonds.
2. Drop by rounded teaspoonfuls onto parchment-lined baking sheets; flatten slightly. Bake at 350° for 10-12 minutes or until bottoms are lightly browned. Cool cookies for 1 minute before removing from pans to wire racks.
1 COOKIE: 54 cal., 3g fat (0 sat. fat), 0 chol., 18mg sod., 6g carb. (3g sugars, 1g fiber), 1g pro. **DIABETIC EXCHANGES:** ½ starch, ½ fat.

GLUTEN-FREE ANGEL FOOD CAKE

My daughter can't have gluten and my husband is diabetic, so there are a lot of special recipes at our house. This is one of them.
—*Anne Wiebe, Gladstone, MB*

Prep: **15 min.**
Bake: **45 min. + cooling**
Makes: **16 servings**

- 1½ cups egg whites (about 10)
- ¾ cup plus ½ cup sugar, divided
- ¼ cup cornstarch
- ¼ cup white rice flour
- ¼ cup tapioca flour
- ¼ cup potato starch
- 1½ tsp. cream of tartar
- ¾ tsp. salt
- ¾ tsp. vanilla extract
  Assorted fresh fruit, optional

1. Place egg whites in a large bowl; let stand at room temperature for 30 minutes. Sift ¾ cup sugar, cornstarch, flours and potato starch together twice; set aside.
2. Add cream of tartar, salt and vanilla to the egg whites; beat on medium speed until soft peaks form. Gradually add the remaining sugar, about 2 Tbsp. at a time, beating on high until stiff peaks form. Gradually fold in flour mixture, about ½ cup at a time.
3. Gently spoon into an ungreased 10-in. tube pan. Cut through the batter with a knife to remove air pockets. Bake on the lowest oven rack at 350° for 45-50 minutes or until lightly browned and entire top appears dry. Immediately invert the pan; cool completely, about 1 hour.
4. Run a knife around the side and center tube of pan. Remove cake to a serving plate. Top cake with fresh fruit if desired.
1 PIECE: 101 cal., 0 fat (0 sat. fat), 0 chol., 149mg sod., 23g carb. (16g sugars, 0 fiber), 3g pro.

1. Preheat oven to 325°. In a large skillet, melt butter over medium heat. Add celery and onions; cook and stir until tender, 8-10 minutes. Stir in parsley, salt, sage, poultry seasoning, thyme and pepper. In a large bowl, toss bread cubes with vegetable mixture. Combine eggs and broth; add to bread mixture and toss to coat.

2. Transfer to a greased 13x9-in. baking dish. Cover and bake for 40 minutes. Uncover and bake until a thermometer inserted in center reads 160°, 15-20 minutes.

¾ CUP: 146 cal., 5g fat (2g sat. fat), 31mg chol., 561mg sod., 22g carb. (2g sugars, 3g fiber), 3g pro.

THE SKINNY

For a vegan option, use an egg replacer according to the package directions. Or, omit the eggs and increase the amount of broth slightly to add more moisture. For a dairy-free version, substitute your favorite vegan butter. Of course, if you don't need to adhere to a gluten-free diet, this recipe will work with regular bread as well.

GLUTEN-FREE STUFFING

Gluten-free eaters, rejoice! Now you can enjoy everyone's favorite Thanksgiving dish, too. This easy side has all the classic stuffing flavor minus the gluten.
—Taste of Home *Test Kitchen*

Prep: **20 min.** • Cook: **55 min.**
Makes: **16 servings**

- ¼ cup butter, cubed
- 4 celery ribs, chopped
- 2 medium onions, chopped
- ¼ cup minced fresh parsley
- 1½ tsp. salt
- 1½ tsp. rubbed sage
- 1 tsp. poultry seasoning
- 1 tsp. dried thyme
- ½ tsp. pepper
- 1½ lbs. day-old gluten-free bread, cubed
- 2 large eggs, lightly beaten
- 1 can (14½ oz.) chicken broth or vegetable broth

GLUTEN-FREE PIZZA CRUST

You don't need to visit a health food store to find the specific flours for this recipe. I'm able to buy both at two local grocery stores here in my small town in Wyoming. This is an ideal dough for those who are gluten intolerant but also crave pizza.
—*Sylvia Girmus, Torrington, WY*

Prep: **20 min. + standing**
Bake: **20 min.**
Makes: **6 servings**

- 1 **Tbsp. active dry yeast**
- ⅔ **cup warm water (110° to 115°)**
- ½ **cup tapioca flour**
- 2 **Tbsp. nonfat dry milk powder**
- 2 **tsp. xanthan gum**
- 1 **tsp. unflavored gelatin**
- 1 **tsp. Italian seasoning**
- 1 **tsp. cider vinegar**
- 1 **tsp. olive oil**
- ½ **tsp. salt**
- ½ **tsp. sugar**
- 1 **to 1⅓ cups brown rice flour**
  Pizza toppings of your choice

1. Preheat oven to 425°. In a small bowl, dissolve the yeast in warm water. Add the tapioca flour, milk powder, xanthan gum, gelatin, Italian seasoning, vinegar, oil, salt, sugar and ⅔ cup brown rice flour. Beat mixture until smooth. Stir in enough remaining brown rice flour to form a soft dough (dough will be sticky).
2. On a floured surface, roll dough into a 13-in. circle. Transfer to a 12-in. pizza pan coated with cooking spray; build up edges slightly. Cover and let rest 10 minutes.
3. Bake crust until golden brown, 10-12 minutes. Add toppings of your choice. Bake 10-15 minutes longer, until the crust is crisp and the toppings are lightly browned and heated through.
1 PIECE: 123 cal., 1g fat (0 sat. fat), 0 chol., 217mg sod., 25g carb. (1g sugars, 2g fiber), 3g pro.

THE SKINNY

You can also use almond flour in place of the tapioca flour. Substituting these flours for one another is easy. There's no need to alter the amounts because they're very similar in taste and texture.

GLUTEN-FREE SUGAR COOKIES

These cakelike goodies are wonderful with a cold glass of milk. You can also use this recipe as a base and mix in dried cranberries or cherries, nuts or other extracts.
—Taste of Home *Test Kitchen*

Prep: **25 min.** • Bake: **10 min./batch**
Makes: **3 dozen**

- ⅔ cup butter, softened
- 1 cup sugar
- 2 large eggs, room temperature
- ¼ cup unsweetened applesauce
- 4 tsp. grated lemon zest
- 1 tsp. almond extract
- 1⅓ cups potato starch
- 1⅓ cups garbanzo and fava flour
- 1 cup tapioca flour
- 1 tsp. salt
- 1 tsp. xanthan gum
- ½ tsp. baking soda
- ⅓ cup coarse sugar

1. In a large bowl, cream butter and sugar until light and fluffy, 5-7 minutes. Beat in the eggs, applesauce, lemon zest and extract. Combine potato starch, garbanzo and fava flour, tapioca flour, salt, xanthan gum and baking soda; gradually add to the creamed mixture and mix well.
2. Shape into 1½-in. balls and roll in coarse sugar. Place 2 in. apart on baking sheets coated with cooking spray. Bake at 350° for 7-9 minutes or until lightly browned. Remove from pans to wire racks.
1 COOKIE: 110 cal., 4g fat (2g sat. fat), 21mg chol., 116mg sod., 18g carb. (8g sugars, 1g fiber), 1g pro.

GLUTEN-FREE SPICED SWEET POTATO MUFFINS

I have a family member with special dietary needs, so I came up with this muffin recipe that we could all enjoy. Gluten-free muffins can sometimes have an unpleasant texture, but these gems are just as good as any traditional recipe. If you don't have sweet potato on hand, canned pumpkin may be used instead.
—*Kallee Krong-Mccreery, Escondido, CA*

Prep: **20 min.** • Bake: **25 min.**
Makes: **1 dozen**

- 2¼ cups gluten-free all-purpose baking flour
- ¼ cup sugar
- 1 tsp. baking powder
- 1 tsp. ground cinnamon
- ½ tsp. baking soda
- ½ tsp. salt
- ¼ tsp. ground allspice
- ¼ tsp. ground ginger
- 3 large eggs, room temperature
- 1 cup mashed sweet potatoes
- ⅔ cup honey
- 2 Tbsp. coconut oil, melted
- 1 Tbsp. olive oil
- 1 tsp. vanilla extract
TOPPING
- 3 Tbsp. sugar
- ¼ tsp. ground cinnamon

1. Preheat oven to 350°. In a large bowl, whisk the first 8 ingredients. In another bowl, whisk eggs, sweet potatoes, honey, coconut oil, olive oil and vanilla until blended. Add to the flour mixture; stir just until mixture is moistened.
2. Fill 12 greased or paper-lined muffin cups three-fourths full. Combine topping ingredients; sprinkle over batter. Bake until a toothpick inserted in center comes out clean, 25-30 minutes. Cool for 5 minutes before removing from pan to a wire rack. Serve warm.
1 MUFFIN: 231 cal., 5g fat (3g sat. fat), 47mg chol., 217mg sod., 44g carb. (25g sugars, 3g fiber), 4g pro.

GLUTEN-FREE BISCUITS

Basic gluten-free biscuits are marvelous with brunch, dinner or even a bowl of soup. This recipe is perfect for tweaking—stir in your favorite ingredients like shredded cheddar and garlic powder, Swiss and chives, or Parmesan and Italian seasoning.
—Taste of Home *Test Kitchen*

Takes: **25 min.** • Makes: **9 biscuits**

- 2¼ **cups gluten-free all-purpose baking flour**
- 2½ **tsp. baking powder**
- 2 **tsp. sugar**
- ½ **tsp. baking soda**
- ½ **tsp. salt**
- ½ **cup cold butter, cubed**
- 1 **cup buttermilk**

1. Preheat oven to 425°. In a large bowl, whisk the first 5 ingredients. Cut in the butter until the mixture resembles coarse crumbs. Add the buttermilk; stir just until moistened. Turn onto a lightly floured surface; knead gently 8-10 times.

2. Pat or roll the biscuit dough to ¾-in. thickness; cut with a floured 2½-in. biscuit cutter. Place 2 in. apart on a greased baking sheet. Bake for 10-12 minutes or until golden brown. Serve warm.

1 BISCUIT: 205 cal., 11g fat (7g sat. fat), 28mg chol., 467mg sod., 24g carb. (3g sugars, 3g fiber), 4g pro.

THE SKINNY

Flours that are gluten free include almond, amaranth, bean, buckwheat, coconut, corn, millet, oat, quinoa, rice, sorghum and teff. You can also buy gluten-free flour mixes. Or make your own gluten-free flour mix using the recipe on page 243.

BEST GLUTEN-FREE CHOCOLATE CAKE

This gluten-free chocolate cake is a yummy treat that everyone can enjoy. Sometimes I stir in gluten-free chocolate chips or chopped nuts for a little variety.
—*Nichele McCague, Poway, CA*

Prep: **20 min.**
Bake: **50 min. + cooling**
Makes: **16 servings**

- 3 Tbsp. plus 2 cups gluten-free all-purpose baking flour, divided
- 2 cups sugar
- ¾ cup baking cocoa
- ¼ cup ground flaxseed
- ¼ cup chia seeds
- 2 tsp. baking powder
- 1½ tsp. baking soda
- 1 tsp. salt
- 1 to 2 tsp. instant espresso powder
- ½ tsp. xanthan gum
- 1 cup boiling water
- 1 cup unsweetened almond milk
- 1 cup canola oil
- 4 tsp. vanilla extract
  Confectioners' sugar

1. Preheat oven to 350°. Grease and flour a 10-in. fluted tube pan using 3 Tbsp. gluten-free flour.
2. In a large bowl, whisk remaining 2 cups flour and next 9 ingredients. In another bowl, combine water, almond milk, oil and vanilla until well blended. Gradually beat flour mixture into milk mixture.
3. Transfer to prepared pan. Bake until a toothpick inserted in center comes out clean, 50-55 minutes.

Cool cake in pan 15 minutes before removing it to wire rack to cool completely. Dust with confectioners' sugar before serving.
1 PIECE: 310 cal., 17g fat (1g sat. fat), 0 chol., 339mg sod., 41g carb. (26g sugars, 4g fiber), 3g pro.

MAKE IT YOUR OWN
Instead of dusting the cake with confectioners' sugar, try frosting it with homemade buttercream (naturally gluten free). Avoid store-bought canned frosting, as some brands may contain gluten.

INDEX